The Glen Canyon
Reader

The Glen Canyon Reader

EDITED BY
Mathew Barrett Gross

The University of Arizona Press   Tucson

The University of Arizona Press
© 2003 The Arizona Board of Regents
First Printing
All rights reserved

∞ This book is printed on acid-free, archival-quality paper.
Manufactured in the United States of America

08   07   06   05   04   03   6   5   4   3   2   1

Library of Congress Cataloging-in-Publication Data

The Glen Canyon reader / edited by Mathew Barrett Gross.
p. cm.
Includes bibliographical references.
ISBN0-8165-2242-1 (pbk. : acid-free paper)
1. Glen Canyon (Utah and Ariz.)
2. Glen Canyon (Utah and Ariz.)—Description and travel.
I. Gross, Mathew Barrett, 1972–
F832.G5 G56 2003
917.92'59—dc21
2002010529

British Library Cataloguing-in-Publication Data
A catalogue record for this book is available from the British Library.

Contents

Acknowledgments

A N ANTHOLOGY, BY ITS VERY DEFINITION, is the work of more than one person, and I have been lucky to have many generous people assisting me in the production of this book. Hank Harrington of the Environmental Studies Department at the University of Montana, Missoula, offered a warm and encouraging reception to the concept when I first shared it with him. The faculty of that fine program (I recommend it; everyone should attend) were universally generous; Tom Roy, Len Broberg, Bill Chaloupka, and Pat Williams have all earned my gratitude and respect. Daniel Kemmis of the Center for the Rocky Mountain West and Dan Flores of the University of Montana History Department served as diligent members of my thesis committee, and any strengths of this collection are no doubt a result of their insightful advice and guidance. Deepest thanks go to their committee chair and my advisor, Don Snow. A raconteur, mentor, sometime agent, and true friend, Don's enthusiasm for this anthology never wavered; without him, this book would not have come into existence.

I was lucky enough to briefly befriend Jared Farmer while at Missoula. I gave him a ride once from Provo to Montana, and he returned the favor by letting me ride on his expertise when I first became interested in Glen Canyon. His help no doubt saved me countless hours in the library stacks. Others offered support in a variety of ways. My parents, Gary and Rosalie Gross, helped make Montana a financial viability. My wife, Mel Gilles, endured the long winters and underemployment of Missoula on my behalf— not to mention more rants about Glen Canyon than any reasonable person should be expected to entertain. Katie Lee lent me her memories and her address book when it came time to track down various authors in this anthology. The authors and their families were invariably courteous, and I thank them all, particularly Floyd Dominy, Charles Eggert, Myrthle Griffin,

Ellen Meloy, Mary Page Stegner, and Ann Weiler Walka. Richard Shelton and Vaughn Short were prompt in returning my inquiries; I regret that they were not ultimately included in this collection. H. L. Weber was generous in helping to prepare the manuscript, and of course I am indebted to Patti Hartmann at the University of Arizona Press for taking on the anthology.

Financial assistance with permissions, for which I am eternally grateful, was provided by Peter Lawson for the S. J. and Jessie E. Quinney Foundation. Many of the historical essays would not have made it into the anthology without the financial support of the Utah Humanities Council. I have been honored by the support of the council and its director, Cynthia Buckingham, though it should be noted that any editorializing outside of the historical literature is entirely my own, and not representative of the views of any agency of the state of Utah.

In advance, I'd like to thank Mr. José Knighton of Back of Beyond Books in Moab, Utah, for the year-round window display.

This book is dedicated to all those who would again see a free-flowing Colorado River. To paraphrase Vaughn Short: Fight. Fight to win. Win.

The Glen Canyon
Reader

Clear Creek: An Introduction

I FIRST WENT TO LAKE POWELL during the particularly radiant autumn of 1999. I had spent the previous two years immersed in books, surveying the literature of Glen Canyon—the literary and historical record of what lies beneath the waters of the second largest reservoir in the Western Hemisphere. That October, I had been hired by an outdoor education center to lead a group of adults on a four-day kayaking trip on Lake Powell.

I approached the task with a mixture of professionalism and entrenched cynicism. There were eleven of us: me, the director of the education center, six of the center's major donors (the "students"), and three guides who worked for the sole independent outfitter on Lake Powell. I reminded myself that I was the educator, that my charges were paying customers, and I decided to hold my personal opinions close.

For I had pursued my study of the literature of Glen Canyon with a certain bias: I was a river runner, a former boatman (albeit briefly) of the Colorado. Having run most of the upper river on private and commercial trips, it seemed a natural extension for me to spend two years of graduate study exploring the one part of the river that could no longer be visited by anyone—the 170 miles of the Colorado River through Glen Canyon, which had been inundated by the waters of Powell reservoir since 1963.

Like many river guides on the Colorado, I had spent nights within the upper canyons, lounging in the sand beside a wind-troubled fire, discussing Glen Canyon and imagining all the spectacular ways it could come to us again. Reared on Abbey to despise the reservoir, I accepted the lost Glen as an Eden, an Elysium, a Shangri-La, and I wanted, above all else, to see Glen Canyon as it was—a sinuous ribbon of water in a stone desert, a place where the meandering Colorado had sculpted an enchanted landscape of umber sandstone, where towering cliffs and secret crevices dazzled the clearest of skies. While guiding trips on the indolent stretches of the Upper Colorado, I would often imagine how it would feel to be on the river when the dam gave way: how the river would speed up, lift our boats in a cartoon's oceanic wave, and whip us about like children being pulled around on the edge of a blanket. Of course, it was only fantasy—a fantasy that defied the laws of hydrology. Yet whenever I was on the river I would retire to my sleeping bag spread out on the beach, lie down beneath blankets of stars, and, in Vaughn Short's memorable phrase, "dream of a mighty boom and quake," and of "a houseboat running Dominy Falls at a million second feet."

It was hardly what educational theorists would call a "neutral bias." I decided to keep my opinions to myself, despite the many opportunities offered to point out the ironies of a river-lover leading an environmental journey to a reservoir.

For example: The entrance sign at Hall's Crossing was etched in a style that I call "Classic NPS"—an unimaginative assemblage of geometric shapes that barely passes as an artistic representation of the landscape. On the Hall's Crossing sign, a red rectangle is, ostensibly, a butte; a dun-colored trapezoid, I can only assume, is meant to represent a mesa; and at the bottom of the sign, a wide swath of baby blue signifies the lake. What's most interesting—to cynics like me, at least—is the location of the name. Someone, perhaps being so cleverly subversive that it passed the Park Service's notice, had the wit to put "Glen Canyon" *beneath* the swath of baby blue, as if to eliminate any confusion as to where the mysterious and majestic Glen Canyon of lore now lies.

I left such observations to myself as we boarded the little runabout that would take us to our base camp. In the air drifted the fresh smell of gasoline; around the bay a half dozen houseboats chugged and sputtered their way out into the old river channel. We stowed our waterproof bags in the bow and soon were off, skipping across the surface of the reservoir. The cliffs of Navajo sandstone bore the tell-tale white "bathtub ring" left by higher water levels, but they maintained their majesty, I had to admit. Try as I might, however, I simply could not appreciate the combination of red rock and blue water that so many have cited as the principal appeal of the reservoir. To me the transposition of colors felt artificial; any fool knows that rivers on the Colorado Plateau should have the color and consistency of baby shit. I'll have no exceptions.

We roared downriver, past the cliffs that soon became monotonous. I felt my protestations dwindling in the bright sun; the rhythmic punch of the water against the bow dulled my objections to the reservoir. "We're six hundred feet above Lake Canyon!" our guide yelled. A brief memory of the photographs I'd studied flashed through my mind, but bore limited resemblance to the truncated cliff before us. We passed the Rincon, an abandoned meander of the river that was, forty years ago, perched hundreds of feet above the Colorado, but which now was lapped by the waters of the reservoir and thus no longer of the remotest interest to anyone.

I was not prepared for this. I had expected to feel anger, sadness, cynicism, grief—but I had made no plans for this encroaching disinterest.

And then we turned up the Escalante, and for the first time I could see what people loved about Lake Powell; it was much the same as what people had loved about Glen Canyon. We cruised 250 feet above what had once been a six-inch deep river that you could walk in, beside what had once been grand cliffs of Navajo sandstone stained and streaked with the patina of desert varnish. We swung around bends and s-turns, capturing glimpses of side canyons that wound back through the molded desert into mystery. All my life, every canyon that I had ever seen had elicited in me the same desire to discover what lay beyond each bend in the canyon wall. These canyons, to my surprise, were no different.

In retrospect this recognition seems banal. Yet I had convinced myself that Glen Canyon had been stolen from me, reduced to nothing more than books and photographs and the reminiscences of an older and dying generation. That Lake Powell was *still* Glen Canyon had been heresy to me. Glen Canyon was gone, I believed, as surely as if it had been picked up by an alien spaceship and transported to another planet.

Yet here I was, looking at the landscape that surrounded Lake Powell, and what I saw was Glen Canyon. The tattered edges of Glen Canyon, to be sure, but Glen Canyon all the same.

In an area that had once been the high cirque of a cliff—but which was now a cove—we made our camp. A houseboat moored to the slickrock provided our supplies and the sea-kayaks that we would use to get around. I grabbed a folding cot and my waterproof bag and found a narrow sandy pocket above the cove in which to set my camp. I had a view down the Escalante River and across the channel into a side canyon. Above the canyon were the Straight Cliffs and the Kaiparowits Plateau, some of the wildest country in the lower forty-eight states.

A powerboat zoomed by, up the Escalante arm.

Down by the boats the guides were cooking steaks and opening bags of wine. They waved me off when I tried to lend a hand. As a guide I'd resented the steady transformation of boatmen into waiters and maids—there were some outfits that literally set up tents, rolled out the sleeping bags, and fluffed the customers' pillows before bedtime—but these men refused my assistance. I consoled myself that they had it easy, what with the running water and electric power of the houseboat.

Into evening we talked about Glen Canyon, about some of the reasons for its construction. Bruce Berger offers a fair explanation in this volume, far better than the one offered by tour guides at the Carl Hayden Visitor Center at Glen Canyon Dam. ("The dam was built for flood control," they intone, which immediately begs the question: What within a three-hundred-mile radius was in danger of flooding? The canyon itself?)

In truth, explaining why the dam was built in any definitive way is a difficult proposition. I offered my students as fair a history as I could manage: The seven states of the Colorado River Basin had overextended the river when they drew up the Colorado River Compact in 1922. By the time Hoover Dam was completed in 1935, California was using its full share of water, which, because of the Compact's erroneous assumptions, meant the Upper Basin states were being *deprived* of their water. In the west, you either use water or lose it. Impoundment is a use, so the Upper Basin states lobbied Congress to build them a dam. They didn't actually *need* the water, they just didn't want California to get it first. Hell, they still don't *need* the water, I said, filling up my mug from the bag of wine. A point of fact: Lake Powell to this day does not irrigate a single acre of land. 'Cept for the Page golf course, that is.

The explanation didn't suit me. Too pithy, after all. I mumbled something about the juggernaut of industrial progress-or-what-have-you and how we really didn't know what we were doing back in the fifties, how we didn't have the National Environmental Policy Act or any of the means to question the Bureau of Reclamation. Then I sat down and poked at the campfire.

Nobody knew this place, somebody said. It was the place no one knew.

I squeezed the bag of wine, which was getting skinny. Well . . . I said. That's a bit of a myth, you know. Eliot Porter published a book by that name in 1963, with David Brower's help. *The Place No One Knew.* Obviously you've heard of it. (I threw a fresh piece of convenience-store white pine onto the fire.) It was the second in the Sierra Club's Exhibit Format series of photo books—what Jared Farmer calls "coffee table propaganda." The first was *This*

Is Dinosaur, about the proposed dam at Echo Park in Dinosaur National Monument. Both Echo Park and Glen Canyon, as well as Flaming Gorge on the Green River, were slated to be dammed by the Colorado River Storage Project (CRSP) legislation that went before Congress in January of 1953. The Sierra Club and the Wilderness Society launched a campaign to remove Echo Park from the legislation, arguing that the national park system was an inappropriate place to build dams. "Shall We Let Them Ruin Our National Parks?" Bernard Devoto asked in *The Saturday Evening Post.* The nation answered back, no. Hell no. But Glen Canyon wasn't a park, though it almost became one back in the 1930s, and only a handful of people fought to preserve it. Not because it was "the place no one knew," but because it didn't have a line drawn around it on the map, and because when the whole battle started to save Echo Park nobody believed there was a chance of defeating the entire CRSP. The modern environmental movement in the United States was largely born from the battle to save Echo Park. In retrospect, maybe Glen Canyon could have been saved before the CRSP passed by a slim Congressional majority on March 1, 1956. It probably could have been saved, but nobody thought that was feasible until later.

And "the place no one knew?" I said. Naw—the place the Sierra Club didn't know, maybe. Compared to the Catskills, sure, no one knew it. But Glen Canyon was as well known, if not better, as many other places on the Colorado Plateau in the 1950s. A whole slew of writers knew Glen Canyon and its history, and knew it well. It's hard to buy the notion that Glen Canyon was ever "the place no one knew." The Anasazi were here in the twelfth century, the Spanish in the eighteenth, and Anglo Americans by the nineteenth. In 1880, the most celebrated Mormon mission in history—what became known as the Hole-in-the-Rock expedition—built the worst road in America through Glen Canyon. In 1882, gold fever hit, and by the turn of the twentieth century virtually every side canyon in the Glen had been panned for gold. By the 1920s, commercial operators were running tours to both Glen Canyon and Rainbow Bridge. In 1942, Boy Scouts from Salt Lake City began annual canoe trips down the canyon. A list of luminaries who "knew" Glen Canyon and its ancillary, Rainbow Bridge, would include Wallace Stegner, Barry Goldwater, Zane Grey, Theodore Roosevelt, Georgia O'Keefe, Stewart Udall, and Cecil B. DeMille. Even that most celebrated section of "the place no one knew"—Music Temple—had a hiker's registry placed in it by the U.S. Government in 1950, and it was filled with the scribbled names of people who knew the place existed very well, thank you. The fact is, when the diversion tunnels of Glen Canyon Dam were finally closed in January of 1963, and the canyon began to fill with the impounded waters of the river and transform itself into Lake Powell, more people had run the course of the Colorado River through Glen Canyon than through the Grand Canyon by a factor of one hundred.[1]

I'd been pacing; I sat down again beside the fire. There was a long silence, punctuated only by the steady lap of water against the sandstone. I began again. The truth is that you can search and search and search, I said, but if you believe Lake Powell was a mistake, you'll never find a satisfactory reason as to why they flooded Glen Canyon. It was a historical mindset, maybe. The states wanted water for future growth. California was a hog. Heck, blame it on mean people. But all the historical explanations in the world will never fully justify the loss. Blaming ourselves by saying it was an unknown place is crap; David Brower can carry that guilt, perhaps, but what about me? I was born in 1972. I might as well feel guilty for the extinction of the giant sloth. It was wrong, I believe that, and we have a moral obligation to bear witness to the wrongs of history. But we have to know our history.

The flame was flickering out. I sighed, my neutrality blown to shreds on my very first evening with the group. So much for steady employment. I nudged the sand and looked beyond the faces at the white cloud of the Milky Way in the night sky above. This was an astounding place to view the stars: the sickle sliver of a new moon hung low in the west, Orion was rising in the east. I cleared my throat.

Who drank all the wine? I said.

We can dream of what was. We can dream of putting our rafts in at Hite, with the high laccolithic peaks of the Henry Mountains in the northwest. The river will take us down, past White and Red Canyons and past the bank of Ticaboo, where Cass Hite lived and prospected for gold. We'll drift on by Tapestry Wall, that long cliff of Navajo sandstone draped with desert var-

1. See Jared Farmer, *Glen Canyon Dammed;* Gary Topping, *Glen Canyon and the San Juan Country;* also annual visitation figures for Grand Canyon and Rainbow Bridge National Monuments, National Park Service. The total number of visitors to Grand Canyon was, of course, higher, but it must be remembered that rafting the Grand Canyon did not blossom until the late 1960s. In 1959, for example, of the 1,168,807 visitors to Grand Canyon, a mere 70 ran the river, compared to an estimated 4,000 who ran the Glen during the same year.

nish, and continue on past the houses, watchtowers, and granaries of Moqui Canyon. We'll be startled by the remains of the Hoskaninni Gold Dredge, we'll slumber past Hall's Crossing and Lost Eden Canyon, we'll eddy out above Lake Canyon before passing beneath the Rincon high above us. At the Escalante we'll get out and walk, our feet in the shallow river, up Clear Creek to Cathedral in the Desert or on to Davis Gulch, where the ghost of Everett Ruess is etched into stone.

On down, past Hole-in-the-Rock, past the confluence of the San Juan. We'll almost miss Hidden Passage, but we'll be prepared for Music Temple, where we'll sign our names in musical notes inside the hiker's registry. There will be Mystery and Oak Creek and Twilight Canyons and then Forbidding. We'll walk—yes, we'll walk—hot, dusty, dry and tired to Rainbow Bridge, where a canteen will await us, full of clean clear water, beneath a running spring.

The names of the canyons will flow past like the river: Cathedral, Little Arch, Balanced Rock, Dangling Rope, Grotto, Dungeon, and half a dozen more. Screw Kane Creek, we'll say, cursing the billboard that orders us to disembark or face federal prosecution for trespassing. Trespassing! On we'll go, past Crossing of the Fathers, past Labyrinth Canyon and on to Wahweap, where Sentinel Rock will rise two hundred feet above us. And on down, on down, deeper into the canyon, past the willows and the cottonwoods, beneath the high enclosing cliffs, beneath the cloudless sky, the oars resting in the tuck of a bended knee, drifting for weeks on end.

Morning dawned clear and bright, a relief after a chilly night in the open desert. The smell of coffee brought me down to the camp. Only the guides were awake.

"Those sleeping bags you supplied are rather thin," I said.

"We don't normally go out this late in the season."

"It was like sleeping between two pieces of Kleenex," I said.

The sun reached above the surrounding slickrock and lit the camp with a golden glow. There wasn't a cloud or contrail in the sky.

"What's that side canyon across the river?" I asked.

"Clear Creek."

My heart jumped. "The Clear Creek where Cathedral in the Desert was?"

"Never heard of it."

I was surprised. Cathedral in the Desert had been one of the crowning glories of Glen Canyon. In the days before the dam you could walk up Clear Creek Canyon, in the creek itself, following the lush green ribbon of willows and reeds as it wound beneath the cliffs. A final turn in the canyon wall would bring you to a massive grotto, a rounded chamber of Navajo sandstone as large as several football fields. From a narrow cleft high above fell a lovely waterfall, at the base of which had formed a lovely green pool. In pictures a person was a dot within the chamber.

"Are we going up there?" I asked.

"Doubt it."

For the next several days we explored the Escalante arm. Glen Canyon is such a compelling intellectual topic because it is full of contradictions: it has been destroyed, and yet a movement is afoot to bring it back; it is known as "the place no one knew," and yet it has produced a body of literature that rivals the literature of any other natural place in the world; it was a place perhaps equal in grandeur to Grand Canyon, and yet it was dammed and inundated with only the faintest puff of dissent; it is despised by many in its present form, and yet fiercely loved in this form by many more. Surely it is not the only beautiful place to have been lost to "progress," but few other places have so twisted the human soul with the agony of its contradictions.

The reality of Lake Powell reinforces those contradictions. The base of Willow Creek, for example, is an ecological nightmare. On a lone island, six young tamarisk are hesitantly taking hold, as if unsure whether even weeds such as themselves should deserve the terrible fate of having to watch a million knuckleheads on Sea-doos scoot by. Yet Willow Creek itself, we discovered, is stupendous. The walls of the canyon tilt inward, suggesting that the sculpted forms of places like Cathedral were not a random freak of erosion but an embodiment of the highest aspiration of the sandstone. Out in the main channels one is indeed on a motorized playground; but by walking a hundred yards up a side canyon, one is in a place as wild and remote as any in the lower United States. In the past these stretches may have been "run-of-the-mill Glen Canyon," pale comparisons to the majesties that now lie flooded. But in the present, for those of us living in this simplified world, they remain a culmination of heartbreaking beauty and mind-boggling contradiction—a singularly verdant hideaway in a landscape of barren stone.

And so I came to terms with Lake Powell. The aesthetic dichotomy of a lost Eden simply didn't hold up. Glen Canyon is diminished, to be sure, but ultimately one must turn for solace in what remains. I still believe Lake Powell should be drained, and I believe it eventually will be, but it will be drained because we can't countenance the loss of water to evaporation; it will be drained because we'll recognize the biological and economic importance of free-flowing rivers. It won't be drained because the aesthetic beauty of what lies underwater surpasses the beauty of what remains on its shores.

And yet, and yet—the Cathedral in the Desert still called to me. On our final afternoon I slipped a kayak into the reservoir and paddled out alone across the channel. The cliffs were alight in the radiance of an autumn afternoon. Up the canyon I went, around the bend in the wall, scores of feet above the old cobbled riverbed. Where the water met the vertical stone there was no life—no odor of sage nor the sweet smell of wet sand in the desert—but as the walls closed in and the channel narrowed, I pushed on, somehow content. The canyon meandered tightly to the left, and a sense of recognition and remembrance rose within me. Was this Cathedral? A deep alcove extended to my left, reaching back into the stone for thirty yards and creating a watery cave. No, this wasn't it.

The reservoir had ended. A small shelf led into the narrow canyon. I pulled the kayak up onto the stone and walked on around the bend, through a cool glen of gambel oak, to a muddy pool beneath a high choke stone surrounded by willow and ash. The stone was the size of a two-story house, a massive boulder, and at the top a narrow and winding flume had been sculpted out by the intermittent stream that fed the dark pool below. Was this, then, what remained of Cathedral—a dark pool covered in sand? The flume above resembled the photographs I'd seen of the waterfall that poured into the lost chamber. Had it silted up? Was I standing above it?

Of course not. I must have passed Cathedral while on the reservoir and not noticed it. And how would I notice it? It was underwater, after all. You couldn't expect to remember a place from a forty-year-old photograph. And yet I knew the canyon would narrow before I came to Cathedral, and it had narrowed abruptly less than three hundred yards back. A crazed notion came to me. What if? I wondered. What if the Cathedral in the Desert still lay farther ahead?

I became mad with hope. "Never heard of it," the guides had said, when I'd asked them about Cathedral. Surely it was a trick. Hell, I did the same thing whenever tourists asked me about a place that I considered special. ("Delicate Arch? Never heard of it.") Perhaps Cathedral hadn't been flooded after all. Perhaps it still lay before me, farther up the canyon, unknown to all those who wouldn't wander far enough. A map I had examined earlier that morning had shown it far into the reaches of the plateau. Perhaps I had been wrong in assuming that it was within a mile of the Escalante?

To the left of the massive choke stone lay a high dune of fine sand. I wandered up the dune, following a loose trail. At the top the canyon continued, disappearing around a bend to the right. My heart raced. Farther I went. Pools of water in the intermittent streambed reflected the cerulean sky. The air grew chill as the narrow canyon plunged into shade. Around the final bend the canyon opened up into a large amphitheater bright in the slanting sun of afternoon.

Cathedral? I wandered through the stands of willow, following the thin creek that had appeared amongst the thick foliage. At the end was another deep pool, fed by a spring that percolated forth from the rock, surrounded by maidenhair fern. One hundred feet above me the cliff tilted inward, but the lip of the canyon was smooth, uncut by water. There was too much sky above; the top of the amphitheater was wide open. The only way out of the chamber was the way I had come—there was no going further—and that meant that Cathedral indeed had been behind me, back in the reservoir, flooded and gone. Of course.

I stayed for a time in that lovely grotto, listening to the sound of the spring as it fed the pool, feeling the sand grow cold beneath my feet, watching the shadows creep down the luminous sandstone walls. In the distance I heard a low moaning, a sound I couldn't make out. I headed back, around the bend in the canyon, over the dune, beside the choke stone. How could I have imagined that this narrow pool was Cathedral? The low moaning grew louder, an eerie siren song of foreign voices, punctuated by drums. And then, when I rounded the last bend to my kayak, the source of the sound became apparent—out in the water, two young couples lounged on a powerboat in the remaining sun. Rock and roll blared from an onboard stereo, and the sound of music reverberated in the low watery cave.

I launched the kayak. At the edge of the reservoir, just beneath the surface, an ornately sculpted flume plunged down into the depths. This was Cathedral. It had to be. I paddled out past the young couples on their boat and recognized the song from the stereo. It was a good song. I called out to them.

"Any idea how deep it is here?"

The young man, shirtless and tan, blipped his sonar. "Sixty-five feet," he said.

I peered down over the edge of the kayak. Sixty-five feet! Sixty-five feet and forty years was all that separated me from the Glen Canyon that once was. Sixty-five measly feet, I thought—further my god from thee. I tried in vain to block the glare of the sun as I looked down into the water. I could see nothing but the reflection of my own face.

The volume you hold in your hands is the culmination of my first exploration of Glen Canyon, an exploration pursued solely in the literary world. Obsessed by the Glen Canyon that once was, I spent two years tracking down almost every essay, poem, or book about the canyon that has been published. In part this collection was born from the difficulty of my pursuit, and from the belief that the best writing about Glen Canyon should not remain forever scattered in incidental chapters in various essay collections by disparate writers—or nearly lost to history, as was Frank Griffin's "Visit to a Drowning Canyon," in a dog-eared 1966 copy of *Audubon* magazine.

It should be noted that this book is meant to be enjoyed regardless of the reader's position on the controversy surrounding Glen Canyon's future. Many people quite rightly find Lake Powell to be as glorious and majestic as the Glen Canyon contained in these pages, and it is my hope that this book will serve to enrich and enliven one's present adventures upon the reservoir. Any bias to the collection is due solely to the mystifying lack of a pro-Lake Powell perspective in the body of work that makes up the literature of Glen Canyon—houseboating, one supposes, being less conducive to literary composition than other outdoor activities.

Thus, while I believe that the end result is a fair and representative sample of the literature of Glen Canyon, I must confess at the outset that these selections are by no means complete.

For example, no poetry has been included in this collection, yet surely Vaughn Short's river poems and Richard Shelton's "Glen Canyon on the Colorado" occupy a revered place in the literature of the Glen. Several fine histories of the canyon and the Colorado River are also noticeably absent, including Gary Topping's *Glen Canyon and the San Juan Country* and Marc Reisner's *Cadillac Desert*. And many of the writers included in the anthology—most notably Wallace Stegner and Edward Abbey—returned several times to Glen Canyon as a literary subject, yet each author appears only once.

Although many of the authors contained herein were chosen in part for either their historical significance (Domínguez-Escalante, John Wesley Powell, Barry Goldwater, David Brower, Floyd Dominy) or their literary merit (Wallace Stegner, Edward Abbey, Zane Grey, John McPhee), all of the selections were ultimately chosen for their power to convey the story of Glen Canyon, both as history and as place.

The anthology is organized in a chronological fashion, beginning with the discovery of Glen Canyon by Padres Escalante and Domínguez, and with the accounts of other early explorers such as John Wesley Powell. The anthology then proceeds to collect a sampling of the many pieces written about or around the time of the dam's construction. Finally, the anthology concludes with a selection of writing that addresses the present day Glen Canyon, and, to a limited extent, the controversy of draining Lake Powell.

One may read the anthology straight through, as one would read any history. Perhaps more pleasurable, however, is to flip through these pages, to poke around and explore, as one would have done in Glen Canyon, and many still do at Lake Powell and elsewhere on this magnificent plateau of the Colorado River—to visit and revisit the places contained in this book, these cool glens and embracing alcoves and hidden grottos, these canyons and dreams and ghosts that will always, always be with us.

Mathew Barrett Gross
Moab, Utah

THE FIRST KNOWN WRITTEN ACCOUNT of Glen Canyon appears in the journal of Fathers Francisco Atanasio Domínguez and Silvestre Vélez de Escalante. In 1776, Fray Domínguez was charged with discovering a direct route from Santa Fe to the new Spanish town of Monterey, on the coast of California. Fray Vélez, widely though incorrectly known as "Escalante," served as second-in-command on the expedition. Although the expedition failed to make it to Monterey, Escalante and Domínguez succeeded in providing the first written documentation of much of the Colorado Plateau, the eastern Great Basin, and the Rocky Mountains. The following is taken from *The Domínguez-Escalante Journal,* translated by Fray Angelico Chavez and edited (including the footnotes contained herein) by Ted J. Warner.

The Domínguez-Escalante Journal

October 27

ON THE 27TH DON JUAN PEDRO CISNEROS went through the canyon of El Río de Santa Teresa, to see if he could find a passage through it in order to get across the east mesa and return to El Río Grande over more open country where it could be forded by taking advantage of its width, or at least where the horse herd could get across without the danger, which existed here, of its getting buried underneath the waters. He traveled all day and part of the night and found no passage. He saw one incline very near here where one might get across the mesa, but it looked too difficult to him. Others went to explore in different directions and found nothing but insuperable obstacles for getting to the ford without retracing much terrain.

October 28

On the 28th we repeated the same attempts, and all in vain. A wood raft was put together in short order, and Padre Fray Silvestre with the servants tried to cross the river by means of it; but since the poles used for pushing it, even though more than five yards long, did not touch bottom a short distance away from shore, it was held back by the waves raised by the contrary wind. And so it thrice came back to the shore it had left, without getting even as far as the river's middle. This, besides being deep and wide, here has quicksands on either bank, in the likes of which we could lose all or the better part of the horse herd.

The Yubuincariri and Pagampachi Indians had assured us that the entire river was very deep except at the ford, for when they went across the water reaches up to the waist or a little more. Because of this, and from other indications they had given us, we guessed that the ford was farther upstream. And so we dispatched Andrés Muñiz and his brother Lucrecio with orders to proceed until they found a place where we could get across the mesa previously mentioned and, when they returned to the river, to look for a good crossing or at least some section where, after we went over by raft, the horse herds could get across without peril.

October 29

On the 29th, not knowing when we would be able to get out of here, and when the meat from the first horse and the piñon nuts and other things we had bought had run out, we ordered another horse killed.

October 30–31

On the 30th and 31st we remained waiting for those who went to look for a ford and a way out.

November 1

On the 1st of November they returned when it was already one in the afternoon, saying that they had found a passage, although a difficult one, and a ford in the river. The way over the mesa was the incline which Cisneros had seen, and, since this was very high and steeply rugged, we decided to get next to it this afternoon. We left the bank of El Río Grande and the distressful Paraje de San Benito de Salsipuedes, went along El Río de Santa Teresa, and, after going a league northwest, halted by its edge at the base of the incline mentioned. Today one league.[1] This afternoon, from sundown to seven in the morning, we were exceedingly cold.

1. Only 2.63 miles today up the shallow, winding Paria River. At Lee's Ferry the Shinarump ledge, against which they had camped, forms a vertical escarpment that dips gradually to the north. At the point where this cliff finally disappears at river level is where the ascent was to begin the next day. Camp was made along the Paria at this spot, probably in a nearby grove of cottonwood trees.

On the 2nd we left El Río de Santa Teresa and went up the incline, which we named Las Ánimas and which must have been half a league long. It took us more than three hours to climb it because it has a very sloping sand dune for a start, and afterward extremely difficult stretches and most dangerous ledges, and is at the very last impassable. After we had climbed it heading east with utmost difficulty, we went down the other side through cliff-lined gorges as we headed north, and after one league turned east for half a one over a stretch of red sand which was quite troublesome for the horse herds. We ascended a small elevation[2] and, likewise going northeast for two leagues and a half, went down into an arroyo which had water running in places, but brackish even though drinkable. There was also pasturage here, and so we halted in it, naming it San Diego.[3] Today four leagues and a half.[4]

Today we stopped about three leagues northeast in a direct line from San Benito de Salsipuedes, close to a multitude of earthen embankments, small mesas, and peaks of red earth which look like ruins of a fortress at first sight.[5]

NOVEMBER 3

On the 3rd we set out from San Diego, headed east-southeast, and after going two leagues came to the river a second time, that is, at the edge of the

2. This difficult climb led to a low spot in the east rim of Paria Canyon. The pass is now known as "Domínguez Pass."

3. Slightly north of the present Arizona-Utah border, although today it lies submerged by two hundred feet of water of Lake Powell. The nearest shore of the lake is the site of the Wahweap Swim Beach.

For the first half mile of this day's travel their route twisted between bleak formations of Chinle shale. This was followed by a steep climb of about 400 vertical feet to a sloping bench covered with large areas of loose red sand. Some of this sand could be avoided, some could not, as they climbed slowly across the bench to the southeast. At a point about 1,000 feet above the Paria the terrain forced them to turn up another very steep slope covered with loose soil and boulders. Finally, about 300 feet from the top, they reached a series of baldrock sandstone ledges that were not only narrow but were dangerously rounded on the outside edge. Switchbacking over and across these ledges, which the journal describes as "impassable," they reached the top through a shallow notch about 150 yards long. In their ascent toward the southeast they were actually approaching Lee's Ferry, so that they crested the ridge only about two miles from San Benito Salsipuedes; yet they were 1,700 vertical feet above the Colorado River.

4. Slightly over 11.8 miles.

5. The formation now carries the name Castle Rock.

canyon[6] which here serves as its box channel. The descent to the river is very long, steep, rugged, and precipitous, consisting of such terrible rock embankments that two pack animals which descended the first one could not make it back, even without the equipment. Those who had come by here before had not informed us of this slope, and here we learned that they had not found the ford either, nor in so many days made the necessary exploration of so small a space of terrain, for their having wasted the time looking for those Indians who live hereabouts, and accomplished nothing.

The river was very deep, although not as much as at Salsipuedes, but the horse herds had to swim for a long distance. The good thing about it is that it was not quicksand, either going in or getting out. The companions kept insisting that we should descend to the river, but since there was no way on the other side to go ahead after one crossed the river, except a deep and narrow canyon of another small one which joins it here—and since we had not learned if this one could be negotiated or not—we feared finding ourselves obliged (if we went down and crossed the river) to do the necessary backtracking which on this precipice would be extremely difficult. So as not to have to risk it, we halted above and sent the genízaro Juan Domingo to go across the river and find out if the said canyon had an exit, but if he did not find it this afternoon to return so that we might continue upstream along this side until we found the Indians' ford and trail.

After the latter was dispatched on foot, Lucrecio Muñiz said that if we let him he would also go bareback on a horse, taking along the things needed for making a fire and sending up smoke signals in case he found an exit, so that with this message we would try finding our way down and shorten the delay. We told him to go, but reminded him that we expected him back this afternoon, whether he found the exit or not. They did not return, and so we passed the night here without being able to water the horse herds while being so adjacent to the river. We named the place El Vado de los Chamas, or San Carlos.[7] Today two leagues[8] east-southeast.

November 4

On the 4th, day broke without our learning about the two whom we had dispatched yesterday on the reconnaissance mentioned. The meat from the

6. Navajo Creek Canyon.

7. "The Hill of the Chamas," or "Saint Charles." The campsite was on the west rim of the canyon opposite the mouth of Navajo Creek. The site is now covered by Lake Powell.

8. About 5¼ miles.

second horse had run out, we had not eaten a thing today, and so we break-fasted on toasted pads of low prickly pear cactus and gruel made from a tiny fruit[9] they brought from the riverbank. This tiny fruit of itself has a good taste but, crushed and boiled in water the way we had it today, is very insipid. On seeing how late it was and that the two aforementioned ones did not show up, we ordered that an attempt be made to get the animal herd down to the river and on the bank to slaughter another horse. They got them down with great difficulty, some of the mounts injuring themselves because, when they lost a foothold on the big rocks, they rolled down a long distance.

A little before nightfall, the genízaro Juan Domingo returned, asserting that he had found no way out and that the other one, leaving the horse midway in the canyon, had kept on following some fresh Indian tracks. And so we decided to continue upstream until we found a good ford and passable terrain on one and the other side.

NOVEMBER 5

On the 5th we left San Carlos, no matter if Lucrecio had failed to return, his brother Andrés remaining behind with orders to wait for him until evening, and for him to try to overtake us tonight. We went along this western side and over many ridges and gullies a league and a half to the north; we went down into a dry arroyo[10] and very high-walled canyon where there was a great deal of copper sulphate. In it we found a little-used trail; we followed it and by means of it came out of the canyon, passing over a brief shelf of soft [white?] rock, difficult but capable of improvement. We kept on going and, after we went a league and a quarter toward the north-northeast, found water, even though a little, and enough pasturage; and since it was almost dark, we halted close to a high mesa, naming the place Santa Francisca Romana.[11] Today three short leagues.[12]

Tonight it rained heavily here, and it snowed in some places. It was raining at daybreak and kept it up for some hours. About six in the morning

9. Probably hackberries.

10. Warm Creek. At the upper end of the trail out of Warm Creek to the east, researchers found a rock cairn marking the spot.

11. Near the base of Ramona Mesa, near the head of Cottonwood Wash, one of the tributaries of Warm Creek.

12. As they measured only "short leagues," this date they probably made something less than 7.5 miles.

Andrés Muñiz arrived, saying that his brother had not turned up. This news caused us plenty of worry, because he had been three days without provisions and no covering other than his shirt, since he had not even taken trousers along—for, even though he crossed the river on horseback, the horse swam for a long stretch and the water reached almost to the shoulders wherever it faltered. So when the genízaro mentioned decided to go and look for him for this reason, by following the tracks from where he saw him last, we sent him on his way with meat for provision and with orders to leave the mount behind if it could not get out of the canyon and to proceed on foot; and should he find him on the other side, for them to look along it for signs of us and to come after us—and if on this one, to try to overtake us as quickly as possible.

November 6

On the 6th, after it had stopped raining, we left Santa Francisca and headed northeast, and after we had gone three leagues we were stopped for a long time by a strong blizzard and tempest consisting of rain and thick hailstones amid horrendous thunder claps and lightning flashes.[13] We recited the Virgin's Litany, for her to implore some relief for us, and God willed for the tempest to end. We continued east for half a league and halted near the river because it kept on raining and some rock cliffs blocked our way. We named the place San Vicente Ferrer.[14] Today three leagues and a half.[15]

Don Juan Pedro Cisneros went to see if the ford lay around here and came back to report having seen how very wide the river was hereabouts and that he did not think it was deep according to the current, but that we could get to it only through a nearby canyon. We sent two others to inspect it and to ford the river, and they came back saying that everything was difficult to negotiate. We did not give much credence to the latters' report, and so we decided to examine it ourselves next day along with Don Juan Pedro Cisneros. Before night came the genízaro arrived with the said Lucrecio.

13. They were in Gunsight Canyon, probably on the west bank of that gulch, when the storm broke with all its fury, sending a flash flood down the canyon and causing the party to stop until the storm and flood had cleared.
14. The site was within a mile of the Colorado River just southeast of the base of Gunsight Butte on the west side of Padre Creek, but not in sight of either it or the Colorado.
15. Slightly over nine miles.

On the 7th we went out very early to inspect the canyon[16] and ford, taking along the two genízaro, Felipe and Juan Domingo, so that they might ford the river on foot since they were good swimmers. In order to have the mounts led down to the canyon mentioned, it became necessary to cut steps with axes on a stone cliff for the space of three yards or a bit less.[17] Over the rest of it the horse herds were able to get across, although without pack or rider.

We got down to the canyon, and after going a mile we reached the river[18] and went along it downstream for about as far as two musket shots, now through the water, now along the edge, until we came to the widest part of its currents where the ford[19] appeared to be. One man waded in and found it all right, not having to swim at any place. We followed him on horseback, entering a little farther down, and in its middle two mounts which went ahead missed bottom and swam through a short channel. We held back, although with some peril, until the first one who crossed on foot came back from the other side to lead us, and we successfully passed over without the horses on which we were crossing ever having to swim.[20]

We notified the rest of the companions, who had stayed behind at San Vicente, to hoist with lassos and ropes—down a not very high cliff to the

16. On the west rim of Glen Canyon overlooking the likely fording place.

17. Access to the floor of Padre Creek was over a steep sandstone slope which a man could negotiate without danger. However, lest the horses lose their footing and tumble to the canyon floor, the expedition hacked out some shallow footholds, or steps, for about ten feet in one of the most dangerous places, making it less hazardous for the animals. This used to be one of Utah's most historic sites. It is now covered with 550 feet of water from Lake Powell.

18. That is, the Colorado River. The distance was actually not more than a quarter of a mile.

19. This is located where a permanent sandbar was found at the base of the west canyon wall. Diagonally across from that bar was a similar one on the opposite side of the river. A ripple in the water surface indicated the shallowest point leading directly to that sandbar. It was evidently from this point that the camp gear was lowered over the cliff to the sandbar. The journal statement that the ford was a mile wide would have to mean from Padre Creek to the sandbar at the east side of the river. The water at the ripple was not more than three feet deep. The actual fording place probably changed slightly from time to time, depending on the shifting sandbar.

20. This marks the famous "Crossing of the Fathers." Most of the area traversed by the 1776 Spanish party now lies beneath the waters of Lake Powell. At the point where the padres crossed, the lake is now about 550 feet deep. Several research teams explored this region in 1938, 1950, and 1958, prior to the construction of the Glen Canyon Dam. See David E. Miller, "Discovery of Glen Canyon, 1776," *Utah Historical Quarterly*, 26 (1958):221–37.

ford's bend—the equipment, saddles, and other effects and to bring the horse herd along the route we had come. They did it that way and finished crossing the river about five in the afternoon, praising God our Lord and firing off some muskets in demonstration of the great joy we all felt in having overcome so great a problem, one which had caused us so much labor and delay—even when the main cause of our having suffered so much, ever since we entered Parussi country, was our having no one to guide us through so much difficult terrain. For through the lack of expert help we made many detours, wasted time from so many days spent in a very small area, and suffered hunger and thirst.

And now that we had undergone all this, we got to know the best and most direct route where the water sources helped in the planning of average day's marches, and we kept on gathering reports about the others, especially when we stopped going south the day we left San Dónulo or Arroyo del Taray[21]—because, from this place, we could have gone to the bounteous water source that we found on the plain which came after; from here we could have conveniently reached another copious water source which lies some three leagues northeast of San Ángel. From this one to Santa Gertrudis; from here we could have gone three leagues, to halt in the same arroyo having sufficient water and pastures, gain as much distance as possible during the afternoon by heading northeast, and, by following the same direction and entirely avoiding the sierra, arrive next day at El Río de Santa Teresa, three or four leagues north of San Juan Capistrano; from this river to San Diego toward the east-southeast, and from this place to the ford without any special inconvenience while evading many detours, inclines, and bad stretches.

But God doubtless disposed that we obtained no guide, either as merciful chastisement for our faults or so that we could acquire some knowledge of the peoples living hereabouts. May His most holy will be done in all things, and may His holy name be glorified.

The river's ford is very good. Here it must be a little more than a mile wide. Already here the rivers Navajó and Dolores flow joined together,[22] along with the rest which we have said in this diary enter either one or the other; and in all that we saw around here no settlement can be established along their banks, nor can one even go one good day's march downstream or

21. That is, October 15, 1776.
22. The Colorado River.

upstream along either side with the hope of their waters being of service to the people and horse herd, because, besides the terrain being bad, the river flows through a very deep gorge. Everything else adjacent to the ford consists of very tall cliffs and precipices. Eight or ten leagues to the northeast of it rises a round mountain, high but small, which the Payuchis—who begin from here onward—call Tucane, meaning Black Mountain,[23] and the only one to be seen hereabouts. The river passes very close to it.

On this eastern side at the ford itself, which we named La Purísima Concepción de la Virgen Santísima,[24] there is a small bend with good pasturage. We spent the night in it and took a bearing of its latitude by the North Star, and it is 36° 55'.[25]

BRIEF ACCOUNT OF THE PEOPLES WHOM, FROM EL VALLE DEL SEÑOR SAN JOSÉ TO EL VADO DEL RÍO GRANDE DE COSNINA, INCLUSIVE, WE SAW, HAD DEALINGS WITH, AND LEARNED ABOUT FROM REPORTS

In this land—which, although we traveled over it for a hundred long leagues[26] because of the detours we made, must be sixty Spanish leagues from north to south and forty from east to west[27]—there reside a great number of peoples, all of pleasing appearance, very engaging, and extremely timid. For this last reason, and because all whom we saw speak the Yuta language in the same manner as the westernmost Payuchis, we named all these of whom we are now speaking Yutas Cobardes.[28] The name of each comes from the area it inhabits, whereby they are distinguished according to several provinces or territories—not according to nations, as all the Yutas known heretofore compose a single nation, or let us call it kingdom, divided into five provinces which are the ones known by the common name of Yutas: the Muhuachi Yutas, the Payuchi Yutas, the Tabehuachis, and the Sabuaganas.

So, in the same way, are the Yutas Cobardes divided into Huascaris, who inhabit El Valle del Señor San José and its vicinity; Parussis, who come next toward the south and southwest and inhabit the banks and vicinity of

23. This high but small, round mountain, called Tucane by the Payuchis (Southern Paiute) and *cerro negro* by the padres, is known today as Navajo Mountain.

24. "The Immaculate Conception of the Most Holy Virgin."

25. Here their calculation is too low; they were slightly above 37°, about three miles north of the present Utah-Arizona boundary.

26. Something over 263 miles.

27. That is, 157.8 miles by 105.2 miles.

28. Apparently refers to the Southern Paiutes.

the small Río de Nuestra Señora del Pilar and are the only ones from among all these we saw who devote themselves to the cultivation of maize; the Yubuincariris, who live almost to the south of the Parussis and hereabouts are the closest to El Río Grande; the Ytimpabichis, who live on mesas and cliffs standing near El Paraje de Santa Bárbara toward the north; and the Pagampachis, who likewise inhabit bad terrain of sterile mesas and embankments, for, although they have a spacious valley and El Río Grande, as we already said, runs through it, they cannot avail themselves of the latter's waters for irrigating.

According to the Yubuincariris' account, downstream from them to the south-southwest there dwell others whom they call Payatammunis. We also learned that to the west and west-northwest of the Huascaris there lived other peoples of the same language as themselves. All the rest (who are many), who live upstream on this eastern or northern side all over the sierra which comes down from the Lagunas—and the country lying between them and the last northern rivers we crossed before they came together—are, according to the reports we got, of this same kind of Indians and belong partly to the Yutas Barbones, partly to the Huascaris, and partly to the Lagunas, depending on what proximity these are to each other for the greater similarity with which those closest speak the common language.

November 8

On the 8th we left the ford and stopping point of La Concepción and climbed the river's box canyon over a not too troublesome reclining cliff. We headed south-southeast by following a well-beaten path and traveled five leagues over sandy terrain with some gullies. We turned east for a league and halted near the last standing cliff in a chain of them extending from the river up to here,[29] naming the place San Miguel.[30] In it there was good pasturage and plenty of rainwater. Today six leagues.[31]

29. These are the magnificent cliffs of Tse Tonte. Tse Tonte is prominently visible from Wahweap Marina on Lake Powell or from Page, Arizona. En route the party had passed along the west base of Padre's Butte, thence along the east side of the outstanding "Domínguez Buttes" before crossing westward from Face Canyon drainage into that of Labyrinth Canyon by way of a relatively low and wide pass that separates Tse Tonte from the Domínguez Buttes.

30. It lies in a pocket of large boulders at the south foot of the thousand-foot-high Tse Tonte. One wonders why the padres failed to mention the spectacular setting of this campsite.

31. About 15¾ miles.

Today we found many footprints of Indians but did not see any of them. Wild sheep breed hereabouts in such abundance that the tracks look like those of great droves of tame sheep. They are larger than the domestic ones, of the same shape as theirs, but very much swifter. Today we finished the horsemeat we had with us, and so we ordered another one killed. Tonight we were very cold, more so than on the other side.

J OHN WESLEY POWELL (1834–1902), immortalized forever as a one-armed adventurer in wax museums throughout the West, led the first expeditions down the Green and Colorado Rivers, in 1869 and 1872. His *Exploration of the Colorado River and Its Canyons* (1875), excerpted here, set the standard for literary and scientific writing about the Colorado Plateau. Having just traversed the dangers of Cataract Canyon, Powell's journals here assume a tone of idleness, and it is interesting to note the nearly-poetic reverie that overcomes him as he surveys Glen Canyon.

⚜

The Exploration of Glen Canyon

JULY 29

WE ENTER A CANYON TO-DAY, with low, red walls. A short distance below its head we discover the ruins of an old building on the left wall. There is a narrow plain between the river and the wall just here, and on the brink of a rock 200 feet high stands this old house. Its walls are of stone, laid in mortar with much regularity. It was probably built three stories high; the lower story is yet almost intact; the second is much broken down, and scarcely anything is left of the third. Great quantities of flint chips are found on the rocks near by, and many arrowheads, some perfect, others broken; and fragments of pottery are strewn about in great profusion. On the face of the cliff, under the building and along down the river for 200 or 300 yards, there are many etchings. Two hours are given to the examination of these interesting ruins; then we run down fifteen miles farther, and discover another group. The principal building was situated on the summit of the hill. A part of the walls are standing, to the height of eight or ten feet, and the mortar yet remains in some places. The house was in the shape of an L, with five rooms on the ground floor,—one in the angle and two in each extension. In the space in the angle there is a deep excavation. From what we know of the people of the Province of Tusayan, who are, doubtless, of the same race as the former inhabitants of these ruins, we conclude that this was a *kiva,* or underground chamber in which their religious ceremonies were performed.

We leave these ruins and run down two or three miles and go into camp about mid-afternoon. And now I climb the wall and go out into the back country for a walk.

The sandstone through which the canyon is cut is red and homogeneous, being the same as that through which Labyrinth Canyon runs. The smooth, naked rock stretches out on either side of the river for many miles, but curiously carved mounds and cones are scattered everywhere and deep holes are worn out. Many of these pockets are filled with water. In one of these holes or wells, 20 feet deep, I find a tree growing. The excavation is so narrow that I can step from its brink to a limb on the tree and descend to the bottom of the well down a growing ladder. Many of these pockets are potholes, being found in the courses of little rills or brooks that run during the rains which occasionally fall in this region; and often a few harder rocks, which evidently assisted in their excavation, can be found in their bottoms. Others, which are shallower, are not so easily explained. Perhaps where they are found softer spots existed in the sandstone, places that yielded more readily to atmospheric degradation, the loose sands being carried away by the winds.

Just before sundown I attempt to climb a rounded eminence, from which I hope to obtain a good outlook on the surrounding country. It is formed of smooth mounds, piled one above another. Up these I climb, winding here and there to find a practicable way, until near the summit they become too steep for me to proceed. I search about a few minutes for an easier way, when I am surprised at finding a stairway, evidently cut in the rock by hands. At one place, where there is a vertical wall of 10 or 12 feet, I find an old, rickety ladder. It may be that this was a watchtower of that ancient people whose homes we have found in ruins. On many of the tributaries of the Colorado, I have heretofore examined their deserted dwellings. Those that show evidences of being built during the latter part of their occupation of the country are usually placed on the most inaccessible cliffs. Sometimes the mouths of caves have been walled across, and there are many other evidences to show their anxiety to secure defensible positions. Probably the nomadic tribes were sweeping down upon them and they resorted to these cliffs and canyons for safety. It is not unreasonable to suppose that this orange mound was used as a watchtower. Here I stand, where these now lost people stood centuries ago, and look over this strange country, gazing off to great mountains in the northwest which are slowly disappearing under cover of the night; and then I return to camp. It is no easy task to find my way down the wall in the darkness, and I clamber about until it is nearly midnight when camp is reached.

July 30

We make good progress to-day, as the water, though smooth, is swift. Sometimes the canyon walls are vertical to the top; sometimes they are vertical below and have a mound-covered slope above; in other places the slope, with its mounds, comes down to the water's edge.

Still proceeding on our way, we find that the orange sandstone is cut in two by a group of firm, calcareous strata, and the lower bed is underlaid by soft, gypsiferous shales. Sometimes the upper homogeneous bed is a smooth, vertical wall, but usually it is carved with mounds, with gently meandering valley lines. The lower bed, yielding to gravity, as the softer shales below work out into the river, breaks into angular surfaces, often having a columnar appearance. One could almost imagine that the walls had been carved with a purpose, to represent giant architectural forms. In the deep recesses of the walls we find springs, with mosses and ferns on the moistened sandstone.

July 31

We have a cool, pleasant ride to-day through this part of the canyon. The walls are steadily increasing in altitude, the curves are gentle, and often the river sweeps by an arc of vertical wall, smooth and unbroken; and then by a curve that is variegated by royal arches, mossy alcoves, deep, beautiful glens, and painted grottoes. Soon after dinner we discover the mouth of the San Juan, where we camp. The remainder of the afternoon is given to hunting some way by which we can climb out of the canyon; but it ends in failure.

August 1

We drop down two miles this morning and go into camp again. There is a low, willow-covered strip of land along the walls on the east. Across this we walk, to explore an alcove which we see from the river. On entering, we find a little grove of box-elder and cottonwood trees, and turning to the right, we find ourselves in a vast chamber, carved out of the rock. At the upper end there is a clear, deep pool of water, bordered with verdure. Standing by the side of this, we can see the grove at the entrance. The chamber is more than 200 feet high, 500 feet long, and 200 feet wide. Through the ceiling, and on through the rocks for a thousand feet above, there is a narrow, winding skylight; and this is all carved out by a little stream which runs only during the few showers that fall now and then in this arid country. The waters from the bare rocks back of the canyon, gathering rapidly into a small channel have eroded a deep side canyon, through which they run until they fall into the farther end of this chamber. The rock at the ceiling is hard, the rock below, very soft and friable; and having cut through the upper and harder portion down into the lower and softer, the stream has washed out these friable sandstones; and thus the chamber has been excavated.

Here we bring our camp. When "Old Shady" sings us a song at night, we are pleased to find that this hollow in the rock is filled with sweet sounds. It was doubtless made for an academy of music by its storm-born architect; so we name it Music Temple.

AUGUST 2

We still keep our camp in Music Temple today. I wish to obtain a view of the adjacent country, if possible; so, early in the morning the men take me across the river, and I pass along by the foot of the cliff half a mile upstream and then climb, first up broken edges, then 200 or 300 yards up a smooth, sloping rock, and then pass out on a narrow ridge. Still, I find I have not attained an altitude from which I can overlook the region outside of the canyon; and so I descend into a little gulch and climb again to a higher ridge, all the way along naked sandstone, and at last I reach a point of commanding view. I can look several miles up the San Juan, and a long distance up the Colorado; and away to the northwest I can see the Henry Mountains; to the northeast, the Sierra La Sal; to the southeast, unknown mountains; and to the southwest, the meandering of the canyon. Then I return to the bank of the river. We sleep again in Music Temple.

AUGUST 3

Start early this morning. The features of this canyon are greatly diversified. Still vertical walls at times. These are usually found to stand above great curves. The river, sweeping around these bends, undermines the cliffs in places. Sometimes the rocks are overhanging; in other curves, curious, narrow glens are found. Through these we climb, by a rough stairway, perhaps several hundred feet, to where a spring bursts out from under an overhanging cliff, and where cottonwoods and willows stand, while along the curves of the brooklet oaks grow, and other rich vegetation is seen, in marked contrast to the general appearance of naked rock. We call these Oak Glens.

Other wonderful features are the many side canyons or gorges that we pass. Sometimes we stop to explore these for a short distance. In some places their walls are much nearer each other above than below, so that they look somewhat like caves or chambers in the rocks. Usually, in going up such a gorge, we find beautiful vegetation; but our way is often cut off by deep basins, or "potholes," as they are called.

On the walls, and back many miles into the country, numbers of monument-shaped buttes are observed. So we have a curious *ensemble* of wonderful features—carved walls, royal arches, glens, alcove gulches, mounds, and monuments. From which of these features shall we select a name? We decide to call it Glen Canyon.

Past these towering monuments, past these mounded billows of orange sandstone, past these oak-set glens, past these fern-decked alcoves, past these mural curves, we glide hour after hour, stopping now and then, as our attention is arrested by some new wonder, until we reach a point which is historic.

In the year 1776, Father Escalante, a Spanish priest, made an expedition from Santa Fé to the northwest, crossing the Grand and Green, and then passing down along the Wasatch Mountains and the southern plateaus until he reached the Rio Virgen. His intention was to cross to the Mission of Monterey; but, from information received from the Indians, he decided that the route was impracticable. Not wishing to return to Santa Fé over the circuitous route by which he had just traveled, he attempted to go by one more direct, which led him across the Colorado at a point known as El Vado de los Padres. From the description which we have read, we are enabled to determine the place. A little stream comes down through a very narrow side canyon from the west. It was down this that he came, and our boats are lying at the point where the ford crosses. A well-beaten Indian trail is seen here yet. Between the cliff and the river there is a little meadow. The ashes of many camp fires are seen, and the bones of numbers of cattle are bleaching on the grass. For several years the Navajos have raided on the Mormons that dwell in the valleys to the west, and they doubtless cross frequently at this ford with their stolen cattle.

AUGUST 4

To-day the walls grow higher and the canyon much narrower. Monuments are still seen on either side; beautiful glens and alcoves and gorges and side canyons are yet found. After dinner we find the river making a sudden turn to the northwest and the whole character of the canyon changed. The walls are many hundreds of feet higher, and the rocks are chiefly variegated shales of beautiful colors—creamy orange above, then bright vermilion, and below, purple and chocolate beds, with green and yellow sands. We run four miles through this, in a direction a little to the west of north, wheel again to the west, and pass into a portion of the canyon where the characteristics are more like those above the bend. At night we stop at the mouth of a creek coming in from the right, and suppose it to be the Paria, which was described to me last year by a Mormon missionary. Here the canyon terminates abruptly in a line of cliffs, which stretches from either side across the river.

FREDERICK SAMUEL DELLENBAUGH (1853–1935) was seventeen years old when he began serving as expedition artist and assistant topographer on John Wesley Powell's second journey down the Colorado River (1871–1873). An accomplished artist, he later studied painting in France before settling in New York City to write and lecture about the American West. Later in life, he served as librarian to the National Geographic Society and founded the Explorer's Club. His memoir of the second Powell Expedition, *A Canyon Voyage* (1908), remains a classic adventure story, and is excerpted here.

Into Glen Canyon

THE NEXT MORNING, the 2d of October, at eight o'clock, we continued our voyage, now entering a new canyon, then called Mound, but it was afterwards consolidated with the portion below called Monument, and together they now stand as Glen Canyon. In about three and one half miles we ran several sharp little rapids, but they were not of much consequence, and we stopped to examine a house ruin we saw standing up boldly on a cliff on the left. It could be seen for a long distance in both directions, and correspondingly its inmates in the old days could see every approach. Doubtless the trail we had seen on the right had its exit on the other side near it. The walls, neatly built of thin sandstone slabs, still stood about fifteen feet high and fifteen inches thick. The dimensions on the ground were 12 × 22 feet outside. It had been of two or three stories, and exhibited considerable skill on the part of the builders, the corners being plumb and square. Under the brink of the cliff was a sort of gallery formed by the erosion of a soft shale between heavy sandstone beds, forming a floor and roof about eight or ten feet wide, separated by six or seven feet in vertical height. A wall had been carried along the outer edge, and the space thus made was divided by cross walls into a number of rooms. Potsherds and arrow-heads, mostly broken ones, were strewn everywhere. There were also numerous picture-writings, of which I made copies.

As we pulled on and on the Major [John Wesley Powell] frequently recited selections from the poets, and one that he seemed to like very much, and said sometimes half in reverie, was Longfellow's:

> "Often I think of the beautiful town
>   That is seated by the sea;
> Often in thought go up and down

The pleasant streets of that dear old town,
    And my youth comes back to me.
And a verse of a Lapland song
    Is haunting my memory still:
    'A boy's will is the wind's will,
And the thoughts of youth are long, long thoughts.' "

He would repeat several times, with much feeling:

"A boy's will is the wind's will,
And the thoughts of youth are long, long thoughts."

Another thing he enjoyed repeating was Whittier's *Skipper Ireson's Ride:*

"Old Floyd Ireson, for his hard heart,
Tarred and feathered and carried in a cart
By the women of Marblehead!"

Towards evening we came to another Shinumo [Anasazi] ruin, where we made camp, having run altogether sixteen miles, with ten rapids, all small, between walls of red, homogeneous sandstone, averaging about one thousand feet in height. The river, some three hundred and fifty feet wide, was low, causing many shoals, which formed the small rapids. We often had to wade alongside to lighten the boats, but otherwise these places were easy. A trifle more water would have done away with them, or at least would have enabled us to ignore them completely. The house ruin at our camp was very old and broken down and had dimensions of about 20 x 30 feet. Prof. [Almon Harris Thompson, Powell's brother-in-law and chief topographer of the second expedition] climbed out to a point 1215 feet above the river, where he saw plainly the Unknown Mountains, Navajo Mountain, and a wide sweep of country formed largely of barren sandstone. Steward felt considerably under the weather and remained as quiet as possible.

In the morning we were quickly on the water, pushing along under conditions similar to those of the previous day, making twenty-seven miles and passing eleven very small rapids, with a river four hundred feet wide and the same walls of homogeneous red sandstone about one thousand feet high. The cliffs in the bends were often slightly overhanging, that is, the brink was outside of a perpendicular line, but the opposite side would then generally be very much cut down, usually to irregular, rounded slopes of smooth rock. The vertical portions were unbroken by cracks or crevices or ledges, being extensive flat surfaces, beautifully stained by iron, till one could imagine all manner of tapestry effects. Along the river there were large patches of alluvial soil which might easily be irrigated, though it is probable that at certain periods they would be rapidly cut to pieces by high water.

Prof. again climbed out at our noon camp, and saw little but naked orange sandstone in rounded hills, except the usual mountains. In the barren sandstone he found many pockets or pot-holes, a feature of this formation, often thirty or forty feet deep, and frequently containing water. Wherever we climbed out in this region we saw in the depressions flat beds of sand, surrounded by hundreds of small round balls of stone an inch or so in diameter, like marbles—concretions and hard fragments which had been driven round and round by the winds till they were quite true spheres.

The next day, October 4th, we ran into a stratum of sandstone shale, which at this low stage of water for about five miles gave us some trouble. Ledge after ledge stretched across the swift river, which at the same time spread to at least six hundred feet, sometimes one thousand. We were obliged to walk in the water alongside for great distances to lighten the boats and ease them over the ridges. Occasionally the rock bottom was as smooth as a ballroom floor; again it would be carved in the direction of the current into thousands of narrow, sharp, polished ridges, from three to twelve inches apart, upon which the boats pounded badly in spite of all exertions to prevent it. The water was alternately shallow and ten feet deep, giving us all we could do to protect the boats and at the same time avoid sudden duckings in deep water. With all our care the *Nell* got a bad knock, and leaked so fast that one man continually bailing could barely keep the water out. We repaired her at dinner-time, and, the shales running up above the river, we escaped further annoyance from this cause. Even with this interference our progress was fairly good, and by camping-time we had made twenty-one miles.

We had a rapid shallow river again the following day, October 5th, but the water was not so widely spread out and there were fewer delays. The walls were of orange sandstone, strangely cut up by narrow side canyons some not more than twenty feet wide and twisting back for a quarter of a mile where they expanded into huge amphitheatres, domed and cave-like. Alcoves filled with trees and shrubs also opened from the river, and numerous springs were noted along the cliffs.

Twelve miles below our camp we passed a stream coming in on the left through a canyon about one thousand feet deep, similar to that of the Colorado. This was the San Juan, now shallow and some eight rods [132 feet] wide. We did not stop till noon when we were two miles below it near one of the amphitheatres or grottoes to which the first party had given the name of "Music Temple." The entrance was by a narrow gorge which after some distance widened at the bottom to about five hundred feet in diameter leaving the upper walls arching over till they formed a dome-shaped cavern about two hundred feet high with a narrow belt of sky visible above. In the farther end was a pool of clear water, while five or six green cottonwoods and some bushes marked the point of expansion. One side was covered with bright ferns, mosses, and honeysuckle. Every whisper or cough resounded. This was only one of a hundred such places but we had no time to examine them. On a smooth space of rock we found carved by themselves the names of Seneca Howland, O. G. Howland, and William Dunn, the three men of the first party who were killed by the Shewits [Shivwits] in 1869.[1] Prof. climbed up eight hundred feet and had a fine view of Navajo Mountain which was now very near. We then chiefly called it Mount Seneca Howland, applied by the Major in memory of that unfortunate person but later, the peak already having to some extent been known as Navajo Mountain, that name was finally adopted. No one had ever been to it, so far as we knew, and the Major was desirous of reaching the summit.

Leaving the Music Temple, which seemed to us a sort of mausoleum to the three men who had marked it with their names, we soon arrived at a pretty rapid with a clear chute. It was not large but it was the only real one we had seen in this canyon and we dashed through it with pleasure. Just below we halted to look admiringly up at Navajo Mountain which now loomed beside us on the left to an altitude of 10,416 feet above sea level or more than 7100 feet above our position, as was later determined. The Major contemplated stopping long enough for a climb to the top but on appealing to Andy for information as to the state of the supplies he found we were near the last crust and he decided that we had better pull on as steadily as possible towards El Vado [Crossing of the Fathers]. We ran down a considerable distance

1. The three men were killed after leaving the first Powell expedition on August 28th, 1869—two days before the expedition came to an end. Exhausted, hungry, and faced with a series of seemingly impassable rapids at the foot of the Grand Canyon, Dunn and the Howland brothers decided to abandon Powell and search for sanctuary from nearby Mormon settlements. A historical controversy continues as to whether the men were killed by Shivwits Indians or by Mormons who may have mistaken the men for federal spies.—Ed.

through some shallows and camped on the left having accomplished about twenty miles in the day towards our goal. Here the remaining food was divided into two portions, one for supper, the other for breakfast in the morning. Though we were running so close to the starvation line we felt no great concern about it. We always had confidence in our ability somehow to get through with success. Andy [Hattan], particularly, never failed in his optimism. Generally he took no interest in the nature of a rapid, lying half asleep while the others examined the place, and entirely willing to run anything or make a portage or even swim; he cared not. "Nothing ever happens to any outfit I belong to," he would declare shifting to an easier position, "Let her go!" and now so far as Andy's attitude was concerned we might have possessed unlimited rations. Jack [Hillers] lightened the situation yet more with his jolly songs and humorous expressions and no one viewing that camp would have thought the ten men had before them a possibility of several days without food, except what they might kill in the barren country, and perhaps a walk from El Vado over an unknown trail about one hundred miles out to Kanab. In the morning, Friday, October 6th, we got away as quickly as we could and pulled down the river hoping that El Vado was not far ahead and feeling somewhat as Escalante must have felt a century before when he was trying to find it. He had the advantage of having horses which could be eaten from time to time. Of course we knew from the position of the San Juan and of Navajo Mountain, that we could reach El Vado in at most two days, but the question was, "would we find anyone there with rations?" The Major apparently was unconcerned. . . .

As we rowed along the Major sang softly another of his favourites:

> "Flow gently, sweet Afton! among thy green braes,
> Flow gently, I'll sing thee a song in thy praise;
> My Mary's asleep by thy murmuring stream—
> Flow gently, sweet Afton, disturb not her dream."

The almost vertical walls ran from two hundred to one thousand feet in height, cut by many very narrow side canyons opening into large glens or alcoves. On and on we steadily pulled till noon, making 13 1/2 miles when we stopped on the right on a sandstone ledge against a high cliff. Andy had a few scraps left, among them a bit of bacon which Jack enterprisingly used for baiting a hook and soon drew out several small fish, so that after all we had quite a dinner. The walls became more broken as we went on apparently with numerous opportunities for entrance from the back country, though the sandstone even where not very steep was so smooth that descent over it would be difficult. We had gone about three miles after dinner when we saw a burned place in the brush on the right where there was quite a large piece of bottom land. We thought this might be some signal for us but we found there only the tracks of two men and horses all well shod proving that they were not natives. About three miles farther down we caught a glimpse of a stick with a white rag dangling from it stuck out from the right bank, and at the same moment heard a shot. On landing and mounting the bank we found Captain Pardyn Dodds and two prospectors, George Riley and John Bonnemort, encamped beside a large pile of rations. Dodds was one of the men with Old Jacob who had tried desperately to reach the mouth of the Dirty Devil with our supplies. He thought he had arrived at a point where he could see it and went back to inform Jacob when they received an order from the Major to come to this place, El Vado de los Padres, by September 25th, and here he was. Jacob had come with him but had gone on to Fort Defiance, the Navajo Agency, to settle some Indian business, leaving him to guard the rations. Having left Kanab early in September they had no late news. They had become discouraged by our nonappearance and concluded that we would never be heard from again. . . . [The crew spends the next day packaging maps, fossils, letters, etc. to be shipped off to Kanab, Utah; on the 10th of October, Powell and Jack Hiller leave with the pack train for Kanab, with plans to rendezvous with the remaining members 35 miles downstream, at the mouth of the Paria River.—Ed.]

Before leaving this point Prof. wanted some observations from the heights, and he and Cap. [E. O. Beaman, the expedition's photographer] tried to climb the near-by cliffs, but failed. They then took a hammer and chisel, and by cutting "holds" in the sandstone after the manner of the old Shinumos, they got up 850 feet and secured the bearings Prof. desired. The following day [October 12th] they went out on the trail toward Kanab five miles, trying to find another point of exit to the summit, but did not succeed. While they were gone we heard a sudden shout, and saw an Indian standing on the rocks not far away. We beckoned for him to come, and thereupon he fell back to another, and together they approached. We saw by their dress, so different from the Ute (red turbans, loose unbleached cotton shirts, native woven sashes at the waist, wide unbleached cotton trousers reaching to a little below the knee and there slashed up on the outer side for seven or eight inches, bright woven garters twisted around their red buckskin leggins below the knee, and red moccasins with turned up soles and silver buttons), that they were Navajos. They indicated that they were father and son, the father announcing himself in a lordly way as "Agua Grande." He was over six feet tall and apparently sixty or seventy years old. The son was a fine young lad of about fifteen. Their bearing was cordial, yet proud and dignified. They had not long been with us when Prof. came in, and during the next hour seven more Navajos arrived, all dressed very much as the first ones were. They expressed great friendliness by embracing us after their custom and delivering long speeches, of which we understood not a word. One had a short black mustache which came straight out sidewise and then turned at right angles down past the corners of his mouth. I never had heard of an Indian with a mustache before. They had no visible firearms, being armed with strong bows and cougar-skin quivers full of iron-headed arrows. Old Agua Grande became much interested in our sick man [John F. Steward, the expedition geologist, who had been ill for a number of days], and made signs by placing two spread fingers of one hand inverted upon one finger held horizontally of the other hand, and moving them north-westerly to indicate that he ought to ride out to the Mormon settlement, whither they were bound, and that they would take him along. As the chief had exhibited a document, signed by the agent at Fort Defiance, to the effect that he and his band were peaceable and going on a trading expedition to the Mormon settlements, we felt certain they would take good care of the invalid, but Steward said he preferred to remain with us.

We now had no further work for this immediate locality, and concluded to run down a mile or so to separate ourselves from the Navajos, one having disclosed a tendency to surreptitiously appropriate small articles belonging to us. A bed was made on the middle deck of one of the boats for Steward, and when all was ready we carried him down to it. The Navajos ranged themselves along the bank to see us off, and Clem [Walter Clement Powell, Powell's young cousin], with his customary urbanity, went down the line all smiles, shaking each one cordially by the hand, and requesting him to "Give my love to all the folks at home," and "Remember me, please, to Eliza Jane," and similar expressions. The Navajos did not understand the words, but being themselves great jokers they saw that it was fun, and they all laughed, making remarks which doubtless were of the same kind. Just below was El Vado de los Padres by which these Navajos had now come across. It was also sometimes called the Ute Ford. The necessary route was indicated by a line of small piles of stones showing above water. It was not an easy crossing, feasible only at low water, and quite impossible for waggons, even had there been a road to it. A shoal was followed up the middle of the river half a mile with deep channels cutting through it, reached from the south over a steep slope of bare sandstone and from the north through a very narrow, small canyon, not over ten feet wide. Escalante in 1776, after the failure of his attempt to reach California, had great difficulty in finding the place, which for centuries has been known to all the tribes of the region. About three miles below our last camp we landed on the left on a very pretty piece of bottom land, inaccessible except by river, being bounded behind by a high, vertical, unscalable wall. Here we made Camp 80, with plenty of food, water, and wood, and all were comfortable by a fine fire; all but Steward, who, feeling very sick, was lying on the bed we had prepared for him. He had another bad night, but after this his condition seemed gradually to improve.

Prof.'s favourite quotation now was Charles Fenno Hoffman's poem:

"We were not many—we who stood
    Before the iron sleet that day;
Yet many a gallant spirit would
Give half his years if but he could
    Have been with us at Monterey."

In the morning he went with Jones across the river and climbed out while the rest of us did nothing but lie around camp doing what was possible to make Steward comfortable. It was Sunday as well and whenever practicable we rested the whole or part of that day. Monday we started late and ran only a short distance before dinner which we ate on the right. Steward still was unable to sit up and he was carried on the middle deck of the Nell where he had a rope to cling to so that he should not roll off into the water when the boat lurched. Toward evening we camped at the head of a small rapid near a fine little stream coming in from the left which we named Navajo Creek. The river was about four hundred feet wide with walls on each side of four hundred feet in height. The next morning Prof., Cap. and I climbed out for bearings reaching an altitude a mile or so back from the river of 875 feet. Everywhere we discovered broken pottery, fragments of arrow-heads, and other evidences of former Shinumo occupancy. Even granting only a few persons at each possible locality, the canyons of the Colorado and Green must have been the former home of a rather large population. In the afternoon we ran the little rapid and kept on for about six miles making twenty in all from El Vado, when we camped on a heavy talus on the left. The following morning, October 18th, we had not gone more than a mile when we came to a singular freak of erosion, a lone sandstone pinnacle on the right, three hundred or four hundred feet high, the river running on one side and a beautiful creek eight feet wide on the other. We named these Sentinel Rock and Sentinel Creek and camped there for Beaman to get some photographs. Prof. and I went up the creek and tried to climb out for observations, but though we made three separate attempts we had to give it up. Steward grew so much better that he was able to walk a little, but now Jones began to feel more pain in his injured leg. On Thursday, the 19th, we made nearly seven miles between walls about eight hundred feet high and one quarter of a mile apart, so nearly vertical that we could not get out.

The next day we ran six miles more with walls one thousand feet high, camping at a place where there was a wide bottom with many signs of old native camps, probably Navajo. In the morning Prof., Cap., and I climbed a steep slope of bright orange sand a little below our camp, a rather hard task as the sand was loose, causing us to slip backward at every step. After twelve hundred or fifteen hundred feet of this kind of climbing we reached the base of three rocky peaks several hundred feet higher. We had considerable difficulty in surmounting one of these, being forced around to the opposite side, where there was a sheer descent from our position of some fifteen hundred feet, with sharp black rocks at the bottom where anyone slipping would fall. There were some narrow transverse crevices in the rock by means of which we got up. One man, having been pushed aloft from the solid ledge by the two below, would lie back against the slope, brace himself with one heel in a transverse fissure, and lower the free foot as a handhold for the others to mount by. The next trouble was a crevice wide enough for us to pass through to the top, but holding exactly midway a large rock lodged in such a manner that we could not crawl under and yet seeming in danger of rolling down if we went over it. It was precarious not only for the man ahead who tried to pass but for those below waiting for results, but it was more firmly wedged than it appeared to be and each one in turn climbed over it. Emerging from this crack we were on the summit 2190 feet above the river and 5360 above the sea, with standing room no more than six or eight feet square. The view was superb. The peaks formed the northern end of a long line of cliffs running back to the south at the end of Glen Canyon, and we looked out across a wonderful region, part of that on the south being the "Painted Desert," so called by Ives. Mountains solid and solitary rose up here and there and line upon line of strangely coloured cliffs broke across the wide area, while from our feet stretching off to the south-west like a great dark dragon extending miles into the blue was the deep gorge of Marble Canyon, its tributary chasms appearing like mighty sprawling legs. Far away west were the San Francisco Mountains, and the Kaibab [Plateau], while behind we saw Navajo Mountain and others.

This peak, or cluster of peaks, of course had never been named, had never been climbed before, but they soon named themselves. For amuse-ment I tried to shoot into the river with Cap.'s 44 Remington revolver. As I pulled the trigger the noise was absolutely staggering. The violent report was followed by dead silence. While we were remarking the intensity of the crash, from far away on some distant cliffs northward the sound waves were hurled back to us with a rattle like that of musketry. We tried again with the same result, the interval between the great roar and the echo being twenty-four seconds by the watch. We could call the place nothing but Echo Peaks, and since then the name has been applied also to the line of cliffs breaking to the south. Our descent was easy and we reached camp without any incident except the loss of my sheath knife.

Nobody did anything the next day, for it was Sunday, so when Monday morning came we were eager to be off for the mouth of the Paria, which we had seen from the top of Echo Peaks. Two or three miles down we reached it; a small river coming through a great canyon on the right. The cliffs of Glen Canyon broke back south-westerly and south-easterly in a V form with the point at the foot of Glen Canyon, leaving a wide platform of different rock rising gently from under them and mounting steadily toward the south. Into the middle of this the river immediately slashed a narrow gorge very much as a staircase might be cut through a floor, beginning the next canyon of the series, called Marble, through which we would not descend till the following year. We went into camp on the left bank of the Paria and the right of the Colorado, Camp 86, in the tall willows. A rough scow lay there, which the Major had built the year before when on his way from Kanab to the Moki Towns, for there is no ford.

We were to wait here for our pack-train which the Major, on arriving at Kanab, was to start back with rations and some extra horses. Our altitude was 3115 feet, showing a total descent for the season of 2952 feet, 930 feet from Gunnison Crossing. Our work on the water for the present was now over; we would operate with mule and pack instead of with boats, and return next year in warmer weather to finish the river job.

Z ANE GREY (1872–1939) largely invented the western as a new literary genre in novels such as *Riders of the Purple Sage* and *The Spirit of the Border*. The prolific author of more than eighty books, Grey first visited the Glen Canyon area in the spring of 1913 when he traveled to Rainbow Bridge with John Wetherill. Although this account of his journey, collected in his nonfiction *Tales of Lonely Trails* in 1922, mistakes Glen Canyon for the Grand Canyon, his sense of unfathomable awe upon seeing Rainbow Bridge set the tone for writing about the natural span for generations to come; it is repeated almost verbatim in Edward Abbey's *Desert Solitaire*.

Nonnezoshe

JOHN WETHERILL, ONE OF THE FAMOUS Wetherill brothers and trader at Kayenta, Arizona, is the man who discovered Nonnezoshe, which is probably the most beautiful and wonderful natural phenomenon in the world. Wetherill owes the credit to his wife, who, through her influence with the Indians finally after years succeeded in getting the secret of the great bridge.

After three trips to Marsh Pass and Kayenta with my old guide, Al Doyle of Flagstaff, I finally succeeded in getting Wetherill to take me in to Nonnezoshe. This was in the spring of 1913 and my party was the second one, not scientific, to make the trip. Later this same year Wetherill took in the Roosevelt party and after that the Kolb brothers. It is a safe thing to say that this trip is one of the most beautiful in the West. It is a hard one and not for everybody. There is no guide except Wetherill, who knows how to get there. And after Doyle and I came out we admitted that we would not care to try to return over our back trail. We doubted if we could find the way. This is the only place I have ever visited which I am not sure I could find again alone.

My trip to Nonnezoshe gave me the opportunity to see also Monument Valley, and the mysterious and labyrinthine Canyon Segi with its great prehistoric cliff-dwellings.

The desert beyond Kayenta spread out impressively, bare red flats and plains of sage leading to the rugged vividly-colored and wind-sculptored sandstone heights typical of the Painted Desert of Arizona. Laguna Creek, at that season, became flooded after every thunderstorm; and it was a treacherous red-mired quicksand where I convinced myself we would have stuck forever had it not been for Wetherill's Navajos.

We rode all day, for the most part closed in by ridges and bluffs, so that no extended view was possible. It was hot, too, and the sand blew and the dust rose. Travel in northern Arizona is never easy, and this grew harder and steeper. There was one long slope of heavy sand that I made sure would prove too much for Wetherill's pack mules. But they surmounted it apparently less breathless than I was. Toward sunset a storm gathered ahead of us to the north with a promise of cooling and sultry air.

At length we turned into a long canyon with straight rugged red walls, and a sandy floor with quite a perceptible ascent. It appeared endless. Far ahead I could see the black storm-clouds; and by and bye began to hear the rumble of thunder. Darkness had overtaken us by the time we had reached the head of this canyon; and my first sight of Monument Valley came with a dazzling flash of lightning. It revealed a vast valley, a strange world of colossal shafts and buttes of rock, magnificently sculptored, standing isolated and aloof, dark, weird, lonely. When the sheet lightning flared across the sky showing the monuments silhouetted black against that strange horizon the effect was marvelously beautiful. I watched until the storm died away.

Dawn, with the desert sunrise, changed Monument Valley, bereft it of its night gloom and weird shadow, and showed it in another aspect of beauty. It was hard for me to realize that those monuments were not the works of man. The great valley must once have been a plateau of red rock from which the softer strata had eroded, leaving the gentle league-long slopes marked here and there by upstanding pillars and columns of singular shape and beauty. I rode down the sweet-scented sageslopes under the shadow of the lofty Mittens, and around and across the valley, and back again to the height of land. And when I had completed the ride a story had woven itself into my mind; and the spot where I stood was to be the place where Lin Slone taught Lucy Bostil to ride the great stallion Wildfire.

Two days' ride took us across country to the Segi. With this wonderful canyon I was familiar, that is, as familiar as several visits could make a man with such a bewildering place. In fact I had named it Deception Pass. The Segi had innumerable branches, all more or less the same size, and sometimes it was difficult to tell the main canyon from one of its tributaries. The walls were rugged and crumbling, of a red or yellow hue, upward of a thousand feet in height, and indented by spruce-sided notches.

There were a number of ruined cliff-dwellings, the most accessible of which was Keet Seel. I could imagine no more picturesque spot. A huge windworn cavern with a vast slanted stained wall held upon a projecting ledge or shelf the long line of cliff-dwellings. These silent little stone houses with their vacant black eye-like windows had strange power to make me ponder, and then dream.

Next day, upon resuming our journey, it pleased me to try to find the trail to Betatakin, the most noted, and surely the most wonderful and beautiful ruin in all the West. In many places there was no trail at all, and I encountered difficulties, but in the end without much loss of time I entered the narrow rugged entrance of the canyon I had named Surprise Valley. Sight of the great dark cave thrilled me as I thought it might have thrilled Bess and Venters, who had lived for me their imagined lives of loneliness here in this wild spot. With the sight of those lofty walls and the scent of the dry sweet sage there rushed over me a strange feeling that "Riders of the Purple Sage" was true. My dream people of romance had really lived there once upon a time. I climbed high upon the huge stones, and along the smooth red walls where Fay Larkin once had glided with swift sure steps, and I entered the musty cliff-dwellings, and called out to hear the weird and sonorous echoes, and I wandered through the thickets and upon the grassy spruce-shaded benches, never for a moment free of the story I had conceived there. Something of awe and sadness abided with me. I could not enter into the merry pranks and investigations of my party. Surprise Valley seemed a part of my past, my dreams, my very self. I left it, haunted by its loneliness and silence and beauty, by the story it had given me.

That night we camped at Bubbling Spring, which once had been a geyser of considerable power. Wetherill told a story of an old Navajo who had lived there. For a long time, according to the Indian tale, the old chief resided there without complaining of this geyser that was wont to inundate his fields. But one season the unreliable waterspout made great and persistent endeavor to drown him and his people and horses. Whereupon the old Navajo took his gun and shot repeatedly at the geyser, and thundered aloud his anger to the Great Spirit. The geyser ebbed away, and from that day never burst forth again.

Somewhere under the great bulge of Navajo Mountain I calculated that we were coming to the edge of the plateau. The white bobbing pack-horses disappeared and then our extra mustangs. It is no unusual thing for a man to use three mounts on this trip. Then two of our Indians disappeared. But Wetherill waited for us and so did Nas ta Bega, the Piute who first took Wetherill down into Nonnezoshe Boco. As I came up I thought we had indeed reached the end of the world.

"It's down in there," said Wetherill, with a laugh.

Nas ta Bega made a slow sweeping gesture. There is always something so significant and impressive about an Indian when he points anywhere. It is as if he says, "There, way beyond, over the ranges, is a place I know, and it is far." The fact was that I looked at the Piute's dark, inscrutable face before I looked out into the void.

My gaze then seemed impelled and held by things afar, a vast yellow and purple corrugated world of distance, apparently now on a level with my eyes. I was drawn by the beauty and grandeur of that scene; and then I was transfixed, almost by fear, by the realization that I dared to venture down into this wild and upflung fastness. I kept looking afar, sweeping the three-quarter circle of horizon till my judgment of distance was confounded and my sense of proportion dwarfed one moment and magnified the next.

Wetherill was pointing and explaining, but I had not grasped all he said.

"You can see two hundred miles into Utah," he went on. "That bright rough surface, like a washboard, is wind-worn rock. Those little lines of cleavage are canyons. There are a thousand canyons down there, and only a few have we been in. That long purple ragged line is the Grand Canyon of the Colorado [*sic*]. And there, that blue fork in the red, that's where the San Juan comes in. And there's Escalante Canyon."

I had to adopt the Indian's method of studying unlimited spaces in the desert—to look with slow contracted eyes from near to far.

The pack-train and the drivers had begun to zigzag down a long slope, bare of rock, with scant strips of green, and here and there a cedar. Half a mile down, the slope merged in what seemed a green level. But I knew it was not level. This level was a rolling plain, growing darker green, with lines of ravines and thin, undefined spaces that might be mirage. Miles and miles it swept and rolled and heaved, to lose its waves in apparent darker level. Round red rocks stood isolated. They resembled huge grazing cattle. But as I gazed these rocks were strangely magnified. They grew and grew into mounds, castles, domes, crags, great red wind-carved buttes. One by one they drew my gaze to the wall of upflung rock. I seemed to see a thousand domes of a thousand shapes and colors, and among them a thousand blue clefts, each of which was a canyon.

Beyond this wide area of curved lines rose another wall, dwarfing the lower; dark red, horizon-long, magnificent in frowning boldness, and because of its limitless deceiving surfaces incomprehensible to the gaze of man. Away to the eastward began a winding ragged blue line, looping back upon itself, and then winding away again, growing wider and bluer. This line was

San Juan Canyon. I followed that blue line all its length, a hundred miles, down toward the west where it joined a dark purple shadowy cleft. And this was the Grand Canyon of the Colorado. My eye swept along with that winding mark, farther and farther to the west, until the cleft, growing larger and closer, revealed itself as a wild and winding canyon. Still farther westward it split a vast plateau of red peaks and yellow mesas. Here the canyon was full of purple smoke. It turned, it closed, it gaped, it lost itself and showed again in that chaos of a million cliffs. And then it faded, a mere purple line, into deceiving distance.

I imagined there was no scene in all the world to equal this. The tranquillity of lesser spaces was here not manifest. This happened to be a place where so much of the desert could be seen and the effect was stupendous. Sound, movement, life seemed to have no fitness here. Ruin was there and desolation and decay. The meaning of the ages was flung at me. A man became nothing. But when I gazed across that sublime and majestic wilderness, in which the Grand Canyon was only a dim line, I strangely lost my terror and something came to me across the shining spaces.

Then Nas ta Bega and Wetherill began the descent of the slope, and the rest of us followed. No sign of a trail showed where the base of the slope rolled out to meet the green plain. There was a level bench a mile wide, then a ravine, and then an ascent, and after that, rounded ridge and ravine, one after the other, like huge swells of a monstrous sea. Indian paint brush vied in its scarlet hue with the deep magenta of cactus. There was no sage. Soap weed and meager grass and a bunch of cactus here and there lent the green to that barren, and it was green only at a distance.

Nas ta Bega kept on at a steady gait. The sun climbed. The wind rose and whipped dust from under the mustangs. There is seldom much talk on a ride of this nature. It is hard work and everybody for himself. Besides, it is enough just to see; and that country is conducive to silence. I looked back often, and the farther out on the plain we rode the higher loomed the plateau we had descended; and as I faced ahead again, the lower sank the red-domed and castled horizon to the fore.

It was a wild place we were approaching. I saw piñon patches under the circled walls. I ceased to feel the dry wind in my face. We were already in the lee of a wall. I saw the rock squirrels scampering to their holes. Then the Indians disappeared between two rounded corners of cliff.

I rode round the corner into a widening space thick with cedars. It ended in a bare slope of smooth rock. Here we dismounted to begin the ascent. It was smooth and hard, though not slippery. There was not a crack. I did not see a broken piece of stone. Nas ta Bega and Wetherill climbed straight up for a while and then wound round a swell, to turn this way and that, always going up. I began to see similar mounds of rock all around me, of every shape that could be called a curve. There were yellow domes far above and small red domes far below. Ridges ran from one hill of rock to another. There were no abrupt breaks, but holes and pits and caves were everywhere, and occasionally deep down, an amphitheater green with cedar and piñon. We found no vestige of trail on those bare slopes.

Our guides led to the top of the wall, only to disclose to us another wall beyond, with a ridged, bare, and scalloped depression between. Here footing began to be precarious for both man and beast. Our mustangs were not shod and it was wonderful to see their slow, short, careful steps. They knew a great deal better than we what the danger was. It has been such experiences as this that have made me see in horses something besides beasts of burden. In the ascent of the second slope it was necessary to zigzag up, slowly and carefully, taking advantage of every bulge and depression.

Then before us twisted and dropped and curved the most dangerous slopes I had ever seen. We had reached the height of the divide and many of the drops on this side were perpendicular and too steep for us to see the bottom.

At one bad place Wetherill and Nas ta Bega, with Joe Lee, a Mormon cowboy with us, were helping one of the pack-horses named Chub. On the steepest part of this slope Chub fell and began to slide. His momentum jerked the rope from the hands of Wetherill and the Indian. But Joe Lee held on. Joe was a giant and being a Mormon he could not let go of anything he had. He began to slide with the horse, holding back with all his might.

It seemed that both man and beast must slide down to where the slope ended in a yawning precipice. Chub was snorting or screaming in terror. Our mustangs were frightened and rearing. It was not a place to have trouble with horses.

I had a moment of horrified fascination, in which Chub turned clear over. Then he slid into a little depression that, with Joe's hold on the lasso, momentarily checked his descent. Quick as thought Joe ran sidewise and down to the bulge of rock, and yelled for help. I got to him a little ahead of Wetherill and Nas ta Bega; and together we pulled Chub up out of danger. At first we thought he had been choked to death. But he came to, and got up, a bloody, skinned horse, but alive and safe. I have never seen a more magnificent effort than Joe Lee's. Those fellows are built that way. Wetherill has lost horses on those treacherous slopes, and that risk is the only thing about the trip which is not splendid.

We got over that bad place without further incident, and presently came to a long swell of naked stone that led down to a narrow green split. This one had straight walls and wound away out of sight. It was the head of a canyon.

"Nonnezoshe Boco," said the Indian.

This then was the Canyon of the Rainbow Bridge. When we got down into it we were a happy crowd. The mode of travel here was a selection of the best levels, the best places to cross the brook, the best places to climb, and it was a process of continual repetition. There was no trail ahead of us, but we certainly left one behind. And as Wetherill picked out the course and the mustangs followed him I had all freedom to see and feel the beauty, color, wildness and changing character of Nonnezoshe Boco.

My experiences in the desert did not count much in the trip down this strange, beautiful lost canyon. All canyons are not alike. This one did not widen, though the walls grew higher. They began to lean and bulge, and the narrow strip of sky above resembled a flowing blue river. Huge caverns had been hollowed out by water or wind. And when the brook ran close under one of these overhanging places the running water made a singular indescribable sound. A crack from a hoof on a stone rang like a hollow bell and echoed from wall to wall. And the croak of a frog—the only living creature I noted in the canyon—was a weird and melancholy thing.

"We're sure gettin' deep down," said Joe Lee.

"How do you know?" I asked.

"Here are the pink and yellow sego lilies. Only the white ones are found above."

I dismounted to gather some of these lilies. They were larger than the white ones of higher altitudes, of a most exquisite beauty and fragility, and of such rare pink and yellow hues as I had never seen.

"They bloom only where it's always summer," explained Joe.

That expressed their nature. They were the orchids of the summer canyons. They stood up everywhere star-like out of the green. It was impossible to prevent the mustangs treading them under foot. And as the canyon deepened, and many little springs added their tiny volume to the brook, every grassy bench was dotted with lilies, like a green sky star-spangled. And this increasing luxuriance manifested itself in the banks of purple moss and clumps of lavender daisies and great mounds of yellow violets. The brook was lined by blossoming buck-brush; the rocky corners showed the crimson and magenta of cactus; and there were ledges of green with shining moss that sparkled with little white flowers. The hum of bees filled the fragrant, dreamy air.

But by and bye, this green and colorful and verdant beauty, the almost level floor of the canyon, the banks of soft earth, the thickets and clumps of cottonwood, the shelving caverns and bulging walls—these features were gradually lost, and Nonnezoshe began to deepen in bare red and white stone steps. The walls sheered away from one another, breaking into sections and ledges, and rising higher and higher, and there began to be manifested a dark and solemn concordance with the nature that had created this old rent in the earth.

There was a stretch of miles where steep steps in hard red rock alternated with long levels of round boulders. Here, one by one, the mustangs went lame and we had to walk. And we slipped and stumbled along over these loose, treacherous stones. The hours passed; the toil increased; the progress diminished; one of the mustangs failed and was left. And all the while the dimensions of Nonnezoshe Boco magnified and its character changed. It became a thousand-foot walled canyon, leaning, broken, threatening, with great yellow slides blocking passage, with huge sections split off from the main wall, with immense dark and gloomy caverns. Strangely it had no intersecting canyons. It jealously guarded its secret. Its unusual formations of cavern and pillar and half-arch led me to expect any monstrous stone-shape left by avalanche or cataclysm.

Down and down we toiled. And now the stream-bed was bare of boulders and the banks of earth. The floods that had rolled down that canyon had here borne away every loose thing. All the floor, in places, was bare red and white stone, polished, glistening, slippery, affording treacherous foothold. And the time came when Wetherill abandoned the stream-bed to take to the rock-strewn and cactus-covered ledges above.

The canyon widened ahead into a great ragged iron-lined amphitheater, and then apparently turned abruptly at right angles. Sunset rimmed the walls.

I had been tired for a long time and now I began to limp and lag. I wondered what on earth would make Wetherill and the Indians tired. It was with great pleasure that I observed the giant Joe Lee plodding slowly along. And when I glanced behind at my straggling party it was with both admiration for their gameness and glee for their disheveled and weary appearance. Finally I got so that all I could do was to drag myself onward with eyes down on the rough ground. In this way I kept on until I heard Wetherill call me. He had stopped—was waiting for me. The dark and silent Indian stood beside him, looking down the canyon.

I saw past the vast jutting wall that had obstructed my view. A mile beyond, all was bright with the colors of sunset, and spanning the canyon in the graceful shape and beautiful hues of the rainbow was a magnificent natural bridge.

"Nonnezoshe," said Wetherill, simply.

This rainbow bridge was the one great natural phenomenon, the one grand spectacle which I had ever seen that did not at first give vague disappointment, a confounding of reality, a disenchantment of contrast with what the mind had conceived.

But this thing was glorious. It absolutely silenced me. My body and brain, weary and dull from the toil of travel, received a singular and revivifying freshness. I had a strange, mystic perception that this rosy-hued, tremendous arch of stone was a goal I had failed to reach in some former life, but had now found. Here was a rainbow magnified even beyond dreams, a thing not transparent and ethereal, but solidified, a work of ages, sweeping up majestically from the red walls, its iris-hued arch against the blue sky.

Then we plodded on again. Wetherill worked around to circle the huge amphitheater. The way was a steep slant, rough and loose and dragging. The rocks were as hard and jagged as lava, and cactus hindered progress. Soon the rosy and golden lights had faded. All the walls turned pale and steely and the bridge loomed dark.

We were to camp all night under the bridge. Just before we reached it Nas ta Bega halted with one of his singular motions. He was saying his prayer to this great stone god. Then he began to climb straight up the steep slope. Wetherill told me the Indian would not pass under the arch.

When we got to the bridge and unsaddled and unpacked the lame mustangs twilight had fallen. The horses were turned loose to fare for what scant grass grew on bench and slope. Firewood was even harder to find than grass. When our simple meal had been eaten there was gloom gathering in the canyon and stars had begun to blink in the pale strip of blue above the lofty walls. The place was oppressive and we were mostly silent.

Presently I moved away into the strange dark shadow cast by the bridge. It was a weird black belt, where I imagined I was invisible, but out of which I could see. There was a slab of rock upon which I composed myself, to watch, to feel.

A stiffening of my neck made me aware that I had been continually looking up at the looming arch. I found that it never seemed the same any two moments. Near at hand it was too vast a thing for immediate comprehension. I wanted to ponder on what had formed it—to reflect upon its meaning as to age and force of nature. Yet it seemed that all I could do was to see. White stars hung along the dark curved line. The rim of the arch appeared to shine. The moon was up there somewhere. The far side of the canyon was now a blank black wall. Over its towering rim showed a pale glow. It brightened. The shades in the canyon lightened, then a white disk of moon peeped over the dark line. The bridge turned to silver.

It was then that I became aware of the presence of Nas ta Bega. Dark, silent, statuesque, with inscrutable face uplifted, with all that was spiritual of the Indian suggested by a somber and tranquil knowledge of his place there, he represented to me that which a solitary figure of human life represents in a great painting. Nonnezoshe needed life, wild life, life of its millions of years—and here stood the dark and silent Indian.

Long afterward I walked there alone, to and fro, under the bridge. The moon had long since crossed the streak of star-fired blue above, and the canyon was black in shadow. At times a current of wind, with all the strangeness of that strange country in its moan, rushed through the great stone arch. At other times there was silence such as I imagined might have dwelt deep in the center of the earth. And again an owl hooted, and the sound was nameless. It had a mocking echo. An echo of night, silence, gloom, melancholy, death, age, eternity!

The Indian lay asleep with his dark face upturned, and the other sleepers lay calm and white in the starlight. I seemed to see in them the meaning of life and the past—the illimitable train of faces that had shone under the stars. There was something nameless in that canyon, and whether or not it was what the Indian embodied in the great Nonnezoshe, or the life of the present, or the death of the ages, or the nature so magnificently manifested in those silent, dreaming, waiting walls—the truth was that there was a spirit.

I did sleep a few hours under Nonnezoshe, and when I awoke the tip of the arch was losing its cold darkness and beginning to shine. The sun had just risen high enough over some low break in the wall to reach the bridge. I watched. Slowly, in wondrous transformation, the gold and blue and rose and pink and purple blended their hues, softly, mistily, cloudily, until once more the arch was a rainbow.

I realized that long before life had evolved upon the earth this bridge had spread its grand arch from wall to wall, black and mystic at night, transparent and rosy in the sunrise, at sunset a flaming curve limned against the heavens. When the race of man had passed it would, perhaps, stand there still. It was not for many eyes to see. The tourist, the leisurely traveler, the comfort-loving motorist would never behold it. Only by toil, sweat, endurance and pain could any man ever look at Nonnezoshe. It seemed well to realize that the great things of life had to be earned. Nonnezoshe would always be alone, grand, silent, beautiful, unintelligible; and as such I bade it a mute, reverent farewell.

BARRY GOLDWATER (1909–1998) served as a U.S. senator from Arizona from 1952 to 1987. His failed 1964 bid for the presidency exemplified the conservative Republicanism that made him famous, yet late in life he confounded supporters and critics alike by arguing to remove the ban on homosexuals in the military and by stating that his senatorial vote to dam Glen Canyon was "the one vote . . . that I would change if I had the chance." In 1939, Goldwater joined Norm Nevills as a paying customer on a trip that re-created the journey of John Wesley Powell along the Green and Colorado Rivers, and in doing so became one of the first one hundred people to successfully navigate the Colorado through Grand Canyon. His impressions and wonderfully concise history of Glen Canyon are from his journal, *Delightful Journey: Down the Green and Colorado Rivers,* first published by the Arizona Historical Foundation in 1970. The excerpt begins following their journey through Cataract Canyon; the footnotes are Goldwater's.

꧅

Delightful Journey

*I like to think that all human effort takes place within the context of
something permanent, like that river and its canyons.*
—Barry Goldwater, from the Introduction

Camp 8

SUNDAY, JULY 21
Hite's Crossing, Utah
WEATHER: Hot, 105°

WE STOPPED HERE YESTERDAY and tied up near Mr. [Art] Chaffin's home-made stern-wheeler. Charlie and I slept on the lawn here at the ranch house, and the change from river sand, rocks, and weeds was most welcome.

At five o'clock this morning Chaffin, John, and little Gary, Chaffin's grandson, drove into Hanksville for our mail. They have not returned yet; and while we are waiting for them I will take the time to describe this place.

Hite's Crossing lies downstream six miles from the mouth of the Frémont River, and a mile below White Canyon's mouth in Glen Canyon. Here the canyon is wide and shallow. In 1883 Cass Hite settled here and the mining boom colony became known as a crossing of the Colorado River. In 1926 people simply moved away and the town declined—its ruins lie a mile upstream. Occasionally a few prospectors wandered in, then went their way.

In 1935 A. L. Chaffin and his wife came to this place, which was then nothing but a sandy waste. Here they built a home and a ranch that are a monument to Mr. Chaffin's ingenuity, enterprise, and ambition. He has developed his own water system, and has trees and truck growing. They live in a pleasant ranch house built of logs and driftwood plastered with mud, and with a mud roof. The house is cool and comfortable, and the two of them enjoy living here. They have a radio which told us that England still holds on and that F.D.R. runs again. Mr. Chaffin has horses and cows and chickens, a workshop, and barns. He has built a stern-wheeler, powered with an old auto,—not just its motor—which plies up and down the river with supplies for the few placer miners in the area. In all, they have a wonderful place.

We have enjoyed staying over here—sleeping, talking, and eating their melons. And when the sun rises tomorrow, it will find each of us, I know, reluctant to leave here and to leave the Chaffins. Mrs. Chaffin is inside now, playing her old piano, while Mildred, Doris and Del try to sing. I can't do worse, so I'll join them. . . .

The mail arrived late this afternoon. There were letters from several people, including my mother and my wife. I loved getting them and will read each one many times. Peggy has written a letter for each day, and I will read them that way even though I am strongly tempted to read them all now.

For some time I have suspected that I have too much film, and now I am beginning to think my suspicions are well founded. I returned some unused film to my secretary, Harriet Walker, today by Mr. Chaffin, who will mail it.

My knee has troubled me all day and tonight I have surrounded it with hot packs. It is swollen and hurts like hell. Keeps going out on me when I walk. This is my right knee, now my bad left knee becomes my good one. . . .

Camp 13

MONDAY, JULY 22
Mile 135½, Tapestry Wall
WEATHER: Hot as hell, 110°; no shade
WATER: Shallow, wide, and calm

All of us were reluctant to leave Hite this morning at 9:30 A.M. We have had a good time and the rest was most welcome. In the boats with us were Charles Gerhart and his son Elmer. They operate a mine below Castle Butte, and we took them there. Their mining outfit is unique and again reveals the ingenuity man is capable of in eking out a living from God's earth.

We ate lunch at Cass Hite's old cabin, or rather at what is left of it, at the mouth of Red Canyon.[1] Today is very hot and the measly-leafed cottonwoods of the cabin site afforded slight protection from the heat. We gorged on watermelon fetched from the Chaffin farm, and the little shade we could find to enjoy made us all long for naps, so curl up in the dust we did.

As I lay under my cottonwood, lazily looking at the ruins of the cabin a few yards away, my thoughts wandered to the history of this place and to the man who built it. After Hite had worked fairly successfully the sandbar at Hite's Crossing (so successfully, in fact, that a small gold rush was precipitated), in the late 1880's he moved nearly twelve miles downstream to this spot. Here at the mouth of Red Canyon, across from Ticaboo Creek, Cass Hite built this cabin. In the true spirit of the meaning of the word *Ticaboo* (which is the Ute Indian word for "friendly"), his home became a congenial place for meetings between white men and Indians. Hite spent some time in jail for killing a man in Green River, Utah, in 1891. His health was broken by incarceration and after his release he returned to this cabin to spend the rest of his life.

I could see him wandering around in his little orchard and garden, working at the forge, or tending to the many other tasks that confront a man living alone. Cass Hite was found dead on his cabin floor in 1914 by Alonzo G. Turner. Hite was given an appropriate burial on the grounds of his spread. The grave is here, but my search for it was futile.[2]

A mining man from Telluride, Hite was first lured into this remote section by the sight of ore taken from the fabled mine, Pish-la-ki, whose location was said to be known only to the Navajo chief, Hoskininni. Two white men, Mitchell and Merrick, had gone into the country of the monuments where the mine was supposed to have been and made one trip out with ore. Hite had seen that ore. On the second trip, though, Hoskininni's warning that all men refrain from prospecting in his country was reinforced by the killing of Merrick and Mitchell. Two large formations of rock in Monument Valley now bear the names of these luckless two.

---

1. Later, from Otis Marston, I learned that the cabin at the mouth of Red Canyon was not Cass Hite's place. Cass lived downriver two miles and on the opposite bank, at Ticaboo. The cabin stood about one-half mile from the river; and this is where he lived after being pardoned from his life term in prison after being convicted of murder. The cabin I *thought* was Hite's was built by a man named Adams, was next lived in by Bert Loper, and in 1927, Marston says, by a man named Carpenter.

2. It is no wonder I was unable to locate the grave. I was two miles off!

Cass Hite visited the Indians' camp and made friends with them, but the red men were too shrewd not to see through the white man's friendliness. They led him not to the fabulously rich mine but down to the Colorado River, where, as I have related, he did find placer gold.

Below a small cliff a few hundred yards upstream and near the corral are evidences of cliff ruins. Hugh and Norm explored them and returned with a few shards and arrowheads. They reported seeing snake tracks, but snakes interest me about as much as the scorpion on which I snoozed today.

We made the afternoon run without mishap or any eventful occurrence, and camped at the mouth of Warm Springs Canyon below the towering elegance of Tapestry Wall which stands immediately to the west. This wall, twelve hundred feet high, extends down the river for over a mile, its red face splashed with long, irregular, vertical marks exactly like huge swags of drapery. These marks are a red darker than the face, and undoubtedly they are caused by water dripping over the edge of the cliff.

The sun and dust have made dirty people of us all, so we welcome a bath in the *cool* waters of Warm Springs.

My knee hurt all day, and, to relieve it, I lay on the back deck with my leg draped over a bucket. That helped the knee a great deal, and additional similar treatments should cure it. The hot sun does wonders.

Good night.

Camp 14

TUESDAY, JULY 23
Mile 108
WEATHER: Hot as hell, 110°; no shade, no clouds
WATER: Shallow, sandbars, wide, smooth

Last night was one of those nights when God makes up his mind He is going to be mean about it. First we were afflicted with swarms of damned May flies. They live only twenty-four hours but that is too long. They squish when you swat them, and you have to swat them because they simply roost on you and refuse to leave. Why we have May flies in July, the Lord only knows. A breeze came up and blew them away; then the breeze turned into a gale, and before you could wink, *we* were almost blown away. Sand swirled in copious quantities; and my ears, mouth, and eyes soon were filled with grit.

The wind stopped in the early morning hours, however, and finally, well past midnight, we fell asleep.

We were away at 7:00 A.M. this morning, and even at that early hour the sun gave fair warning of what he had in store for us. Five miles downstream we stopped at Smith's Fork which enters from the right, at Mile 132, to fill canteens and see some pictographs. The water was very good there.

As early as 11:00 A.M., the sun made us say "uncle." We pulled up at Moki Canyon which forks in from the left at Mile 125. We ate lunch there and lolled in the shade for three hours. Refreshed, we tackled the sun again, and Old Sol just smiled and gave us hell.

About three miles below Moki Canyon we passed a big sandbar strewn with the remains of a large dredge that had been used for gold operations. Julius Stone, whose book *Canyon Country* contains some of the finest photographs ever taken of the Colorado, and Robert Brewster Stanton invested a considerable sum of money in this dredge. When he came by here in 1938 a fire supposedly was built from scraps of wood from the machine and coffee was boiled over this fire. Remarks were voiced at the time that it was probably the most expensive cup of coffee ever brewed.

We passed Bullfrog Canyon and Hall's Crossing in the afternoon. An old trail and road that came down Hall Creek used to transit at Hall's Crossing.

At 4:30 P.M., we reached Lake Canyon and made camp. I went one way and the others went another in search of a date reported to be carved on the wall opposite our camp. They found the date, but since I was tired and a great distance from them I did not go across to view the date—1642. Many people doubt the authenticity of the 1642; however, anything could have happened.

Fate *would* have caused me to wander off in the opposite direction. I hope that the next party to pass will take special pains to check the date. The authentication would add impetus to search for additional inscriptions by D. Julien.

We broke three sheer pins on the motorboat today in shallow water and also had to push ourselves off several shoals and bars. This river has less and less water in it each day. I fear the balance of our passage through Glen Canyon will be filled with hours of rowing and shoving boats from shallow water into deep. . . .

Tonight we are camped at an old mine on the left, at Mile 108. The owners are away and they have left indications, in the form of canned shrimp, canned mushrooms, and a good selection of other fancy tinned goods, including sauces of all kinds, that they are not ordinary placer miners. Needless to say, we have used these cans to vary our diet. We have kept a list of what we used, and will send a check to cover the cost of the items.

I am tired tonight. My leg doesn't hurt so much now, but I'll have to be careful with it. So, tired little man, get the hell to bed. Good night. . . .

Camp 17

FRIDAY, JULY 26
Mile 88
WEATHER: Cooler, but windy all day
WATER: Down slightly

This morning we walked up the shallow Escalante looking for a spring, but since then we have done nothing but lie around camp cussing the constant wind. It has blown since early last evening and this is the first calm we have had, and it is now late afternoon. I found some pictographs just below camp on the right side of the canyon while I was rowing this morning. They are about one hundred fifty yards down the right wall from the Escalante.

We have seen nothing of the others as yet, so I don't know what luck they had with the bridge. They probably will return late tonight and we will get an early start on the river again tomorrow.

Glen Canyon from the mine to this point has become increasingly narrower and deeper, and the slopes are stippled with broken rock. There are many coyote tracks. We have also glimpsed white egrets and the inevitable beaver. I am happy we are approaching Arizona.

Norm has just returned and announced that they found the bridge but that it won't beat Rainbow. He says it is eight and one-half miles up Escalante, then one and one-half miles up Forty-mile Canyon into the second canyon on the right. He has named the span Nijoni but we insist upon calling it Gregory in honor of Dr. Herbert Gregory and Norm says he will send in the name. He estimates the thickness at 114 feet, the inside height 192 feet, overall height 306 feet, and the width inside 193 feet. In mentioning the route, Forty-mile Canyon is the third on the left up Escalante.

I have gone back to the site where I found the pictographs, and have made an interesting discovery. There is a large ruin there, with many ash piles and fireplaces. The place may have been an Indian hunting camp, as there are few pottery shards but a great many arrow chips and flint cutters. At this place is the inscription:

L. Harris 1894 April 22

Fifty feet upstream on the right side of the Colorado, are several inscriptions:

A. J. TADJE[3]	T. WILLIAMS
M. Pictures	dec. 25
Dec. −10	1885
1914	
KF	R.R.

Good night.

Camp 18

SATURDAY, JULY 27
Mile 68, Forbidding Canyon
WEATHER: Cooler today, about 95°
WATER: Not a hell of a lot of it

This has been one of the most interesting days of our trip. We got an early start and at 9:00 A.M. we pulled in at Hole-in-the-Rock Canyon. The canyon is short, not over three-quarters of a mile or, at most, a mile to where it tops out. It is most difficult of ascent and descent, even on foot. I spent nearly three hours walking up and down because of my knee and my cameras. On the way down, I slipped and fell about ten feet, landing on my belly on the camera case. Cursing appropriately, I went on, none the worse for my clumsiness.

This narrow slit in the wall of the canyon was the site of one of the most heroic and determined efforts at colonization by pioneers in the West. Mormons, having ever been farmers, soon occupied most of the good land in northern Utah. The one place left for large companies of these industrious people to migrate was the little known country of the San Juan. This was confirmed in 1878 when scouts sent south for the purpose reported back to

3. My friend Dock Marston informs me that August J. Tadje was cameraman with Russell during a run in 1914–15 from Green River, Utah, to Bass Cable in the Grand Canyon.

the successor to Brigham Young, John Taylor, that arable land could be had for the settling along the San Juan River.

Consequently, late in the winter of 1879 a company of Mormons departed, bound for this new land to the south. They were to follow a trail (roughly traced on a map by Taylor) that would lead them through Parowan, Bear Valley, Panguitch to Escalante, then across the Escalante Desert, the Colorado, and on to the vicinity of what is now Bluff, Utah. This brave company was composed of nearly two hundred fifty men, women, and children, traveling in eighty-two covered wagons, and accompanied by nearly one thousand head of cattle. Though little was known of the country that lay between Escalante and the river, the party started with every expectation of arriving at its destination in good time.

They reckoned without knowledge of the miles of deep canyons that had to be crossed or of the labor that traversing this eroded land would entail. The early miles sped by, if miles in a covered wagon can be said to speed by, and the party's spirits remained high. A tremor of concern went through the group, however, when the train had to cross the Sevier. Climbing out of the deep valley of that river taxed man and beast to the utmost.

This concern must have increased when the scouting party that had been sent ahead on November 28 returned with a description of rugged country before them. This news must have particularly disheartened men who had labored hard to construct a passable road between Forty-mile Spring and Fifty-mile Spring. A meeting of the company revealed that everyone was determined to go on. They felt that to retrace their route would have been nearly impossible owing to the scarcity of grass for feed. At this time they had been on the road more than the total number of days they had planned to use for the entire trip, and they had scarcely started on their journey.

I stood on top of the Hole-in-the-Rock, gazing across the desert toward Escalante, and tried to imagine myself jouncing over that rocky, barren country in a covered wagon after having spent nearly two months toiling through canyons, over mountains, across sand, and over rocks. I guess I would be tired but happy, for the going here would be slightly easier than that over which I had come. I would be admiring the great Kaiparowits Plateau that stretched majestically to the west of my wagon. Then my eyes would stray ahead of me, to the rocky buttress of Navajo Mountain and on up to its snowcapped summit. I tried to imagine the surprise, consternation, and then utter despair as I drove up to the narrow crack in the earth's surface and looked down hundreds of feet to the Colorado a mile below. Down this crack that was a few scant feet wide my wagon would have to go . . .

I abandoned my imaginings at that point. The magnitude of the tasks involved in such a descent soared beyond the powers of my imagination.

The company pulled up at Hole-in-the-Rock on December 14, 1879. The people immediately commenced broadening this six-foot crack to a width that would allow the passage of wagons. Steps were cut; a bridge was built halfway down; a dugway road was constructed down the canyon wall to the edge of the river.[4] Supplies were hauled from Escalante sixty miles away. Men labored all day in bitter cold and then gathered around evening fires to sing and dance to bolster their spirits. With typical Mormon zeal, they held religious meetings twice each week. It is a tribute to the faith of those people that their morale remained high in spite of the extreme hardships they were forced to endure.

New Year's Day of 1880 found the group still working at the Hole-in-the-Rock, with part of the company strung out as far back as Forty-mile Spring. Gradually, however, more wagons arrived at the main camp, and the additional manpower accelerated the speed of the work. Finally, on January 26, someone braver than the rest was sought to attempt the first descent. A young man by the name of Kumen Jones volunteered and started down the precipitous trail with nothing more than a prayer and twenty men behind him firmly holding back his perilously tilting wagon with hands and ropes.

Weeks of work were rewarded when the wagon successfully reached the river. It was rolled onto a ferry which they had built and brought with them, and rowed across the stream. On that day twenty-six wagons were lowered and ferried to the opposite shore of the Colorado. The water was freezing cold and ice edged the banks of the river, but across it went the men and women who were making Utah history.

On February 10, all wagons and cattle having been ferried and swum across, the party began the ascent of the eastern bank of the river. There is a low wall about one hundred feet high on the eastern side of the river at this point, and the gentle slope made building a road up the side comparatively easy. (This road is still visible and appears to be in good condition. I did not have sufficient time to examine this road more closely, which I regretted.)

---

4. As described by David H. Miller in *Hole in the Rock*, the first trail was cut by the Silas S. Smith Party in 1879. The steps were cut into the solid stone two decades later by citizens of Escalante establishing an Indian trading post at its base.

On to the east they traveled, over slick rocks, through canyons, over deserts, and through mud. Horses and cattle wasted into skeletons, rations had long ago become meager, but the indomitable pioneer spirit of the Latter-day Saints drove these people forward until, on April 5, 1880, the first wagon reached the San Juan River at the mouth of Comb Wash where Bluff now stands. Many families traveled farther east into Colorado and New Mexico, since there was not enough land at the San Juan to sustain everyone.

As our boats slowly drifted past this spot, I felt a thrill at having stood on ground made historic by these people. I imagined wagons being ferried across the river with cattle swimming after them. I could see the tired faces wreathed with the smiles that come to those who have tried and conquered; and as the current carried us around a bend and out of view of Hole-in-the-Rock, I tipped my hat, not to the beauty of the place—even though it is beautiful—but to the courage, the will, and the zeal that drove these Mormons to accomplish their mission without sacrificing the life of a single man, woman, or beast.

The West has never suffered from the migrations of people like the individuals comprising that Mormon company.

Near lunchtime we stopped on the right bank in Hidden Passage Canyon. This appropriately named canyon is about eight hundred feet deep and only thirty-five feet wide. Its mouth is completely hidden by brush. This width and height prevailed as far back as we went, about three hundred yards; at two hundred yards the canyon makes a sharp turn right and continues in that direction for a long way.

Across the river is Music Temple, the place Powell loved so much. On its wall are inscribed the names of his companions:

F. M. Bishop '71	J. F. Steward '71
F. S. Dellenbaugh '71	W. C. Powell '71
J. K. Hillers '72–'71	
W. D. Johnson '72	

Music Temple is a dead-end canyon that culminates in a tremendous cave containing a large pool under a waterfall. The sun never shines in the temple except for a few hours in the middle of the day. Powell's men sang here, and the singing sounded so good to their ears that they christened the cavern Music Temple.

This afternoon, for the first time, we glimpsed the large, bluish-green mountain rising out of the plateau in northeastern Arizona that is known as

Navajo Mountain. Although the southern base of this mountain is in Arizona, the summit, with an altitude of 10,400 feet, is in Utah. This mountain is the legendary dwelling place of the Navajo war god, and so firmly do the Indians believe this that they go to elaborate extremes to avoid the mountain. I have seen canyon sheep trails on the southern slopes with barriers constructed across them to prevent the sheep from straying up the mountain. If a sheep wandered up the mountain, of course, the Indians would have to go after it. War God Spring is named in honor of the god and is located more than halfway up the mountain on the Arizona side.

Powell named this mountain Mount Seneca Howland in honor of one of the men who left his first expedition, in 1869, farther down the river and was killed by Indians. The name was not adopted officially because for years the place had been called Navajo Mountain. However, on the Macomb-Newberry map of 1859, on the Eckhoff map of 1880, and on the Gregory map of 1916 the peak is referred to as Sierra Panoche. (*Panoche* is the Spanish word for a small loaf of unprocessed brown sugar.)

The view from the summit of this landmark is memorable. Many square miles of the Indian country are visible to the south, and to the north and west stretch seemingly unending canyons. If there remains in this United States a section that may be termed wild or unexplored, the country visible from the summit of Navajo Mountain would include all of it. Peggy and I have explored many of the little mesas around Navajo Mountain, and we have also been in several of the canyons around its base. This, coupled with the fact that our friends Bill and Katherine Wilson live on the southwestern slope of the mountain made Navajo Mountain a most welcome sight. In my mind nothing but pleasantness is associated with this massive mountain.

Today we passed the mouth of the San Juan River which empties in from the left. This river, one of the principal tributaries of the Colorado, had little water in it today. This stream supplies much of the silt carried by the Colorado. Earlier in the year I had occasion to see the San Juan farther upstream when it was running nearly sixteen thousand second feet, and it amazingly resembled a miniature Colorado. Its course is southward from its head in southwestern Colorado and it passes by Farmington, New Mexico, and enters Utah near Four Corners, flowing a little north of west. Most of the river's bed is cut through canyons, many of which, particularly for the fifty miles before the San Juan joins the Colorado, are as deep as many of the canyons through which we have passed.

Tonight we are camped at the mouth of Forbidding Canyon and have made our beds out on the sandbar. Rain appears to be a real possibility, judging from the many dark clouds scudding overhead. Tomorrow we are going up to Rainbow Bridge.

Yes, it has been a good day and now I am ready for a good sleep. Good night. . . .

Camp 23

Last night I was dreaming of an operation and just as the doctor stuck a needle in my arm some damned bug ran his stinger in me. God knows what the insect was, but he ran off and left part of his equipment in my flesh.

We stopped at El Vado de los Padres (the Crossing of the Fathers) at 11:30 A.M. and then walked up Padre Creek to see the steps that Escalante cut in the slick rock when he used this place as a ford to cross the river.

The crossing, as marked by Russell Frazier and party in 1938, is downstream one mile from Kane Creek which enters on the right. Until Frazier and Kelly (who were both members of the Stone party) marked this place with a plaque, the crossing generally was supposed to have been at Kane Creek. I could easily see how this could be believed, and probably many crossings have been made at the mouth of Kane Creek, even by modern travelers. After the careful study these two men have made of this subject by locating landmarks mentioned in the diary of Escalante (who returned this way in 1776 to the Spanish settlements toward the east after attempting—unsuccessfully—to find a short route to Monterey) and by following the route the good priest actually took, I believe that the plaque is accurately situated. The strongest point supporting the acceptance of this canyon as being the route are the steps to be found farther up the canyon, incised with a metal instrument into the stone walls of the canyon. Escalante led his animals down these steps and recorded this feat in his diary along with a mention of the actual cutting of the steps. The river here, as well as at Kane Creek, is wide and evidently very shallow, and the opposite bank is low and sloping, affording easy access and exit.

We walked for about two hours, breaking our way through thick underbrush and knee-deep slime. The view from on top was magnificent, a splendid reward for our efforts to see Escalante's route.

This afternoon at 4:20 we entered my beloved Arizona. The river dips into the state for about half a mile, then loops out again, only to swing back in at Warm Creek Canyon, which comes in from the right (west bank). The time, 4:20 P.M., refers to the latter place. I noticed immediately a more bracing quality in the air; a clearer, bluer sky; a more buoyant note in the song of the birds; a snap and sparkle in the air that only Arizona air has, and I said to myself, without reference to a map, that we were now *home.*

On the downstream wall of Warm Creek Canyon, with the aid of Charles Larabee of Kansas City, I placed in the red sandstone above high-water level the following inscription, chiseled and filled with white lead:

ARIZONA	
WELCOMES	UTAH
YOU	

We took pictures and were off again. The line marked is probably off the actual state line by one hundred feet or so, but we placed the inscription here for practical purposes. This spot is more accessible and easily visible,[5] thus preferable to the spot designated on the map, which is a way back from the river; our efforts would have gone to waste there.

We ran late tonight and have camped on a sandbar. Sleep will be welcome, as we are all tired—and I mean tired out. Good night.

5. No more; it is now inundated by the waters of Lake Powell.

CHARLES EGGERT LED THE LAST EXPEDITION (1955–56) to retrace the route of John Wesley Powell's 1869 journey before the construction of Glen Canyon Dam, an effort that resulted in two films, *A Canyon Voyage* and *Danger River*, as well as an uncompleted written account of the journey, titled *Forbidden Passage*. A retired filmmaker and photographer, Eggert currently resides in New York. His films and photographs are archived at the University of Utah's Marriott Library. This excerpt from the manuscript of *Forbidden Passage*, which originally appeared in the November 1958 issue of the *Sierra Bulletin*, provides an excellent snapshot of the reaction among river-runners to the plans to build Glen Canyon Dam.

Forbidden Passage

TEN MILES BELOW HITE A BUTTE rises from the Colorado River's edge—a great sentinel marking the entrance to Glen Canyon. Here some ancient Indian god must have stood, pointing the way to Paradise. If anywhere, that place was below—through the 147 miles of Glen Canyon. What exquisite and wondrous beauty was there!

If there is weeping to be done, cry over the destruction of this place. As I write, blasts of dynamite are shaking its quiet solitude. Mighty earthmovers are roaring over the desert above, and pneumatic drills are tearing at the walls seeking firm anchorage for the Glen Canyon dam. The reservoir behind it will flood under hundreds of feet of water priceless gems of scenic wonder unequalled on the face of the earth. "The reservoir will make the beauty of Glen Canyon accessible to all," they tell us. We would ask: Is it not accessible now? There is no canyon on the river more accessible to all than this one. What of the beauty will remain? It is all in the bottom of the canyon! Everything will be flooded; there will be no more to see except the desert country—the same kind of country one can now see from a car window on roads already built.

We have protected most of our other priceless scenic areas as national parks, unimpaired, for the benefit and enjoyment of *all* the people. To these places you and I and our children's children can come to look in wonder at our land, uncluttered by hot-dog stands, road signs, jive joints, or even the more handsome aspects of progress. There, spread before us is the awesome wonder of natural things—the things God alone made. Stand on the rim on the canyon of the Yellowstone at dawn sometime and listen to the breeze singing in the pines around you. Smell their fragrance, and the bright crisp air, fresh of the earth God created out of time and space. Feel on your face the spray sent up from the great Lower Falls. Look out across that chasm and up into the sky, still peppered with the brighter stars which outshine the dawn.

Or some night lie at the mouth of a rock-carved amphitheater two or three times the size of anything you've ever been in. Look up the two-thousand-foot wall to the billion stars and listen to the murmuring of the river still carving deeper the slot of canyon you're in. Think of nothing but what you see and feel and hear and smell.

What a campsite we had picked! We were on a high place above the river, on a rock-ledged terrace. The riverbank was a series of mammoth rock steps rising from the water. Each level was flat and large enough to accommodate all of us. We had made our campfire in one of the numerous pot holes eroded in the rock. The one we chose made a perfect shelter for our fire. Beyond us, the river made a lazy curve to the left and there the canyon wall rose straight up a thousand feet. For a mile and a half this cliff followed the river before the wall fell back again. The face of the cliff was stained with long, black streamers from the water which cascaded over the rim in wet weather. It was an imposing sight, a gigantic backdrop—a motionless hanging tapestry—behind us, soft in the light of early evening.

Tony, Don and I stayed behind when the *Brontosaur* set off on the morning run. With the cameras and tripods, we climbed to the highest ledge—over a hundred feet above the river—where we could get an uninterrupted view of the full sweep of the river as it made its path through the red rock and under Tapestry Cliff. How amazingly ephemeral this solid mass of a million tons of sandstone looked.

The river below, almost the color of the surrounding rock, would have been lost in the scene had it not been for the thin line of green tamarisk bushes lining the banks to mark the course. In the boats we knew the river *was* a big stream, but high up where we stood, it was a thin, golden, serpentine thread. We could barely make out the *Brontosaur* as she traveled downstream. Knowing how big she really was, we could understand the scale of things. This country was big.

Another twilight and we were at another good campsite. Nearby was an old deserted cabin; the home, one time, of a gold prospector. All along the way there had been ruins of old mines where men had come and dug with hope. But their sights were aimed too short. The gold was here all right, but it wasn't the kind one can take to the assayer's office and get a price on. If they left in poverty it was because they were unable to see. The gold I speak of surrounded them wherever they chose to look, and those who could see it left this place abundantly rich.

Then we stopped at Navajo Creek, just above the Escalante River. On our map was written, "Waterfalls—lovely pool." We hadn't had a clear-water bath in weeks. "Want to come along for a clean shower?" I asked Cid Sumner.

"No—I'll stay at the boats. You boys just go on. I'll remain here to enjoy my figs in peace!" she laughed. The six of us hiked up the narrow canyon cut by the creek and presently we came to an enchanting emerald pool, crystal clear, surrounded by mammoth boulders. At the far end of the pool Navajo Creek cascaded in graceful leaps of sparkling white water. Around the pool, like a wreath, ferns grew. The place was so inviting, we could hardly get our clothes off fast enough. Clean, clear water! What a relief to get the silt washed off. I stood for a long while under the waterfall, letting the forceful spray pound down upon my head. Then for awhile we all lay on a large rock, sunbathing. The sun felt particularly soothing now that I was clean. I noticed how tanned we all were. The color of our skins nearly matched the brown rocks we were lying on. We had used sun-tan lotion the first week or two, and we were careful not to get burned too quickly. But now we didn't have to worry any longer—except for that conspicuously white patch our shorts had left.

After the sun bath, we jumped into the water again, had a vigorous waterfight which riled up the bottom of the emerald pool, took another shower. Refreshed, we returned to the boats.

"Now wouldn't you like to shower?" Fred asked Cid. "It's really not far to the pool."

Cid was sitting under the shade of a tamarisk bush, her wet nylon veil draped over her head. "No—there's been a nice breeze here in the shade. I'm too lazy to make the effort," she answered. Nevertheless, we sensed, she strongly approved the improvement the pool had made in us.

Our camp, the night of July 7, was again on a series of red-rock ledges rising from the water's edge. Close by was the narrow slit of an entrance to a side canyon. After supper Fred and I hiked below to explore it. To get to the mouth of the canyon we had to climb high above the river, along the top of a steep talus slope. Upon reaching the mouth, we came upon a scene of tremendous violence. A huge section of the canyon wall had fallen and the big boulders that obliterated our path were so newly broken and cracked that the fall must have occurred within the past few days; the leaves of the trees it had taken with it were still fresh, and sap was still running from the twisted broken branches. Tons of rock had come crashing down and there was a mammoth scar on the face of the canyon wall to mark its source. Across the narrow canyon, the walls were scraped where rocks had ricocheted.

Fred and I painstakingly crawled across the rockfall. When we came to the end of the debris we found ourselves buried deep in a narrow passage into the rock beyond. The sides of the canyon were no more than eight feet apart where we stood. They were nearly two thousand feet deep in the sandstone crust of the earth. No sunlight had ever entered the depth of this place. Down the center of the canyon floor ran a trickle of a stream.

The hidden passage twisted and turned as we followed it through the rock, and presently we came to a sharp turn. Here the stream had cut diagonally through the rock. The sky was shut off from our view completely; only the rock hung overhead. The canyon wall on the opposite side of the turn followed upward, parallel to its companion wall, and the two sides were like giant pieces of a jigsaw puzzle jarred slightly apart. Fred and I stood at the middle of the turn where we could look up and down the canyon as it wound its way deep in the earth. As we looked up through the slit the rock wall opposite seemed like the prow of a supernatural ship turned upside down. Behind us, the stream had gouged out a deep cave, and in front of it a soft dune of powdery sand lay piled high. The air was heavy with the green of ferns.

Fred and I wandered on, unable to believe what we saw. In places the bottom of the canyon narrowed, leaving only room enough for the stream to run between the walls. In other places the stream had eroded deep pot holes and we had to work our way along the slanting wall to get around them. At one place there seemed to be a mild enough pitch to the wall to allow us to climb to a ledge above, but we could not. The rock was too slippery, for here small springs gushed from the wall, making the wall wet. Wherever there was a seep in the canyon wall, ferns grew.

It was getting dark by the time we turned back, not yet having come to the end of the narrow passage, even though we had walked a good two miles. We had been so entranced with the place that we forgot the hour. Now we thought of that rock slide with the jagged-edged boulders we'd have to climb over to get back to camp. We hurried out as fast as we could. . . .

A short distance downstream from Hidden Passage we came upon a great alcove in the rock. If we searched the world high and wide and deep, we could find no grander temple. Here was a domed chamber in the yellow-brown sandstone, more than two-hundred feet high, five-hundred feet long and at least two-hundred feet wide. In the center was a high mound of rock and sand on which grew a grove of box elders, cottonwood trees, and ferns. It was like a Japanese garden, and Fred remarked that it could not have been more perfect had it been landscaped deliberately. At the far end of the vast chamber was a clear, still pool in which, we were certain, lived a water sprite, for every few moments a tiny spout of water would break the surface, leaving behind a perfect ring which would slowly enlarge and spread out until it was stopped by the edge of the pool. The pool was deep—so deep we could not see bottom, and around it, on the rock wall, grew a thick bank of maidenhair fern. Above the pool, through the ceiling and up through the rock for a thousand feet there was a narrow, winding skylight which had been carved out by a little stream which runs only when it rains. What a sight it must be to see it cascading in a two hundred-foot free fall to the center of the pool below! And, what a lovely sound it must make here, for the acoustics are perfect.

"We are pleased to find that this hollow in the rock is filled with sweet sounds," Major Powell wrote in his diary on August 1, 1869. "It was doubtless made for an academy of music by its storm-born architect; so we name it Music Temple."

It was here that Powell and his men camped and sang. And here it was, too, that Seneca and Oramel Howland and Bill Dunn, along with the others, carved their names on the rock wall where they remain, almost as distinct as on the day they were made. Powell, on his second journey down the river in 1871, revisited Music Temple. Seeing the names of those three men of his first expedition, Powell thought this place would be a fitting memorial to Dunn and the Howland brothers. They had deserted him in the Grand Canyon, convinced that the party was doomed to disaster. They climbed out, only to be killed by Indians when they reached the plateau above. As we stood looking at those names carved in the rock, we wondered what Powell would think, were he to know that this place, too, would be destroyed by reservoir waters, and later by silt which would cover it forever from men's eyes. Powell was aware of the potential water resources of the Great American Desert, and he believed in utilizing nature in man's behalf. But he was also keenly aware of the resources which feed men's souls. Meeting this need, too, was in man's behalf. How would he have felt about Glen Canyon reservoir?

Five miles below Music Temple we found hundreds of petroglyphs—one of the many sites to be found in Glen Canyon where the prehistoric red men had left their marks in passing.

"An almost universal human wish," Cid remarked, "to leave some sign that will last when we are gone—to hack away at the hard stone with the urgency of our mortality upon us."

Near the petroglyphs another narrow side canyon cut its way back through the rock. We decided to explore it. Perhaps we'd find another hidden passage. Instead we found a hidden amphitheater, unexpectedly. The narrow canyon took a sharp twist and there it was—so big Madison Square Garden could have fit into it without a squeeze. Again, as in Hidden Passage where the creek curved in an almost complete circle, the rock was cut down at a diagonal angle and the far wall had been deeply gouged out.

The great domed roof above us must have been ten stories high and five-hundred feet across, and coming down the center of the chamber was a gigantic rock peninsula. Near its base at the dry creek bed was a flat area, large enough to hold a symphony orchestra and a full chorus. As we sat on the talus which rose high against the wall opposite, Tony and I speculated on what a glorious concert could be held here. "If Stokowski could only see this, I'll bet he would arrange it!" I said. "He has the imagination for such a thing—just the conductor to do it."

"Yes, and we'd haul everyone down in boats. It would be the most magnificent concert ever given," Tony added enthusiastically. We sat back and speculated. A fantastic idea? Perhaps, but a possible one, I thought. It would certainly be the music experience to end all music experiences, what with the build-up the audience would have just getting to the place. I closed my eyes and could imagine the sound of a great orchestra here.

I kept my eyes shut for a long time but opened them when I heard Al call for our attention. His voice seemed to come from everywhere, close to me, yet far, far away. "Where is he?" I asked.

"Over there—on the rock, climbing down. You can just make him out." Don pointed straight across the chamber to the rock peninsula. In the twilight of the place—for here, too, the sun had never entered—I spotted Al: a small spot no bigger than the period at the end of this sentence.

"Come across," Al shouted, "you can see the sky from here." We walked over and looked up to the crescent-shaped slit of blue winding around over us. Above the dome, where the chamber ended, rose a sheer wall of solid sandstone another thousand feet. Up there were millions of tons of rock and we were in the very heart of it. All that weight above, the bigness of the place; it was too much for me—too superhuman, too vast. I had to get out of there, get back to where I was my right size again. I felt as I had a few nights before, when I lay on a rock ledge staring into the sky, where every star that was there was brilliantly lit. The longer I looked up, the more three dimensional the sky became, and I sensed the spatial distances in it. Seeing the universe spread out above and around me that night made me feel as infinitesimally small as the sky was infinitely big. Now I found myself almost running to get out of Twilight Amphitheater. I was glad to be in the open again where I towered above something, even though it might be only a sagebush.

"What a place!" Tony said when he caught up with me. "It was like being in the belly of a whale!"

While we were gone, a strong wind had come up. It kicked up high waves on the river, and we had a hard time fighting our way as we continued downstream. The waves tossed the *No Name* about and the motor's propeller alternately dug into the water and whirled futilely in the air. The sun beat down on us relentlessly. When we could hardly endure it much longer, we saw Navajo Mountain hovering in the distance. We knew we were nearing the mouth of Aztec Creek, the entrance from the river to Rainbow Bridge.

"Almost there!" Don shouted from the small boat, "think you can stand it a little farther?"

"Yes, yes—go on!" Cid shouted back to him from behind the piled-up duffle in the middle of the *Brontosaur* where she sheltered herself against the wind.

It must have been another half hour before we pulled into a quiet bay which was sheltered momentarily from the wind by a sheer, high wall on the opposite side of the river. We dragged the food boxes across the sandy beach to a wide, flat shelf of rock. Here the campfire was built in the shelter of a small crevice and the table set up as the sun went behind the cliff on the other side of the river. "At least we'll be in the shade," Don remarked caustically.

That hot night we huddled in our sleeping bags like pupae in cocoons. The blowing sand was more uncomfortable than the heat.

A climax was ahead. Well hidden up the side canyon was one of the wonders of the world—Rainbow Bridge; Nonnezoshie, it was called by the Indians. A rock arch like a rainbow in the sky, a place held sacred and secret by the ancient Indians; I dare not be so close and miss it. As I lay huddled in my sleeping bag thinking of that place, the wind suddenly stopped and all was at once quiet; so quiet I could again hear the murmur of the river beyond. I popped my head out of my bag to listen to that soothing sound and breathe the clear air again. When I looked up I saw the stars. To the northeast was the Big Dipper that had followed us all those 650 river miles we had come. Only one night had it deserted us—back in Cataract [Canyon], where we had slept on the rocks below the Big Drop. The 3,500-foot cliff above us had hidden it from our view. It hadn't occurred to me until now that every night except that one I had looked into the night sky and had seen that one familiar thing in this unfamiliar world, and I had felt at peace, at home in the universe—secure. This night, seeing the Big Dipper there, I felt in place again after the day of incredulities.

Strange that one should walk so far and suffer so much to see a mass of stone arched across the sky. Perhaps this was why it was such a thrill. It was something one had to exert oneself to see. I wonder whether we aren't making a big mistake in making it so easy for people to see things. Nearly every week I receive press releases informing me that this road or that one in our national parks is being "improved," widened, paved, made into a highway. It is getting so that almost everything can be seen from the car window. People boast about how many parks they have "covered" during their vacation. Only recently I spoke to a couple who, in the course of their auto trip across the country, had seen Yosemite, Sequoia, Death Valley, the Grand Canyon, Bryce and Zion canyons, the Tetons, Yellowstone! *Seen* them? I wondered. *Felt* them? *Understood* them? Hardly. Their pictures showed a two-dimensional experience, all seen either from their car window or from an overlook beside the road. They could almost as well have stayed home and looked at pictures in a travel magazine. Their appreciation of what they had seen was in exact proportion to the time they had spent. One has to get out of the car and walk—feel the ground beneath, the earth around, smell the air, hear the sounds. What is a waterfall without the spray in your face? What is a forest without the spongy feel of the thick layer of needles cushioning your feet? What is a desert without the sand burning through the soles of your shoes or the cactus spine pricking your leg? All these are a part of the whole. And if there is effort involved, the more the appreciation.

Most of what we walked through, and that set the stage for the deep appreciation we would feel, is soon to be erased by the fluctuating reservoir behind Glen Canyon dam. Power boats will zoom the most casual traveler into the canyon—indeed right under Rainbow Bridge itself if some of the proponents of ease should have their way and forestall the steps proposed to keep the last half mile from a silty grave. We were among the last to know this approach as God made it. Our sons would not know it, and we tried to forget how rich an experience was being taken from them. They would be deprived of it here, and also up along the main Colorado, in such sweetly quiet and peaceful places as Twilight Amphitheater, Hidden Passage, and Music Temple.

We walked toward the Bridge, stopping at every new vista to sit and look. The closer we got, the more beautiful and graceful it became. There was a simple explanation of how the arch had been formed but that didn't matter; the arch was *there,* spread across the canyon, framing all of Navajo Mountain in its span, and the beauty of it transcended its geology. We spent a long time at its foot, resting there, feeling its presence. Then we climbed to the abutment where the National Park Service had placed a register. We signed in and read a few of the two-thousand-odd names of those who had come before, most of them on horseback by a fourteen-mile trail from the one-time lodge. One man had written "Not worth it" after his name. Had he become so bogged down with the contrivances of civilization that he could no longer focus on beauty and wonder?

I think of him often. Perhaps now, his blisters healed and muscle soreness gone, he sits on his foam rubber and looks past the air conditioner upon the crush of humanity, fighting its way across streets, bucking traffic, hating to have to rush back to jobs. Trapped in the maze of the world whose face man has changed, perhaps this man will think back to Rainbow Bridge and the soon-to-be-forbidden passage—and wish he could erase what he wrote there.

F RANK L. GRIFFIN (1909–1990) graduated from Reed College in 1931. Following military service in the Second World War, Griffin worked as an actuarial consultant in Chicago. A lifelong conservationist, Griffin was a fierce proponent of the early anti-dam movement in the 1950s. Following retirement in the early 1970s, he became the publisher and editor of the Gardner, Nevada *Record Courier.* "Visit to a Drowning Canyon" provides the reader with a dramatic account of the loss felt by many as the level of Powell reservoir rose. It originally appeared in the January 1966 issue of *Audubor* magazine.

Visit to a Drowning Canyon

THE WATERS BEHIND THE NEW Glen Canyon Dam in Utah were rising steadily by the spring of 1965. The Colorado River, interrupted on its journey to the sea, was recoiling, as if in anger, to form massive Lake Powell. Soon the great scenic wonders of the canyon would be covered by water, lost forever to the eye and appreciation of man.

When I learned that the magnificent work of nature known as the Cathedral in the Desert would be inundated by June, I decided to beat the rising waters to it. Never again would it be possible to see this and other scenes of natural grandeur which took a billion years to create but which take man only a few years to destroy.

On completion of business in Phoenix, Ariz., on April 1, I drove to Escalante, Utah, where arrangements had been made for a guide. My plan was to proceed from there by truck, horse and on foot to a spot near the junction of the Escalante and Colorado rivers. There, a motor-powered rubber boat would enable us to tour a number of canyons tributary to Glen Canyon on the Colorado.

After several adventures and near-misadventures, which took me through a snowstorm in Oak Creek Canyon, a blizzard in Flagstaff, hail and rainstorms between Page and Kanab, and brief camera stops at Bryce Canyon and other points, I reached Escalante a little over a day and some 500 miles later.

Escalante is a town of about 1,000 people, mostly devoted to cattle raising, minor oil operations and tourists. It's the end of the line, except for dirt roads leading into the canyon country toward Hanksville.

Much to my surprise, Ken Sleight, my intended guide, wasn't in town. Ken is president of the Utah Guides Association. He had been called to a meeting in Los Angeles but had made arrangements to have me flown to Hall's Crossing on the Colorado, about 20 miles above its confluence with the Escalante River. There, a veteran riverman, Frank Wright, was to serve as my guide and furnish his power boat for our canyon trip.

The next morning there were clouds and snow on the mountains, but Bill Wells, the "Flying Bishop," was at the crude airstrip with his Cessna 172. He got his nickname from flying rescue missions. Bill looked more cowboy than pilot in his eight-gallon hat and Mackinaw.

We took off down the rough gravel strip, climbed over Ten Mile Wash and Coyote Gulch, and headed toward the lower Escalante canyons. Bill made a nice landing on a high plateau overlooking the Colorado River.

While the Hall's Crossing airstrip was only a few hundred yards from Wright's place, as the crow flies, it was probably a mile in the pickup truck, which had to negotiate a steep and winding route around and through gullies and washes.

Bad weather now was blowing up the river from the south. Heavy black clouds obscured the mountains and moved toward us. Frank Wright was a little doubtful about going, but his concern was primarily for me— how I would react to the venture in bad weather, whether I would blame him later for taking me out (at his rates!) on a damp camera expedition.

After I assured him that I had been wet before on salmon expeditions, we set off in his power boat with supplies for two days. The original plan with Ken Sleight had been for a four-day expedition, but nothing would be lost by the change in plans. One day already had been saved by flying in, and another would be saved by using the higher-speed boat to cover the distance to Rainbow Bridge and back, with side trips.

We spent the balance of the morning exploring Hall's Creek and the ruins of Indian cliff dwellings in Lake Creek, on our way down-river. In reacting to the novelty of these impressive cliffs, I found myself taking too many pictures. Later I was to wish that I had saved more exposures. We spied several black-crowned night heron's nests high on the cliff (the heron are being driven out), photographed Paul Bunyan's Potty, and made our way carefully up Lake Creek between the tops of drowned and dying trees to the Indian ruin which was to be below water in a matter of days or weeks.

Capt. Wright said that thousands of beavers had been trapped and drowned by the rising waters. They had stayed in their habitat too long and then had been forced to swim in the narrow canyons until exhausted. The deer had been forced out, and the birds were leaving, too, as the vegetation was inundated. Soon all land life between these walls would be virtually gone.

We stopped for lunch at Shock Bar, a sandstone formation, large, rounded and leading gently up to a niche and overhang containing the ruins of an Indian village high above the water. This ruin, fortunately, will survive the expected rise in Lake Powell.

Setting out again down the lake (one must become accustomed to saying "the lake" rather than "the Colorado"), we found our next diversion at the Escalante River estuary. We moved upstream between the patterned cliffs guarding the river's serpentine course, passed large dunes of orange sand (which, Capt. Wright explained, had blown over the rim from the mesa above) and passed the spot where Ken Sleight's rubber boats were moored. These were at the foot of the trail we would have come down according to the original plan. As it was raining again, I was thankful to be operating from Capt. Wright's boat rather than from the slower, unprotected, rubber variety.

We continued up the Escalante to the creek crossed by Gregory Arch. Winding slowly and skillfully up the canyon, avoiding driftwood and flooded vegetation, Capt. Wright eased us around many bends before we arrived at this beautiful span, soon to be inundated.

The rain increased and was driven by occasional gusts of wind. On the way back to the Colorado, we entered Clear Creek, which runs through the canyon of the Cathedral in the Desert. The sky was gray, and I suggested that we leave the trip to the Cathedral until the next day, hoping for better photographic conditions.

We revved up the motor and bounced over a heavy chop toward Rainbow Bridge canyon, many miles down-river, our intended destination for camp. Frank pulled into a small bay a short distance below Jackass Beach to look for a convenient place out of the weather to refill the gas tanks. But we found no shelter for the boat, and the weather did not break.

As we drifted there without the sound of the motor, a roar of water became audible above the rain pelting on the canvas overhead. We looked out to see several waterfalls, 800 to 1,000 feet in height, cascading over the cliffs. These cataracts were falling on a wide shelf of ledge rock some 30 feet above, and as we wondered where all this water was going, suddenly a series of lower falls began to appear. At one point about a dozen falls were in view.

We watched, fascinated. Frank Wright said that in all his years on the river, he had witnessed such a sight only three times. Few persons have ever photographed it. I was extremely fortunate to have had that opportunity during my one brief experience on the river.

Later, we pulled into a large cave to refuel the tanks. Water cascaded down the face of the cliff and fell in a narrow ribbon at the center of the cave's mouth. This place housed ancient Indian ruins which already have been drowned.

Next we entered Music Temple to see what was left after the flooding. Frank remarked that the sight was nothing compared to what it was when the water was 100 feet lower. The temple once resembled the "Cathedral," he said, and it would be even less impressive as days passed.

The entrance to Rainbow Canyon was breath-taking. After rounding several bends we entered a narrow side opening and proceeded up Bridge Canyon a few dozen yards. We camped at the foot of a trail leading a mile and a half up the creek to the arch, the highest point boats could reach on April 3, 1965. I understand that later it will be possible to take a motorboat almost into the shadow of Rainbow Bridge. Some of our lazy cousins may hail this, but many others will decry it. True outdoorsmen, including Wright, view these "civilized" changes with sad feelings.

We moored the boat to a drowned mountain ash and set up our cooking gear on the grassy beach, near the overhang of a 20-foot bank. Rain was sporadic, and there were enough lulls to permit a comfortable cookout and an excellent steak dinner with all the trimmings, prepared by Chef Wright. Our spirits were far from dampened in this beautiful, boxlike canyon, surrounded by magnificent, towering pink walls splashed with "desert varnish."

At first I planned to place my bedroll at the entrance to a cleft in the rock, but as the rain mounted we decided to bunk aboard the boat, where the canvas cover would afford partial protection.

During the night I awoke at intervals to the sound of a heavy downpour, each downpour followed shortly by the sound of five separate waterfalls around the sides of the canyon. These continued to run for some time after the downpour had ceased.

About 6:30 A.M. I managed to revive the almost dead fire and took a picture of a "desert rill" in the dim light of dawn. After a good breakfast, consisting of canned grapefruit segments, pancakes, bacon and coffee, we tidied up camp—keeping a weather eye constantly on the patch of sky which formed our roof. About eight o'clock there were signs that the clouds were breaking up, so we surveyed the creek (which was running high after the storm) to see what the possibilities might be of hiking up to Rainbow Bridge.

Six fordings of the creek are required, but we managed to cut this to two by picking a new route between the first and last of the indicated fords. By the time we reached the arch, the water had gone down enough so that on our return we were able to stay fairly close to the regular trail.

I took three color photographs of Rainbow Bridge—two from below (one showing snow-covered Navajo Mountain through the arch) and one from above. Coming down the canyon I shot one wall detail and two other views showing the creek and some juniper trees. At this point "operation film ration" had to go into effect, for we still had Twilight Canyon, Cathedral in the Desert, and Hole-in-the-Rock ahead of us. (I never did get a shot of the last, my "torture climb.")

Aside from the intricate patterns and mosaics etched on the sides of (Rainbow) Bridge Canyon, colorful as they are with "desert varnish" running down their pink walls, the sheer immensity of the sandstone cliffs and rounded domes, which stand 1,000 to 1,500 feet above the canyon floor, make them breath-taking. They dwarf one with a sense of awe and reverence. It seems positively sacrilegious to deface these canyons with the works of man.

The majesty of these tremendous cliffs will be impaired as their exposed height is lessened and their talus slopes and alcoves are obliterated by the rising waters. If this is true of relatively bare canyon walls, how much truer it will be when the living things which breathe color and sound into this unique world finally are gone.

From Rainbow we cruised to Twilight Canyon, so narrow and twisting as to amaze; and so deep as to inspire wonder. This canyon is almost beyond belief when one realizes that the plateau far above has been divided, by a single, deep, narrow, winding cleft, into two separate worlds between which no direct bridge exists. Passage between them, except by a long and circuitous route, would have been impossible to the ancient Indians.

We made the long run back to Clear Creek and Cathedral in the Desert on schedule. Frank ran the boat up the creek as far as possible and then we set out on foot. Up the creek bed we sloshed for half a mile, mainly on hard ledge rock, detouring occasionally through thickets or over orange sand bars. On either side of the canyon I noticed that the caves high on the face were deeper than most I had seen previously.

Then we rounded a final corner, and I caught my breath! What a fitting climax to this mysterious world of beauty. It was as if this were the end toward which all other wonders had been pointing. And even more, the prayers for sunshine had been answered. A shaft of light shone through a narrow cleft high above the grotto and formed a wedge upon the softly carpeted floor.

The floor of the Cathedral was a smooth and slightly raised mount of sand around which, in a semicircle, flowed a tiny stream. From a pool overhead and out of sight, a narrow jet of crystal clear water fell into a bowl at our feet, wound its way around the far perimeter of the chamber, then flowed into the outer world by the path we had taken.

Near the opening of the chamber, where sunlight must frequently fall, a delicate carpet of emerald-green plants spread over the clean sand. The entire chamber was rounded and domed high above, and its light entered from back of the basin whence the water flowed. A six-foot band of "desert varnish," covered by moist blue-green plants on the wet stone wall, circled half of the lower chamber.

As we faced the waterfall, it seemed, indeed, Nature's altar, lighted by a window to Heaven. In this place, I thought, no attitude of mind or heart would be possible except one of worship.

"Truly an emotional experience," I commented to Frank Wright. Despite the pictures I had seen in the Sierra Club books, I had hardly been prepared for the Cathedral when we came upon it. After slogging upstream and observing numerous, deep alcoves in the dry, sandstone cliffs, somehow I had expected another cave.

I had first become aware of Cathedral in the Desert, Music Temple, Twilight Canyon, and other outstanding scenic spots on the Colorado, through the magnificent Sierra Club book, *The Place No One Knew: Glen Canyon on the Colorado.* This poetic lament—augmented by François Leydet's later classic, *Time and the River Flowing: Grand Canyon*—presented, with beautiful text and superb color photography by Eliot Porter, the story of needless despoliation of the unique natural beauty of the region, and of most of the living things in its side canyons, by the building of Glen Canyon Dam.

Very few persons have ever secured pictures of the Cathedral similar to mine, nor, unfortunately, will they ever do so now that it has been flooded. Frank Wright and Mohr Christiansen both told me they had never seen the waterfall in the Cathedral grotto. Nor would I have done so if we had not gone on this expedition in the face of an unseasonal storm.

There is nothing left to say except that I felt like falling on my knees in thankfulness for having been permitted this experience, and in contrition for the blindness of men who permit the destruction of such handiworks of God.

After a run back to Hole-in-the-Rock, I was to climb out of the canyon to meet Mohr Christiansen at the rim. We had made the arrangement in Escalante because of a suspicion that flying out might mean a two-day wait at Hall's Crossing because of the weather.

Hole-in-the-Rock is a vertical fissure in cliffs which rise approximately 1,000 feet at this point. To get out, one must climb through the crack at close to a 45-degree angle for one-third of a mile, clambering over, around and under huge boulders weighing many tons. In some places the passage is over rocks so smooth and steep that the early Mormons cut steps in them. The climb was an experience I would not care to repeat often, even without my pack and camera case, which complicated things immensely. Several times I weighed the possibility of letting the pack go. Alone in the massive crack between those sheer sandstone walls, among debris which had fallen in earlier centuries, I had time to contemplate the inevitable result of a disablement, and so I exercised due care.

There remained also a possibility that, as a result of the storms, the primitive dirt road from Escalante had become impassable, even for Mohr's four-wheel-drive pickup, and that I would arrive at the top of the cliffs to find nothing but 60 miles of wilderness ahead of me. I took one hour and three-quarters to reach the top, making frequent rest stops and going over parts of the route twice—once to reconnoiter without my luggage and once to carry it or push it up ahead of me through the boulder-strewn chimney.

Frank Wright waited until I had traversed half of the climb, then started out for Hall's Crossing. He had checked to be sure I had matches, and had given me a can of tuna "just in case." I lugged four pounds of water up that slope, too.

Frank had said that he planned to fly down to Page the following day, weather permitting, and would buzz the top of the Hole to see whether I was still there or had picked up my ride.

He had told me that, if I were still there (my blood would have been congealed by that time, I'll wager), they would land the plane on a small strip three miles away and pick me up. He also had said that I would be foolish to start walking to Escalante if my ride wasn't there, because it would take three days to reach civilization.

Fortunately, Mohr showed up just before I emerged from the Hole. I was certainly happy to see him.

Despite a fast run over the last 20 miles, it took us three hours to cover the 62 miles. The road was muddied and rutted in places where clay overlay the sand, and it crossed deep gullies and washes with dangerous grades and curves. There had been eight inches of snow in Escalante that morning.

All I could think of on the way back, in addition to the elation with which the trip had buoyed my spirits, was a hot shower and clean clothes. That was to be much later, for after hot coffee and dinner in Escalante I drove to Panguitch, planning to start for Salt Lake in the morning.

Exhausted and tired as I was, I'm afraid I wasn't prepared for the comments I heard at dinnertime from a man newly arrived from Colorado with a fast buck in mind. He opined that Lake Powell was a great thing and would bring in tourists and fishermen when the government got around to building the promised road from Escalante, and the boat launching facilities on the river some ten miles below Hole-in-the-Rock.

That did it. With new conservationist zeal instilled by my journey into the wilderness with Frank Wright, I gave a strong reply: "It was a terrible mistake, a crying shame," I said, "to destroy so many 'live' canyons in order to provide an overgrown, straight-walled bathtub for the boys to run their motorboats in."

I mentioned the beavers, deer and birds, the trees and creeks which were being destroyed, the ancient ruins being covered, the "go-go" boys throwing empty cans and other litter on the remaining ledges or in the lake. I also mentioned the growing laziness of men who must build roads into every wilderness for themselves and for thousands of careless visitors unconcerned about man's defacement of nature's wonders.

Perhaps I was too wound up. Yet, everything I said was true.

R USSELL MARTIN IS THE AUTHOR and editor of nearly a dozen works, including *Beethoven's Hair, Out of Silence,* and the novel *Beautiful Islands. A Story That Stands Like a Dam: Glen Canyon and the Struggle for the Soul of the West* won the Caroline Bancroft History Prize upon its publication in 1989, and remains the most vivid and engaging history of Glen Canyon and the dam's construction yet written. The following excerpt from the book tells the tale of the Emergency Salvage Project conducted by Jesse Jennings and C. Gregory Crampton, among others, from 1957 to 1963. Although significantly excised, the chapter also gives the reader a glimpse into the two most populous eras in Glen Canyon's history: the era of the Anasazi and the Glen Canyon "Gold Rush" of the late nineteenth century.

The Salvage Seasons

EMBARKING FROM HITE [IN 1950], Crampton and his companions floated the Colorado—so swollen with runoff it was close to flood stage—in the war-surplus rubber rafts that detractors such as Nevills (who used only hard-hulled wooden craft) liked to call "baloney boats." Though the rafts looked like outsized wading-pool toys, they were perfectly suited to desert rivers, and navigating them downstream, Crampton and company quickly were overwhelmed by the glories of Glen Canyon.

But in addition to the beauty of the serpentine river and the high, many-hued walls that contained it, in addition to the enchanting side canyons and legendary landforms like Rainbow Bridge, Gunsight Butte, and Sentinel Rock, Crampton was astonished to find such rich evidence of the human presence in the canyon. There were Fort Moqui, Defiance House, Wasp House, and dozens more easily visible architectural ruins of the Anasazi; there were the chimney remains of the cabin built by the first Anglo settler in the canyon and many, more recent domiciles scattered about in various states of disrepair; there were mining dumps and rusted hand tools; an ancient Model 30 Caterpillar filled with gasoline waited on Gretchen Bar as if it were still ready to go to work, and there in the middle of the current a couple of miles upstream from Bullfrog Creek was the listing wreck of a giant gold dredge. It was fascinating and somehow paradoxical from Crampton's perspective. This was wilderness, to be sure. The canyon was hundreds of miles from the nearest community of even a few thousand people. The river itself was its only avenue, its only accessible pathway. It seemed as wild as any place imaginable, yet it obviously held a whole sweep of human history, of long occupations and short attempts at exploitation. It was at once a naturalist's wonderland and a historian's treasure trove, a riverine world that was utterly empty of people when Greg Crampton floated through it in

1949, but one whose ghosts were almost palpable, a place that he was determined to visit again and again.

Although he managed a second sojourn in Glen Canyon in the summer of 1950, familial and professional demands kept Crampton from returning to it again before he heard in 1956 the crushing news that the canyon would be flooded. The river canyons of the Glen and the San Juan and their side canyons—more than a hundred of them—would begin to go under in only a few years, Crampton's wonderland lost.

Yet perhaps there was an opportunity amid the tragedy. Jesse Jennings, an archaeologist specializing in the prehistoric cultures of the desert Southwest and chairman of the University of Utah's anthropology department, was already at work trying to secure for the university the federal contract to conduct studies of the myriad archaeological resources soon to be inundated by the reservoir that would fill Glen Canyon. The Historic Sites Act of 1935 had charged the Department of the Interior, through the National Park Service, with the preservation and scientific dissemination of the nation's antiquities, and it had called for their "emergency salvage" in situations where major developments threatened to destroy them. The law had been passed too late to result in any sort of antiquities inventory prior to filling Lake Mead behind Hoover Dam, and only minimal salvage work had been undertaken in the intervening years at other Reclamation project sites. But because the Anasazi culture had had such an enormous impact on the Colorado Plateau, because the plateau's dry desert and semidesert environments so successfully preserved physical evidence of the culture, and because Glen Canyon itself had been heavily occupied by early peoples, Jennings was determined that this time the salvage should be comprehensive. It should include basic geological, paleontological, and ecological surveys, as well as extensive archaeological fieldwork, and the resulting data and their interpretations should be made readily available through a series of detailed, if necessarily voluminous, reports.

In concert with Jennings's efforts, Crampton urged the park service to authorize historical investigations in the reservoir area as a critical adjunct to the studies of the canyons' prehistory. And by early 1957 the park service was convinced—the agency entering into formal salvage agreements with the University of Utah and the Museum of Northern Arizona, a privately endowed research institution based in Flagstaff. The museum, with Alexander Lindsay, Jr., acting as field director, was charged with the archaeological investigation of the 74 miles of the San Juan River Canyon that the reservoir would inundate, plus its adjoining side canyons, as well as the 69 miles of the left bank of the Colorado between the confluence with the San Juan and the canyon's terminus at Lee's Ferry. The University of Utah's responsibilities included the archaeological studies of the 130 miles of the upper Glen and its tributaries, the right bank and side canyons below the San Juan's confluence, and the ecological and historical studies of the entire reservoir area. Jennings was named project director, and Crampton happily agreed to head up the historical studies.

There would be seven field seasons, 1957–63, during which time more than 800 miles of sheer-walled canyons would be investigated by boat and on foot, the looming deadline imposed by the dam allowing archaeological sites merely to be sampled rather than entirely excavated. Small teams of researchers—usually composed of ten or fewer professors, students, volunteers, and occasional hired hands—systematically would scour the reservoir area during the summer months, using baloney boats and hiking boots as their principal means of access, spending up to two weeks at a time ensconced in the canyon, roaming, digging, recording their findings before flushing themselves out at Lee's Ferry. Unlike traditional scientific fieldwork, normally undertaken as an inquiry into a specific issue or "problem," the mission of the salvage teams would be no more than to try—as completely as the limitations of time and related resources would allow—to document what was there in those secretive canyons, what once had been.

The first fundamental surprise encountered by the academicians and inveterate diggers was that, even in relatively recent times, Glen Canyon had been a different sort of place. In the late 1950s, the side-canyon streams the researchers observed coursed across bedrock en route to the river, but they cut through remnants of alluvial sediments that once had created broad, flat, and fertile plains in the canyon bottoms. They were astonished to discover that in some cases the silt beds had been as deep as 90 feet. What immediately seemed possible was that agriculture once had flourished in these side canyons, but that much of the evidence of the first farmers—their shelters, fields, ditches, and drainage systems—subsequently had been flushed from the canyons along with the alluvial soils. The ruins of masonry structures that might have been granaries, lookouts, or seasonal dwellings still clung to rocky outcroppings, some of them sheltered by overhanging cliffs, but none seemed to be accompanied by the large, multilayered trash heaps that archaeologists call middens, whose presence strongly would have suggested long-term habitation. The ruins of the first residential structures in Glen Canyon long since might have been washed into the Colorado and away, but there was another possibility. Perhaps these early inhabitants lived on the canyon rims and adjacent uplands and only ventured into the canyons to farm. To try to determine whether that indeed had been the case, the archaeologists would have to extend their investigations laterally onto the plateaus that bounded the canyons, and the salvage would have to become decidedly more complicated as it barely got under way.

The first nomadic inhabitants of the Colorado Plateau belonged to a culture that Southwestern archaeologists have labeled the Desert Archaic. Entering the region perhaps as early as the tenth century B.C., the people of the Desert Culture migrated seasonally, following game and the growing seasons of the plants they foraged. They shaped primitive tools out of stone and wove baskets, but left only scant evidence of themselves in Glen Canyon and elsewhere in the vast region they roamed.

By about 100 B.C., however, the people had begun to be more sedentary, building their first permanent dwellings and experimenting with the exotic business of agriculture. A cultural revolution—an elemental change in living groups, habitation, diet, and geography—subsequently was spawned by the successful cultivation of crops and it became widespread throughout the Southwest, beginning first with the people in the region that is now southern Arizona and New Mexico, then extending north to the peoples who inhabited a great arc of land reaching from the Rio Grande in central New Mexico to the Virgin River in southwestern Utah. It was roughly the same region the unrelated Navajos would begin to occupy 1,500 years later, and the Navajos referred to their predecessors as *Anasazi,* a word variously translated as "Ancient Enemies," "Old Strangers," "Those Who Were Here Before Us."

Anglo settlers in the Four Corners region of the Southwest (where the states of Colorado, New Mexico, Arizona, and Utah meet at a common point) tended first to refer to the Anasazi as *Aztecs,* mistakenly thinking that the physical evidence of them—their ruins were obvious and everywhere—linked them to the ancient culture of central Mexico. Later, the terms *Mo-*

qui, a variant of *Hopi,* and *Pueblo* became current, and finally, archaeologists made a determined effort to establish Anasazi as the best of several possible appellations.

As archaeological investigations of the Anasazi grew intensive early in the twentieth century, it became clear that the culture had had a remarkable fluorescence, one that had lasted more than a millennium before it mysteriously collapsed. During the early years of what was the nascent Christian era on the banks of the Mediterranean, the Anasazi lifeway on this continent quickly began to grow complex, and the Anasazi population burgeoned. The people devoted far more of their time to growing corn, beans, and squash than to foraging and hunting; they wove intricate, excellent baskets, and they constructed pithouses—dwellings dug shallowly into the earth, covered with roofs built from posts and a latticework of branches, brush, grasses, and dirt.

An Anasazi move toward urbanization began between A.D. 700 and 900, at about the same time that technical abilities and aesthetic senses began to flourish. Pithouses began to be closely clustered, sometimes built with adjoining walls. Pottery became commonplace and was carefully and beautifully painted. By the year 1000 or so, houses were built almost exclusively above ground, with upright walls constructed of mortared sandstone, and the clustering of houses increased. For reasons that probably had much to do with their agricultural achievements—their increasing ability to support large numbers of people from carefully tended fields, and the corresponding demand for many field-workers—the Anasazi began to group themselves into larger and larger masonry villages, some several stories tall, built high on mesa tops and, later, in the arching caves in canyon walls. Concerns about defense could have precipitated the moves, but the migrations weren't made hastily. Architecture, in fact, reached its most sophisticated and aesthetic dimensions by about 1100.

At the height of their cultural expansion, the Anasazi were the Southwest's dominant culture. Trading within the Anasazi region and with neighboring cultures located even thousands of miles away became extensive. Elaborate road systems, some hundreds of miles long, were constructed throughout much of the Anasazi region, as well as what appear to have been line-of-sight communications towers. Irrigation, previously limited to the planting of crops in alluvial creekbeds or near intermittent springs, felt the rush of technology as well. Catch basins and dikes were built at the mouths of arroyos and washes to trap periodic runoff. Ditches, long canals, and reservoirs carried and stored the precious water for the fields and the people themselves.

It was evidence of the Anasazi's proficiency as farmers and irrigationists that was among the most important information salvaged in Glen Canyon. Jennings and his young, enthusiastic colleagues—many of whom would go on from the salvage project to establish prominent careers in southwestern archaeology for themselves—identified and excavated an otherwise un-known double-walled masonry dam at a place called Creeping Dune, a relatively sophisticated structure that had caught water which spilled to the surface of the ground where a block of Chinle shale was exposed. A water gate with a notched stone slab that likely was used to regulate flow was built into a corner of the U-shaped dam, and a stone-lined ditch system led from it to a terraced field. In Beaver Canyon, the archaeologists found an extensive ditch-and-field complex where an alluvial fan had been irrigated by water diverted from the intermittent creek and carried in carefully lined ditches. Near Castle Creek, an earthen aqueduct had carried water laterally across a shallow depression, making it possible to irrigate an otherwise inaccessible shelf. Terraced fields, often protected by mortared retaining walls and wa-tered by subterranean seeps, were found on the large bars along the Colo-rado and in several side canyons; and in Lake Canyon, where piling sand had dammed the headwaters of a slender stream to form a lake, numerous sites testified to the fact that the Anasazi had been dependent on the canyons' water resources, water that wasn't available on the arid mesas above.

During their several summers of work, Jennings's and Lindsay's crews were able to identify a variety of trails—precarious toeholds chipped into sweeping slabs of sandstone—connecting the canyon bottoms to the rims. They found exquisite petroglyph panels—pecked and incised figures at the bases of looming walls that depicted mountain sheep, birds, animal tracks, geometric designs, trapezoidal men and women. Collectively, the two in-stitutions mapped and cataloged more than 2,500 canyon sites, and hundreds more on the peripheral tablelands. And before their emergency work was finished, they were able—to the satisfaction of most of their number—to make a basic conclusion about what first had puzzled them.

It seemed certain in the end that the side canyons of the Glen long had undergone a cycle of filling and flushing, sediments washing down and settling on the canyon bottoms for hundreds of years perhaps—perhaps only for decades—before the runoff from violent storms flushed them out and the filling began again. And although it was possible that large Anasazi villages had been constructed on these very tenuous and temporary plains, what seemed far more likely was that the Anasazi never lived in the canyons in great numbers. The trail systems, the ruins of large pueblos (with middens of corresponding size) that were found on adjacent mesa tops, and the Anasazi's long tenure in the Glen Canyon country (making it very likely that they would have known from the experiences and stories of their elders that the alluvial beds could be destroyed) all contributed to the archaeologists' conclusions that Glen Canyon served principally as a kind of garden, but a vitally important one. Water was prevalent in the canyons; the soil was fertile, the growing season long and dependable. But for some reason, the Anasazi never chose or were never forced to build the great fortress cities in Glen Canyon that they had constructed at Chaco Canyon, Canyon de Chelly, Tsegi Canyon, and Mesa Verde. It was hard to know why they did not, and the nature of the emergency salvage meant that these diggers into the dimly understood past, these examiners of bone and stone and painted ceramics, probably would never know.

It may have been the breaching of their fields by floods that led the Anasazi elsewhere; it may have been the depletion of myriad resources after centuries in a fragile landscape; almost certainly, a long and disastrous drought descended on the plateau region in the middle decades of the 1200s. But whatever their mix of reasons, the people began to go. There was no mass exodus from the cities and villages and the fields that had sustained them for so long, but everywhere the emigrations increased. People who for generations had known only intensely communal lives left their houses, their possessions, their buried kin, and wandered away in little bands—drifting south, southwest, southeast, searching for those elements that had made life good in the slickrock north. The Anasazi abandonment reached its peak in the last quarter of the thirteenth century. By the year 1300, most of the Colorado Plateau was empty of human habitation, and no one was left in Glen Canyon. . . .

Although its route was tortuous, the Hole-in-the-Rock trail joining the towns of Escalante and Bluff was used intermittently in the succeeding years [following its "construction" in 1879]. Charles Hall, one of the founders of the town of Escalante and the man who had fashioned the Mormon's Hole-in-the-Rock ferryboat, was optimistic enough about the trail's potential, in fact, that he had stayed behind in Glen Canyon, offering his services to the rare traveler for a full year before he determined that business in that spot probably never was going to be brisk. Thirty-five miles upstream, however, Hall found a ferry-crossing site that seemed far better than Hole-in-the-Rock. The creek that eventually was named after him provided relatively gentle canyon access from the west, and from the east the river was accessible down a series of descending benches. Hall built a 30-foot-long boat out of lumber hauled in from Escalante, reasoned that he would need to charge $5.00 per wagon and $.75 per horse for the ride across the river, then sat down to wait for customers, the first full-time resident in the interior of the canyon since the era of the Anasazi. Two years later, however, Hall had company in the canyon and his river crossing had competition.

Cass Hite was a prospector who had spent years searching the Navajo country for a fabled silver mine. A Navajo headman named Hoskininni, with whom Hite had become acquainted, informed him that although he wouldn't tell him the location of the silver mine, he'd show him where he could find gold, if that particular mineral was of any interest to him. Hite assured Hoskininni that gold would be just fine; the two made their way down White Canyon to the Colorado; and sure enough, Hite found gold in the sand and gravel terraces beside the river. Despite his jubilant mood, Hite also took time to notice that the spot where the two men stood would make a "Dandy Crossing," a name that stuck only a little while before it was replaced by Hite City and then simply by Hite.

But Cass Hite wasn't interested in anything as prosaic as operating a ferry, not when there plainly were fortunes to be made. He never built or brought any boats to the river, but he did do his best to publicize the crossing—certainly the most accessible one between Lee's Ferry and Moab, he claimed, probably correctly—and in letters to the *Salt Lake Tribune* and several newspapers in Colorado, he lauded the Glen Canyon gold discovery, speculating that the canyon would become the site of the nation's next great mining boom.

At first, however, there was anything but a rush to riches in Glen Canyon. Interest in the place was so slim, in fact, that Charles Hall abandoned his ferry business in 1884, aware that Hite, 45 miles upriver, was getting increasing cross-river traffic, convinced as well that this mining business would never amount to much. But soon after Hall had made his retreat from the river, reports of other strikes—big strikes—began to gain currency in the alpine mining camps of Utah's Wasatch and Uinta ranges and Colorado's San Juans. Many a miner decided it wouldn't hurt to go have a look for himself, to see if those crazy canyons really were giant sluice boxes lined with gold.

Dandy Crossing Bar, Ticaboo Bar, Good Hope Bar, California Bar, Klondike Bar, Gretchen Bar, Oil Seep Bar, Boston Bar—before the eighties were out there were dozens of variously productive gold placers in operation along the river. Gold, washed down out of the Rockies for many millennia, so fine it was literally dust, was found along the river from Hite all the way to Lee's Ferry. And when William McKinley's election to the presidency in 1896 meant a victory as well for the gold standard, prospectors began to pour into Glen Canyon—entering at Hite, at Hall's Crossing, at Hole-in-the-Rock, and the Crossing of the Fathers, maniacal men getting into the canyon wherever and however they could, staking claims, establishing mining districts, hauling in sluicing and dredging and drilling equipment, building cabins and camps throughout its length. By 1889, Hite was so prosperous it had a post office, and an estimated 1,000 miners were at work in Glen Canyon, each one sure he soon would be a millionaire.

The fact that Glen Canyon was going to be another Klondike, so lots of fellows said, made a railroad through the canyon all the more attractive, all the more a certain financial success. A rail line already had reached Grand Junction, Colorado; if it could be continued on through the lower canyons of the Colorado River to southern California, what a boon it would be to the whole of the Southwest, what money it would make for its owners! Frank M. Brown, president of the newly incorporated Denver, Colorado Canyon and Pacific Railroad Company, was determined to see it accomplished, and he had hired the well-known railroad engineer Robert Brewster Stanton to design a suitable river-level route. Traveling through Glen Canyon by boat at the end of June 1889, Brown, Stanton, and a crew of sixteen men liked what they saw. Westwater Canyon on the Colorado-Utah border would be difficult to punch a railroad through; Cataract Canyon would be equally intractable; but Glen and the connecting canyons upstream seemed to have been built not by Powell's "storm-born architect," but rather by some sort of celestial engineer. They were perfect for such a plan. Then, having met Cass Hite at Ticaboo Bar—discussing their dream with him while they repaired their Cataract-battered boats—and having made a similar courtesy call on the Mormons operating Lee's Ferry, the men pushed on into Marble Canyon. There, within only a few miles, Frank Brown was caught in a whirlpool and drowned in Soap Creek Rapid. Neither the overweight entrepreneur nor any of his companion travelers had brought along the cork life-preservers that by then had become commonplace.

Stanton eventually was able to complete his survey all the way to the mouth of the Colorado, and although he remained adamant that a railroad through the canyons was both economically and technically feasible, the company never was able to raise enough capital to give the project a try. Daunted, but still convinced that his fortune awaited him along the river, Stanton returned to Glen Canyon in 1897, possessing substantial eastern capital this time and a grand plan indeed, though no longer one concerned with railroads.

Cass Hite and other miners in the Glen had convinced Stanton that the canyon *was* a gigantic serpentine sluice box. All that was required to exploit it, to extract its gold, was an efficient large-scale operation, it seemed. What Stanton wanted to do was to install a series of floating dredges throughout the canyon's length. He would build dams in several side canyons—and perhaps even across the Colorado itself—to generate electricity to operate the dredges. He would stake contiguous claims from Hite clear to Lee's Ferry, more than 150 miles of them, and he would become rich in the process of growing legendary.

Initial tests seemed to prove the abundance of the Glen Canyon gold; crews built primitive roads and improved trails—including the widening of the Hole-in-the-Rock access to the river—in advance of delivering the many dredges; and 145 claims were staked and duly recorded. In June 1900, Stanton's pilot dredge, the machine that would prove the viability of the grand scheme, was shipped in pieces by rail to Green River, Utah, hauled by wagons to Hanksville, then over the flank of the Henry Mountains, and finally down to a dredging site about four miles above Bullfrog Creek. Stanton's men had to cut a dugway in the canyon walls to get the dredge down to the river, but it was finally assembled, floated, and put in operation—five small gasoline engines operating the 46-bucket, 105-foot-long dredge. Yet nothing seemed to go as planned. The dredge tended to get stuck on submerged sandbars; the river's silt gummed up the amalgamating tables; and, somehow, the fine, powdery, almost ethereal gold dust kept escaping back to the river. Stanton's operation had already cost $100,000, and a return on that investment was growing problematic. After his first general cleanup, Stanton recorded in his diary a yield of $30.15 in gold. A second cleanup yielded a whooping $36.80 before Stanton abandoned his dredge in midriver in the summer of 1901 and left Glen Canyon for good.

The mining business wasn't going much better for anyone else at the turn of the century. There had been a brief boom along the banks of the San Juan, but it had played out quickly; Cass Hite was still at work, and so were scores of others, but the gold dust was so light, so flaky, that it simply floated over the amalgamators. No placer-mining technique known to humankind could deal with gold that tended to *float*. Yet before it all went bust, there would be one more flamboyant effort to capture the canyon's riches.

A prospector named Charlie Spencer had already failed dramatically in the San Juan Canyon when he went to the foot of Glen Canyon at Lee's Ferry in 1909 in possession of a pneumatic pipe dredge that surely would be the solution to the problem of the lightweight gold. His high-pressure hoses would force water to dissolve the gold-bearing Chinle shale in the area, and mercury-coated amalgamators then would latch on to the precious mineral and trap it. It was a system that was certain to work, but it would require a lot of coal to produce steam to power the operation.

Spencer and his men found a suitable coal bed on a branch of Warm Creek, 28 miles upstream; they mined the coal, hauled it to the mouth of the creek on ox-drawn wagons, then loaded it onto the *Charles H. Spencer,* the only steamer and the largest boat of any kind ever to float through the canyon. Although the *Spencer* occasionally would beach itself on sandbars as it came downstream heavily loaded with coal, its biggest problem was that it required almost a full load of coal to steam *upstream* to Warm Creek. Charlie Spencer finally surmounted that difficulty when he began to tow a barge behind his steamer, but by that point, it was becoming clear that all the coal in the world couldn't solve a fatal situation: something in the river water, the sand or the Chinle shale, was coating, clogging, gumming the mercury, rendering it unable to absorb the gold, and, as had happened countless times upstream during the preceding thirty years, the gold cavalierly slipped away and then returned to the river.

By 1913, Lee's Ferry was simply a ferry again, owned now by the Arizona county of Coconino; Charlie Spencer had gone on to try to pursue greatness in other places. Cass Hite died at Ticaboo in 1914, and in 1915, the abandoned *Charles H. Spencer* sank. At the end of that same year, Bert Loper, a river man and occasional prospector, left the hermitage he had built for himself at the mouth of Red Canyon, near his diggings at Castle Butte Bar.

Loper had been the last resident in the interior of the canyon. Now Glen Canyon was quiet, its flirtation with industry ended.

The physical evidence of the occupation of Glen Canyon from the time of the Anasazi until early in the twentieth century had been readily visible to Jesse Jennings, Lex Lindsay, Greg Crampton, and their baloney-boat crews. From Hite to Lee's Ferry, masonry ruins, small dams and ditches, astonishing dugways, mysterious petroglyphs and clumsily incised names, cabins and the sentinel chimneys of cabins long since burned, wrecked wagons, steel boilers and the remnants of sluicing equipment, a river-soaked dredge and a steamboat that now rested on the river bottom—all had been in easy evidence, certifying that people had known this place for two thousand years and more.

Yet this was a place that people simply had clambered across, a riverine world they had gone into to farm, to mine, to explore in the name of science and the marketplace. It had always been remote enough, harsh enough despite its myriad delights, that no one had ever gone there plainly and principally because it seemed like a good place to be. The Anasazi had never lived in the canyon in large numbers; the early Mormons, willing to endure the hardships thrown up by almost any other place, weren't even tempted to stay. The canyon had done little more than to get in the way of Utes, Paiutes, Navajos, and the long queues of horseback missionaries and traders. Powell and subsequent explorers at last had seen all of Glen Canyon, but it was only a place through which they slowly were in transit, a place to note in water-stained logs before they reached the next place. The miners, like miners everywhere—equally ignoring difficulty and splendor—had been interested only in rocky treasure.

In 1922, the year E. C. LaRue escorted federal and state water officials through Glen Canyon to show them what a fine environment it would be for a high dam and reservoir, the canyon had appeared much the way it did to the salvagers in 1962. The relics of its history already seemed as old. The trails that cut across it at the Crossing of the Fathers, Hole-in-the-Rock, and Hall's Crossing seemed equally archaic, equally impossible to believe.

At Lee's Ferry at the foot of the canyon, however, much had changed in that forty-year span. In 1929, Navajo Bridge had been built across Marble Canyon, six miles downstream from the ferry, by the Arizona Highway

Department—at that time the only bridge across the Colorado in the more than 600 miles between Moab, Utah, and Needles, California. The fifty-year-old ferry subsequently—and very quickly—had gone out of business.

At Hite, at the head of the canyon, things were different as well. A cable-guided ferry finally had gone into operation in September 1946, when the state of Utah completed a serviceable gravel road connecting the communities of Blanding and Hanksville. Yet Hite had not gone modern; it was still a mere speck of a place set down in God's own outback; it was still an awfully slim excuse for a town, and its minuscule post office, barely bigger than a bread box—officially White Canyon, Utah, on the canceled stamps—was still open for occasional business. Historians and archaeologists, students and summer adventurers wearing T-shirts and sand-battered pith helmets, men like the grinning, impish-faced Greg Crampton, often were wont to mail wish-you-were-here postcards from Hite before they embarked in their rubber boats, headed into splendid Glen Canyon to look again at the old days.

KATIE LEE GAINED FAME IN THE 1950s as a singer and actress in Holly-wood, appearing regularly on NBC's radio and television *The Milton Berle Show.* In the decade preceding its inundation, Lee regularly ran, guided, and explored Glen Canyon. Since the dam's completion, her name has become synonymous with the canyon and efforts to restore it. Ms. Lee currently resides in her native state of Arizona. *All My Rivers Are Gone* (1997) recounts her journeys through Glen Canyon, focusing on her trips with Tad Nichols and Frank Wright from 1954 to 1957, during which the three named nearly twenty-seven of the Glen's side canyons, including Dangling Rope.

All My Rivers Are Gone

SEPTEMBER 26, 1955

NIGHT SETTLES COOL IN GLEN CANYON in September. In the first weeks there's a noticeable brittleness in the air. Waters from up north are already chilled, and there's little chance they'll warm between the high walls, which now cast early shadows on the water. Nearby our camp in the quiet eddy, mist swirls and rises into the willows, as if the river's out on a cold night watching his breath vaporize. I call it "witches' breath" and stare at it for a long time. Tadito [Tad Nichols], the desert rat, sneezes—HORSEshit!—and Bigfeets [Frank Wright], when he thinks nobody's looking, stoically reaches for the small of his back and presses hard.

On a darkly varnished wall near the mouth of Smith Fork [River Mile 132] is an Anasazi story board. It pictures squiggles, dots and spirals, suns and snakes, animals and bugs; human and superhuman figures armed with bows and arrows, others with arrows through them; much game, many hunters; hands, a lot of feet and bird prints; heavy-hung Shaman figures with goofy headdresses, Kokopelli from the mythical (?) world, with his hump and his flute—and things the archaeologists, anthropologists, and other educated guessers will never figure out.

Our campfire near the petroglyph wall pulls the figures into strong relief, making them dance grotesquely in the flickering light. We lie facing them, propped on our bedrolls watching the square-shouldered gods move down through the centuries to join us. I point to one with my big toe.

"See that one there? Reminds me of Barry Goldwater."

"Which one?" asks Tad, "the guy with the large. . ."

"No, sweetie, the one *without* the balls. He's been *down* this river and *still* he writes me stupid letters about how much more beneficial it will be to everyone when it's not here anymore."

Already having my suspicions, I decide now is the time to find out why Tad was late meeting us at the river. Turning from the dancing figures, I nail him with the firelight in my eyes. "What *were* you doing that kept you so long, E.T.?"

Frank feels something coming, gets up and heads for the kitchen box. "Cookies, anyone?"

"I'll have some," answers Tad, "might need to sweeten this exchange." He rolls over, facing me, props on an elbow, and sets his defenses: "I stayed for a meeting with some state officials so I could show them some slides of the canyon—give them some reasons not to build the dam."

"Did you tell them this time the slides were of Glen Canyon, the place they are intending to wipe off the map? Last time I went to one of your showings, you failed to mention that little item."

"Wasn't the time or place for it, sweetie."

"*Everyplace* is the time and place for it now, Tad, or we won't have the chance of a snowball in hell of stopping them. We can't let a single opportunity pass. I write the letters, I show your movie, I sing the songs, I write for newspapers and magazines. If there's a hearing I can get to, I go to protest their insane actions, their idiotic proposals, their greed—but there aren't enough of us to. . ."

"I know, and I've been around when you've had a go at some of the officials, even though I understand exactly why." He puffs slowly on his pipe, making little wheezing noises. "It doesn't help to get them angry."

"Damn it, why are you always defending these people, E.T.?"

"I'm not defending them, but I want you to see that the way you fight for our canyon doesn't always help."

"Yes, dear, I've heard that before—'get your facts down, your statistics up, and your emotions out.' What the hell's wrong with emotion? Without it we'd just be animals."

"Doesn't mix with the oil of politics, is what I infer."

"Neither does reason," offers Frank, opening the cookie tin and handing it around. "Katie's proposal of not building the dam high enough for water to enter the Rainbow Bridge National Monument *is* reasonable. It'd save a lot of beautiful country up here, too."

"Anyway," I persist, still wound up, "what's wrong with the way I fight for our river? I sure use more *reason* than the Wreckers [The Bureau of Reclamation] when I'm at hearings ticking off reasons for keeping it. They've got their goddamn nerve telling me what it *should* be like when half of them *haven't ever seen this place!*"

Tad taps out his pipe on a nearby stone and says, "You aren't going to like this, but say it's left as is. All spring, summer, and fall, boats line the banks. How many beer cans would be sitting here beside us? Where would our freedom be to enjoy this solitude? How long before we'd have to find a new place to get away from all those we've helped lure here?"

"No!" I bark, "that kind of camper excludes himself; he's too lazy to get here. Now it's a river for *outdoor* people. When the Bu-Wreckers are done, it'll be a 'recreation area' for *indoor* people. River people *earn* the thrill of seeing and being in a majestic place. It's the clods who need everything brought to them, packaged, arranged, and spoon-fed, who don't deserve a place like this. Make this . . . this spiritual place a reservoir so they can see less faster? Insane! They'll dump their crap all over, squat and shit on the slick-rock, climb out of their ski boats into their campers and drive away without the faintest notion of where they've been—just another playground with wall-to-wall water!"

Tad plays devil's advocate. "Ah-ha, but it's *progress* to make Glen Canyon a reservoir. Your Bunglers of Resources don't know *why* it's progress, because the word has lost its meaning. What they really mean is it's *money;* in America the words are synonymous."

Still burning inside, I get up to put more wood on the fire, "Well, I *don't* want it to be a stinking puddle, and I have as much right to it as they do, more actually; I know and love it. My very soul is in this canyon, so . . . I think I'll spend the rest of my days figuring a way to blow up their damn dam. Fucking politicians! O-oh, sorry Frank."

Tad pockets his pipe. "*Not* reasonable. *Highly* emotional, as I've said before."

He's right, of course. "Well, Tad-O, when every hidden pocket's been flooded, bulldozed, oil slicked, strip mined or made radioactive, where do we flee the techno-bureaucratic monster?"

"Not to worry, pal, by then our culture will have flown up its own ass, thereby obliterating itself. Have a cookie."

Journal Note: Saturday, October 1, 1955
(We Three [Lee, Nichols, and Wright] Trip, Eighth Day)

Each new discovery surpasses the last. It seems the tougher these canyons are to penetrate, the more beauty they hide. I leave a part of me in the arms of Bowns Canyon; leave blood and tears in exchange for what I've seen and will remember all my life.

Over, under, and around Wingate boulders, through water in tunnels of tumbled rock, past rabbit brush, datura, and stunted cottonwood, we make our way to the base of the Kayenta. Ah-hhh, bedrock at last!

As we round a bend and come over a small rise, I feel like I've been hit in the middle of my everything. I grab for Frank's arm and say, "Wait a minute, Bigfeets, I don't think I can take much more of this. It's *too* beautiful!" Suddenly I'm crying. He nods, takes my hand, and squeezes hard. When I look at him, there are tears in his eyes as well.

I ask myself, *what's here* that triggers an emotion so overwhelming it brings tears? It's not like theater, where our emotions are aroused by what we hear, and we cry over words and evolving situations. This is *rock*—inert—water, air, aromas, silence, light, and shadowplay. Words would mock this scene.

Our tears have come unexpectedly because we're thankful to the point of overflowing. We've just been handed a spectacular gift—rare, flawless, stunning to the senses—and the privilege has touched our hearts in a wash humility and reverence. I am humbled and bow my head before these generous Canyon Gods, glad to be one who can shed tears.

Floyd Dominy would probably stop here and take a piss.

Journal Note: The Following Year—October 14, 1956
(We Three's Second Trip, Nearing Mile 15)

Down below is the horrendous scar on the wall—the machinery and crap that it takes to stop the flow of centuries. At Sentinel Rock the bloody business of the dam's beginning is evident. They've got white lead paint all over the walls, have had for several miles upstream (for coffer dams, I suppose) and below the site itself. This being Saturday, the men are all up at Art Green's lapping up the booze. That'll make Art happy. He doesn't give a shit about this river, only the money he can make from it. He's happy as hell to have a marina (Wahweap) and a big puddle to play in instead! A big gaudy sign—an infringement on our rights, since this part of the Colorado is navigable—blares:

WARNING: No travel beyond this point to Lee's Ferry. Blasting on Canyon walls is dangerous to boat travel.

(To myself quietly, says I: "Fuck you, Junior—try and stop us.") The Wreck-the-nation Bureau has provided no exit road; Colorado river guides have the constitutional right to proceed. Sadly, some are ignorant of the fact and believe the Wrecker's press releases, such as "Today the Department of Interior curtailed boat travel on the Colorado River between . . . ," etc. (Thanks a lot, Mr. Seaton!) If we had the time, I'd cover the whole thing over with mud, like the other graffiti—futile, but I'd do it anyway.

Frank goes up Wahweap a way to see if they've brought a road down to the river. There's one there, but pretty sorry as roads go, and it's for the dam builders (they want *us* to exit twenty-five miles upstream at Kane Creek). A mile farther on, a cable crosses the top of the canyon. Bold white numbers are splattered over the desert varnish, a flyspeck trail of them down both walls where the abutments will eventually go. Dotting the shore are strange boats, flags, survey equipment, tools, and hieroglyphics peculiar to those who drill diversion tunnels into *sandstone* (heh-heh!) to fool the river into escape tunnels while they surreptitiously build a plug in his path. Little men crawl down the walls from the top via rope chairs, all silent and busy, marking it for charges. Tomorrow! President Eisenhower presses a button in Washington, and the first explosion rips away a millennium of the river's patient, enduring caress.

We don't talk much the last few miles, but we *know* a lot, and we're happy inside. We've had a rare experience, and dam or no goddamn dam, they can't take that away from us. We have been what I've discovered very few human beings can be. We've been *free*—utterly, completely *free*—for two weeks, totally independent of anyone but ourselves. Nobody has said a cross word or had a moment's misunderstanding. We've laughed and lived to the fullest here in Glen Canyon, on the luscious banks of the mighty Colorado, and most inviolable of all, we *can* take it with us—because we do, every year. (With this trip I've completed 1,609 miles on the San Juan and Colorado Rivers, and by god, I ain't done yet!)

We dock at Lee's—nobody here to meet us but the truck and trailer, just the way we want it. For lunch we drive to Art's, which is now a bunch of ugly trailers stuck on the land he managed to wrangle above the rim, south of

Wahweap Canyon. Art's not here, and the place is jumpin' with Wreck-the-nation Bureau boobies.

"Kain't understand why y'all is so upset 'bout this dam; why lookit what you'll have—a big . . ."

"Never mind explaining what we'll *have,* Buster," I cut him off. "It's what we *had* that your numb skull will never understand."

I remember a song Josh White taught me and sing my way out the door: "You got a head like a rock, and a heart like a marble stone!"

MUSIC TEMPLE—1956

On our second We Three trip, we had found our way above the twisting mystery that drops into Music Temple's pool. A circuitous route of badly eroded, vertical Moki steps led us above the dome. They were terrifying, especially coming down! But what we found beyond was a place where believers in heaven would surely wish to go.

There was a constant flow of water that did not always run down into the Temple. Strange, but having been below, seen the pool empty, and on the same day played above in the running stream, I didn't question who was in authority there—just knew that the ruins, the waterfalls, and a whole other canyon with cottonwoods, redbuds, and fish swimming in the pools was a Shangri-la, and that those who'd lived there knew they were blessed, and had in turn blessed that place.

I remember well the last song I sang in Music Temple—October 15, 1962—my last trip on The Glen. It was a spiritual that Josh had taught me, *They Crucified My Lord*—only I sang it:

They crucified my river
    And he never said a mumblin' word—
        Not a word . . . Not a word . . . Not a word
They pierced him in the side
    But he never said a mumblin' word . . . not a (etc.)
And the blood came trink-lin' down,
    Still, he never said a mumblin' word . . .
He just hung his head, and he died
    But he never said a mumblin' word . . .

Now wasn't that a pity and a shame—
>> The way they done my River?
>>> Not a word . . . not a word . . . not a word.

Music Temple—May 1967

Half the dome, and most of the spiral that had fed the pool, was under water. I wedged *Screwd river* in between the walls to where the chine rested on rock and I was able to climb the remaining narrows to open canyon. There'd been another drawdown, and for several hundred feet all was scaly, dead, ugly— blurring my vision for the hundredth time.

But above, out of sight and smell of the rez, the cap above Music Temple still had that aura of belonging to the past, and I ran—as fast as slickrock, pools, and stacks of rotting driftwood would let me—to the clear, untouched part of that treasured Shangri-la. I spent the whole day there, in the ruins, under waterfalls, planing around the bowls, listening to frog cantatas, watching iridescent fish in the clear spring water, and tennie-sticking the sides above potholes I couldn't get into . . . or out of. A lesson learned!

I was coiling the bow rope when a shot rang out!

I yelped, but another shot covered the sound, and a ricocheting bullet hit the wall above my head.

A scream tore at my throat. "STOP IT! STOP! You goddamned idiot! There are people up here!!"

No echo—it muted out on the dead water. There was a muttering of voices from round the bend, then silence.

I was shaking so hard with anger, frustration, and the urge to get my hands around some bastard's throat, that fear didn't enter into it. I bellowed at them, "What do you morons think you're doing? It's against the law to have guns here . . ."

I heard their motor cough to a start just as my own cavitated and hit the water. Backing out of those narrows was time consuming, and when I finally got to the chamber, I saw two or three men in a boat much faster than mine, heading out to open water.

Still I yelled after them . . .

"You stupid fools? You're shooting in a Temple . . . Music Temple! THIS IS MUSIC TEMPLE! Muu . . . sic . . . Teh-h-h. . ."

I choked on my sobs.

JOHN McPHEE HAS BEEN A staff writer at *The New Yorker* since 1965. The author of more than twenty-six books of nonfiction, McPhee is widely regarded as among the preeminent journalists of his generation. In 1999, he was awarded the Pulitzer Prize for *Annals of the Former World,* his book on the geology of North America. Excerpted here is the famous exchange that took place between David Brower and Floyd Dominy as they floated the Colorado through Grand Canyon with the author; it is taken from his cult classic, *Encounters with the Archdruid* (1971).

Encounters with the Archdruid

ILE 130. THE WATER IS SMOOTH HERE, and will be smooth for three hundred yards, and then we are going through another rapid. The temperature is a little over ninety, and the air is so dry that the rapid will feel good. Dominy and Brower are drinking beer. They have settled into a kind of routine: once a day they tear each other in half and the rest of the time they are pals.

Dominy is wearing a blue yachting cap with gold braid, and above its visor in gold letters are the words "LAKE POWELL." His skin is rouge brown. His nose is peeling. He wears moccasins, and a frayed cotton shirt in dark, indeterminate tartan, and long trousers secured by half a pound of silver buckle. He has with him a couple of small bags and a big leather briefcase on which is painted the great seal of the Bureau of Reclamation—snow-capped mountains, a reservoir, a dam, and irrigated fields, all within the framing shape of a big drop of water. Dominy has been discoursing on the multiple advantages of hydroelectric power, its immediacy ("When you want it, you just throw a switch") and its innocence of pollution.

"Come on now, Dave, be honest," he said. "From a conservationist's point of view, what is the best source of electric power?"

"Flashlight batteries," Brower said.

Brower is also wearing an old tartan shirt, basically orange, and faded. He wears shorts and sneakers. The skin of his legs and face is bright red. Working indoors and all but around the clock, he has been too long away from the sun. He protects his head with a handkerchief knotted at the corners and soaked in the river, but his King Lear billowing white hair is probably protection enough. He travels light. A miniature duffelbag, eight inches in diameter and a foot long—standard gear for the river—contains all that he has with him, most notably his Sierra Club cup, without which he would be incomplete.

Dominy and Brower are both showing off a little. These organized expeditions carry about a dozen people per raft, and by now the others are thoroughly aware of the biases of the conservationist and the Commissioner. The people are mainly from Arizona and Nevada—schoolteachers, a few students, others from the U.S. Public Health Service. On the whole, I would say that Dominy so far has the edge with them. Brower is shy and quiet. Dominy is full of Irish pub chatter and has a grin as wide as the river.

Cans of beer are known as sandwiches in this red, dry, wilderness world. No one questions this, or asks the reason. They just call out "Sandwich, please!" and a can of Coors comes flying through the air. They catch the beer and drink it, and they put the aluminum tongues inside the cans. I threw a tongue in the river and was booed by everyone. No detritus whatever is left in the canyon. Used cans, bottles—all such things—are put in sacks and go with the raft all the way. The beer hangs in the water in a burlap bag from the rear of the raft, with Cokes and Frescas. The bag is hauled onto the raft before a heavy rapid but rides through the lighter ones.

The raft consists of, among other things, two neoprene bananas ten yards long. These pontoons, lashed to a central rubber barge, give the overall rig both lateral and longitudinal flexibility. The river sometimes leaps straight up through the raft, but that is a mark of stability rather than imminent disaster. The raft is informal and extremely plastic. Its lack of rigidity makes it safe.

This is isolation wilderness: two or three trails in two hundred miles, otherwise no way out but down the river with the raft. Having seen the canyon from this perspective, I would not much want to experience it another way. Once in a rare while, we glimpse the rims. They are a mile above us and, in places, twelve miles apart. All the flat shelves of color beneath them return the eye by steps to the earliest beginnings of the world—from the high white limestones and maroon Hermit Shales of Permian time to the red sandstones that formed when the first reptiles lived and the vermillion cliffs that stood contemporary with the earliest trees. This Redwall Limestone, five hundred feet thick, is so vulnerable to the infiltrations of groundwater that it has been shaped, in the seas of air between the canyon rims, into red towers and red buttes, pillars, caverns, arches, and caves. The groundwater runs for hundreds of miles between the layers of that apparently bone-dry desert rock and bursts out into the canyon in stepped cascades or ribbon falls. We are looking at such a waterfall right now, veiling away from the Redwall, high above us. There is green limestone behind the waterfall, and pink limestone that was pressed into being by the crushing weight of the ocean at the exact time the ocean itself was first giving up life—amphibious life— to dry land. Beneath the pink and green limestones are green-gray shales and dark-brown sandstones—Bright Angel Shale, Tapeats Sandstone—that formed under the fathoms that held the first general abundance of marine life. Tapeats Sea was the sea that compressed the rock that was cut by the river to create the canyon. The Tapeats Sandstone is the earliest rock from the Paleozoic Era, and beneath it the mind is drawn back to the center of things, the center of the canyon, the cutting plane, the Colorado. Flanked by its Bass Limestones, its Hotauta Conglomerates, its Vishnu Schists and Zoroaster Granites, it races in white water through a pre-Cambrian here and now. The river has worked its way down into the stillness of original time.

Brower braces his legs and grips one of the safety ropes that run along the pontoons. He says, "How good it is to hear a living river! You can almost hear it cutting."

Dominy pulls his Lake Powell hat down firmly around his ears. He has heard this sort of thing before. Brower is suggesting that the Colorado is even now making an ever deeper and grander Grand Canyon, and what sacrilege it would be to dam the river and stop that hallowed process. Dominy says, "I think most people agree, Dave, that it wasn't a river of this magnitude that cut the Grand Canyon."

Brower is too interested in the coming rapid to respond. In this corridor of calm, we can hear the rapid ahead. Rapids and waterfalls ordinarily take shape when rivers cut against resistant rock and then come to a kind of rock that gives way more easily. This is not the case in the Grand Canyon, where rapids occur beside the mouths of tributary creeks. Although these little streams may be dry much of the year, they are so steep that when they run they are able to fling considerable debris into the Colorado—sand, gravel, stones, rocks, boulders. The debris forms dams, and water rises upstream. The river is unusually quiet there—a lakelike quiet—and then it flows over the debris, falling suddenly, pounding and crashing through the boulders. These are the rapids of the Grand Canyon, and there are a hundred and sixty-one of them. Some have appeared quite suddenly. In 1966, an extraordinarily heavy rain fell in a small area of the north rim, and a flash flood went down Crystal Creek, dumping hundreds of tons of rock into the river at Mile 99. This instantly created the Crystal Rapids, one of the major drops in the Colorado. In rare instances—such as the rapid we are now approaching—the river has exposed resistant pre-Cambrian rock that contributes something to the precipitousness of the flow of white water. The roar is quite close now. The standing waves look like blocks of cement. Dominy emits a cowboy's yell. My notes go into a rubber bag that is tied with a string. This is the Bedrock Rapid.

We went through it with a slow dive and climb and a lot of splattering water. We undulated. The raft assumed the form of the rapid. We got very wet. And now, five minutes later, we are as dry and warm as if we were wearing fresh clothes straight out of a dryer. And we are drinking sandwiches.

We have a map that is seven inches high and fifty feet long. It is rolled in a scroll and is a meticulously hand-done contemporary and historical portrait of the Colorado River in the Grand Canyon. River miles are measured from the point, just south of the Utah line, where the Paria River flows into the Colorado—the place geologists regard as the beginning of the Grand Canyon. As the map rolls by, it records who died where. "Peter Hansbrough, one of two men drowned, Mile 24, Tanner Wash Rapids, 1889. . . . Bert Loper upset, not seen again, Mile 24, 1949. . . . Scout found and buried in talus, Mile 43, 1951. . . . Roemer drowned in Mile 89, 1948." The first known run of the river was in 1869, and the second shortly thereafter—both the expeditions of Major John Wesley Powell—and even by 1946 only about a hundred people had ever been through the canyon by river. With the introduction of neoprene rafts—surplus from the Second World War—the figure expanded. Five hundred a year were going through by the middle nineteen-sixties, and the number is now in the low thousands.

"As long as people keep on taking out everything that they bring in, they're not going to hurt the Grand Canyon," Brower says. "Rule No. 1 is 'Leave nothing—not even a dam.'"

Dominy does not hear that. He is busy telling a pretty young gym teacher from Phoenix that he played sixty minutes a game as captain of the ice-hockey team at the University of Wyoming. "I liked the speed. I liked the body contact. I developed shots the defense couldn't fathom."

Dominy is in his sixtieth year and is planning an early retirement, but he looks fifty, and it is not at all difficult to imagine him on a solo dash down the ice, slamming the Denver Maroons into pulp against the boards and breaking free to slap the winning shot into the nets. He once did exactly that. He has the guts he says he has, and I think he is proving it now, here on the Colorado. He may be an athlete, but he can't swim. He can't swim one stroke. He couldn't swim across a goldfish pond. And at this moment it is time for us to put things away and pull ourselves together, because although we are scarcely dry from the Bedrock Rapid, the crescendoing noise we hear is Deubendorff, an officially designated "heavy rapid," one of the thirteen roughest in the canyon. Brower goes quiet before a rapid, and he is silent now. He says he is not much of a swimmer, either. We all have life vests on, but they feel as if they would be about as effective against these rapids as they would be against bullets. That is not true, though. Once in a great while, these rafts turn over, and when they do the people all end up bobbing in the calmer water at the foot of the rapid like a hatful of spilled corks. Riding a rigid boat, Seymour Deubendorff was claimed by this rapid on the Galloway-Stone expedition, in 1909. This we learn from our map. Looking ahead, we see two steep grooves, a hundred and fifty yards apart, that have been cut into the south wall of the river gorge. They are called Galloway Canyon and Stone Canyon, and the streams in them are not running now, but each has thrown enough debris into the river to make a major rapid, and together they have produced Deubendorff. Directly in front of us, a mile ahead and high against the sky, is a broad and beautiful Redwall mesa. The river disappears around a corner to the left of it. Meanwhile, the big, uncompromising mesa seems to suggest a full and absolute stop, as if we were about to crash into it in flight, for spread below it in the immediate foreground is a prairie of white water.

There is a sense of acceleration in the last fifty yards. The water is like glass right up to where the tumult begins. Everything is lashed down. People even take hats and handkerchiefs off their heads and tie them to the raft. Everyone has both hands on safety ropes—everyone but Dominy. He giggles. He gives a rodeo yell. With ten smooth yards remaining, he lights a cigar.

There is something quite deceptive in the sense of acceleration that comes just before a rapid. The word "rapid" itself is, in a way, a misnomer. It refers only to the speed of the white water relative to the speed of the smooth water that leads into and away from the rapid. The white water is faster, but it is hardly "rapid." The Colorado, smooth, flows about seven miles per hour, and, white, it goes perhaps fifteen or, at its whitest and wildest, twenty miles per hour—not very rapid by the standards of the twentieth century. Force of suggestion creates a false expectation. The mere appearance of the river going over those boulders—the smoky spray, the scissoring waves—is enough to imply a rush to fatality, and this endorses the word used to describe it. You feel as if you were about to be sucked into some sort of invisible pneumatic tube and shot like a bullet into the dim beyond. But the white water, though faster than the rest of the river, is categorically slow. Running the rapids in the Colorado is a series of brief experiences, because the rapids themselves are short. In them, with the raft folding and bending—sudden hills of water filling the immediate skyline—things happen in slow motion. The projector of your own existence slows way down, and you dive as in a dream, and gradually rise, and fall again. The raft shudders across the ridgelines of water cordilleras to crash softly into the valleys beyond. Space and time in there are something other than they are out here. Tents of water form overhead, to break apart in rags. Elapsed stopwatch time has no meaning at all.

Dominy emerged from Deubendorff the hero of the expedition to date. Deubendorff, with two creeks spitting boulders into it, is a long rapid for a Grand Canyon rapid—about three hundred yards. From top to bottom, through it all, Dominy kept his cigar aglow. This feat was something like, say, a bumblebee's flying through a field of waving wheat at shock level and never once being touched. Dominy's shirt was soaked. His trousers were soaked. But all the way down the rapid the red glow of that cigar picked its way through the flying water from pocket to pocket of air. Actually, he was lucky, and he knew it. "Lucky Dominy," he said when we moved into quiet water. "That's why they call me Lucky Dominy." The whole raftload of people gave him an organized cheer. And he veiled his face in fresh smoke.

We have now moved under and by the big mesa. Brower watched it silently for a long time, and then softly, almost to himself, he quoted Edith Warner: " 'This is a day when life and the world seem to be standing still—only time and the river flowing past the mesas.' "

Wild burros stand on a ledge and look at us from above, right. All burros are on the right, all bighorns on the left. Who knows why? We have entered the beauty of afternoon light. It sharpens the colors and polishes the air.

Brower says, "Notice that light up the line now, Floyd. Look how nice it is on the barrel cactus."

"Gorgeous," says Dominy.

The river is in shadow, and we have stopped for the night where a waterfall arcs out from a sandstone cliff. This is Deer Creek Falls, and it is so high that its shafts of plunging water are wrapped in mist where they strike a deep pool near the edge of the river. The campsite is on the opposite bank. Brower has half filled his Sierra Club cup with water and is using it as a level with which to gauge the height of the falls. His measuring rod is his own height at eye level. Sighting across the cup, he has painstakingly climbed a talus slope behind us, adding numbers as he climbed, and he is now a small figure among the talus boulders at the level of the lip of the waterfall across the river. He calls down that the waterfall is a hundred and sixty feet high. With the raft as a ferry, we crossed the river an hour or so ago and stood in the cool mist where the waterfall whips the air into wind. We went on to climb to the top of the fall and to walk above the stream through the gorge of Deer Creek. The creek had cut a deep, crenellated groove in the sandstone, and for several hundred yards, within this groove, we moved along a serpentine ledge high above the water, which made a great deal of sound below, within the narrow walls of the cut. Brower walked along the ledge— it was sometimes only a foot wide—as if he were hurrying along a sidewalk. At the beginning, the ledge was perhaps fifty feet above the foaming creek, and gradually, up the gorge, the ledge and the creek bed came closer together. Brower just strode along, oblivious of the giddy height. In that strange world between walls of rock, a butterfly flickered by, and he watched it with interest while his feet moved surely forward, never slowing. "Viceroy," he said.

I am afraid of places like that, and my legs were so frozen that I couldn't feel the ledge underfoot. I suggested that we stop and wait for Dominy, who had started later and had said he would catch up. This would obviously provide a good rest, because where Dominy comes from the narrowest ledge is at least three hundred miles wide, and I thought if he was still coming along this one he was probably on his hands and knees. Just then, he came walking around a shoulder of the rock face, balanced above the gorge, whistling. We moved on. Where the ledge met the creek bed, the walls of the gorge widened out and the creek flowed in clear, cascading pools among cactus flowers and mariposa lilies under stands of cottonwood. A scene like that in a context of unending dry red rock is unbelievable, a palpable mirage. Brower walked in the stream and, after a while, stopped to absorb his surroundings. Dominy, some yards behind, had an enameled cup with him, and he dipped it into the stream. Lifting it to his lips, he said, "Now I'll have a drink of water that has washed Dave Brower's feet."

The water was cold and very clear. Brower scooped some for himself, in his Sierra Club cup. "Any kind of water in country like this is good, but especially when man isn't hogging it for his own use," he said.

Watercress grew around the plunge pools of the short cascades—watercress, growing in cool water, surrounded by thousands of square miles of baking desert rock. Brower took a small bunch in his hand. Bugs were crawling all over it, and he carefully selected leaves and ate them, leaving the bugs behind. "I don't mind sharing my cress with them," he said. "I hope they don't mind sharing it with me."

Brower's snack appealed to Dominy. He waded into the same pool, picked two handfuls of cress, and ate them happily, bugs and all. "Paradise," he said, looking around. "Paradise."

Half obscured in the stream under a bed of cress was the distinctive shimmer of a Budweiser can. Brower picked it up, poured the water out of it, and put it in his pocket.

"When people come in, you can't win," Dominy said, and Brower looked at him with both approval and perplexity.

Inside Dominy's big leather briefcase is a bottle of Jim Beam, and now, at the campsite, in the twilight, with the sun far gone over the rimrocks, we are going to have our quotidian ration—and Dominy is a generous man. After dinner, if patterns hold, he and Brower will square off for battle, but they are at this moment united in anticipation of the bourbon. Big steaks are ready for broiling over the coals of a driftwood fire. There is calm in the canyon. The Commissioner steps to the river's edge and dips a half cup of water, over which he pours his whiskey. "I'm the nation's waterboy," he says. "I need water with my bourbon."

Over the drinks, he tells us that he once taught a German shepherd to climb a ladder. We believe him. He further reminisces about early camping trips with his wife, Alice. They were in their teens when they married. He was state Master Counsellor for the Order of DeMolay, and she was the Queen of Job's Daughters. They had married secretly, and she went with him to the University of Wyoming. "We lived on beans and love," he said. "Our recreation was camping. We went up into the Snowy Range and into the Laramie Peak country, where there was nothing but rattlesnakes, ticks, and us. We used to haul wood down from the mountains to burn for heat in the winter."

Jerry Sanderson, the river guide who has organized this expedition, calls out that dinner is ready. He has cooked an entire sirloin steak for each person. We eat from large plastic trays—the property of Sanderson. Brower regularly ignores the stack of trays, and now, when his turn comes, he steps forward to receive his food in his Sierra Club cup. Sanderson, a lean, trim, weathered man, handsome and steady, has seen a lot on this river. And now a man with wild white hair and pink legs is holding out a four-inch cup to receive a three-pound steak. Very well. There is no rapid that can make Sanderson's eyes bat, so why should this? He drapes the steak over the cup. The steak covers the cup like a sun hat. Brower begins to hack at the edges with a knife. Brower in wilderness eats from nothing but his Sierra Club cup.

10 P.M. The moon has moved out in brilliance over the canyon rim. Brower and Dominy are asleep. Dominy snores. Just before he began to snore, he looked at the moon and said, "What's the point of going there? If it were made of gold, we couldn't afford to go get it. Twenty-three billion dollars for landings on the moon. I can't justify or understand that. One, yes. Half a dozen, no. Every time they light a roman candle at Cape Canaveral, they knock four hundred million off other projects, like water storage."

Tonight's fight was about siltation. When Brower finished his steak, he looked across the river at the flying plume of Deer Creek Falls and announced to all in earshot that Commissioner Dominy wished to fill that scene with mud, covering the riverbed and the banks where we sat, and filling the inner gorge of the Colorado right up to within fifty feet of the top of the waterfall.

"That's God-damned nonsense," Dominy said.

Brower explained quietly that rivers carry silt, and that silt has to go somewhere if men build dams. Silt first drops and settles where the river flows into still water at the heads of reservoirs, he said. Gradually, it not only fills the reservoir but also accumulates upstream from the headwaters, and that might one day be the story here at Deer Creek Falls, for Dominy wanted to create a reservoir that would begin only seven miles downstream from our campsite.

"They said Hoover Dam was going to silt up Lake Mead in thirty years," Dominy said. "For thirty years, Lake Mead caught all the God-damned silt in the Colorado River, and Hoover has not been impaired."

"No, but when Mead is low there are forty miles of silt flats at its upper end, and they're getting bigger."

"Not appreciably. Not with Lake Powell three hundred miles up-stream."

"Yes, Lake Powell will fill up first."

"When? Tell me *when?*" Dominy was now shouting.

"In a hundred to two hundred years," Brower said quietly.

"That's crap! The figures you work with aren't reliable."

"They come from reliable people."

"Nonsense."

"Oh."

The Colorado, Brower reminded us, used to be known as Old Red. This was because the river was full of red mud. It would never have been possible for Dominy to dip his cup in it in order to get water to go with his bourbon unless he wished to drink mud as well. On arriving at a campsite, rivermen used to fill their boats with water, so that the mud would settle to the bottom of the boats and they would have water for drinking and cooking. Except after flash floods, the Colorado in the Grand Canyon is now green and almost clear, because Lake Powell is catching the silt, and Glen Canyon Dam—fifteen miles upstream from the beginning of the Grand Canyon—is releasing clean water. "Emotionally, people are able to look only two generations back and two generations forward," Brower said. "We need to see farther than that. It is absolutely inevitable, for example, that Lake Powell and Lake Mead will someday be completely filled with silt."

"Nonsense, nonsense, complete nonsense. First of all, we will build silt-detention dams in the tributaries—in the Paria, in the Little Colorado. And, if necessary, we will build more."

"Someday the reservoirs have to fill up, Floyd."

"I wouldn't admit that. I wouldn't admit one inch!"

"Someday."

"*Some*day! Yes, in geologic time, maybe. Lake Powell *will* fill up with silt. I don't know how many thousands of years from now. By then, people will have figured out alternative sources of water and power. That's what I say when you start talking about the geologic ages."

Brower then began to deliver a brief lecture on the phenomenon of aggradation—the term for the final insult that follows when a reservoir is full of silt. Aggradation is what happens to the silt that keeps on coming down the river. The silt piles up and, in a kind of reverse ooze, reaches back upstream many miles, following an inclined plane that rises about eighteen inches per mile—a figure reckoned from the site of the now mud-packed and obsolete dam.

Brower was scarcely halfway through sketching that picture when Dominy ended his contributions with a monosyllabic remark, walked away, put on his pajamas, delivered to the unlistening moon his attack on the space program, and, forgetting Brower and all the silt of years to come, fell asleep. He sleeps on his back, his feet apart, under the mesas.

5 A.M. The sky is light. The air temperature is eighty degrees. Brower sleeps on his side, his knees drawn up.

7 A.M. Eighty-eight degrees. We will soon be on the river. Dominy is brushing his teeth in the green Colorado. Sam Beach, a big, bearded man from White Plains, New York, just walked up to Dominy and said, "I see God has given us good water here this morning."

"Thank you," Dominy said.

And Brower said to Beach, "I imagine that's the first time you ever heard Him speak."

And Beach said, "God giveth, and God taketh away."

N O BOOK ON GLEN CANYON would be complete without the voice of Floyd Dominy, the controversial commissioner of the U.S. Bureau of Reclamation from 1959 to 1969. Born in Nebraska, Dominy graduated from the University of Wyoming in 1932 and entered the bureau in 1946. As commissioner, Dominy oversaw the most active period of large-dam construction in U.S. history, standing watch over the completion of Glen Canyon, Flaming Gorge, and Navajo Dams in the Colorado River Storage Project. In the following text, originally published by the Government Printing Office in 1965, Dominy co-opts the imagery of wild nature to celebrate the completion of the reservoir.

Lake Powell:
Jewel of the Colorado

Dear God, did you cast down
Two hundred miles of canyon
And mark: "For poets only"?
Multitudes hunger
For a lake in the sun.
—Gordon Michelle, 1952

SIRED BY THE MUDDY COLORADO in magnificent canyon country, a great blue lake has been born in the West.

It is called Lake Powell. When full, it will be 186 miles long. Its shoreline will total 1,860 miles. It formed behind Glen Canyon Dam, which is at the town of Page, Ariz. The lake begins in the northern part of that State. Most of it is in Utah.

Lake Powell holds working water—water for many purposes. And one of those purposes is to provide the people of this country with the finest scenic and recreational area in the Nation.

At intervals along shores of astonishing beauty will be 10 recreation centers developed by the National Park Service. Their names have a tang of the Old West: Wahweap, Lee's Ferry, Warm Creek, Rainbow Bridge, Hole-in-the-Rock, Oil Seep Bar, Hall's Crossing, Bullfrog Basin, Castle Butte, and Hite Crossing.

Five of these will have marinas, four will have airstrips, seven will have complete lodging accommodations, all will have boat docks, supplies, camping sites, and picnic grounds. Work is underway on over half of these sites. Wahweap—nearest to Glen Canyon Dam—is virtually complete.

All you need is a boat—or there are excursion boats for hire if you prefer. Where you go and what you do in this water wonderland is for your personal choice. You are rich with opportunity before you begin.

I'd like to invite you to visit Lake Powell and especially to see that natural marvel Rainbow Bridge. Before Lake Powell, Rainbow Bridge National Monument could be visited only by the rugged few who "packed" in. Now all of you can see it—easily. Your boat will moor to floating docks at the entrance to Rainbow Bridge Canyon. Then you take a walk on a trail along the canyon's side. You'll find the bridge undamaged by Lake Powell's waters—for even when the lake is at maximum elevation its waters can never reach the ledge upon which the bridge rests. And you can marvel at its arched and graceful beauty in the peace and quiet of its natural setting.

How can I describe the sculpture and colors along Lake Powell's shores? Every time I go back, I search again for a new set of words. And they always seem inadequate.

Over eons of time, wind and rain have carved the sandstone into shapes to please ten thousand eyes. The graceful, the dramatic, the grand, the fantastic. Evolution into convolution and involution. Sharp edges, round edges, blunt edges, soaring edges. Spires, cliffs, and castles in the sky.

Colors like a symphony of Nature's music. Bright orange, brick red, ocher, pink, deep brown, vivid purple, granite black, mustard yellow—and a soft, pale green so delicate no artist could ever capture it with paint.

If I sound partisan toward Lake Powell, you are correct. I am proud of this aquatic wonder and want to share it with you.

Do you like to fish? Lake Powell has been stocked with millions of trout and bass. They'll be good fighting size this summer and good eating, too.

Feel like exploring? Hundreds of side canyons—where few ever trod before the lake formed—are yours. They have names like Cathedral and Twilight—the list is long and many are still nameless.

Fun sports? Yes. This is sun country. Water skiing, swimming, scuba diving—all in clean, blue water that looks like deep blue sky.

And if you feel lazy and just want to soak up sun and beauty, this is your place. Don't hike—amble. Lie in the sun. Putter along the shore. You'll never run out of places and space.

If you're tired in mind and soul, in need of restful serenity, I don't know a better place. If you want to be alone, you can be alone. You just can't crowd Lake Powell's 1,860 miles of shoreline—equal in length to our Pacific shoreline from Tia Juana, Mexico, to the Olympic shores of Washington State.

For that grand old American custom of seeing America first, where could be better? The air is dry and bracing, the sun is warm, and there's a prizewinning scene round every bend.

And best of all for some, a campfire with old friends on Powell's shores at dusk. After pan-fried trout, which never taste the same in restaurants.

You have a front-row seat in an amphitheater of infinity. The bright blue sky deepens slowly to a velvet purple and the stars are brilliant—glittering in that vast immensity above. Orange sandstone cliffs fade to dusky red—then to blackest black. The fire burns low—reflected in the placid lake.

There is peace. And a oneness with the world and God.

I know. I was there.

E DWARD ABBEY (1927–1989) wrote more than twenty books of fiction and nonfiction, nearly all of which take place in the American West. A passionate defender of the environment, Abbey is perhaps best known for his novel *The Monkey Wrench Gang,* which introduced an entire generation of readers to the idea that Glen Canyon Dam was an abominable error, and for his nonfiction memoir of life as a ranger at Arches National Monument, *Desert Solitaire,* which contains an account of his only river trip through Glen Canyon. The destruction of Glen Canyon Dam is a recurring theme in a number of his books and essays. "The Damnation of a Canyon" is taken from *Beyond the Wall: Essays from the Outside* (1981).

The Damnation of a Canyon

THERE WAS A TIME WHEN, in my search for essences, I concluded that the canyonland country has no heart. I was wrong. The canyonlands did have a heart, a living heart, and that heart was Glen Canyon and the golden, flowing Colorado River.

In the summer of 1959 a friend and I made a float trip in little rubber rafts through the length of Glen Canyon, starting at Hite and getting off the river near Gunsight Butte—The Crossing of the Fathers. In this voyage of some 150 miles and ten days our only motive power, and all that we needed, was the current of the Colorado River.

In the summer and fall of 1967 I worked as a seasonal park ranger at the new Glen Canyon National Recreation Area. During my five-month tour of duty I worked at the main marina and headquarters area called Wahweap, at Bullfrog Basin toward the upper end of the reservoir, and finally at Lee's Ferry downriver from Glen Canyon Dam. In a number of powerboat tours I was privileged to see almost all of our nation's newest, biggest and most impressive "recreational facility."

Having thus seen Glen Canyon both before and after what we may fairly call its damnation, I feel that I am in a position to evaluate the transformation of the region caused by construction of the dam. I have had the unique opportunity to observe firsthand some of the differences between the environment of a free river and a power-plant reservoir.

One should admit at the outset to a certain bias. Indeed I am a "butterfly chaser, googly eyed bleeding heart and wild conservative." I take a dim view of dams; I find it hard to learn to love cement; I am poorly impressed by concrete aggregates and statistics in the cubic tons. But in this weakness I am not alone, for I belong to that ever-growing number of Americans, probably a good majority now, who have become aware that a fully industrialized, thoroughly urbanized, elegantly computerized social system is not suitable for human habitation. Great for machines, yes. But unfit for people.

Lake Powell, formed by Glen Canyon Dam, is not a lake. It is a reservoir, with a constantly fluctuating water level—more like a bathtub that is never drained than a true lake. As at Hoover (or Boulder) Dam, the sole practical function of this impounded water is to drive the turbines that generate electricity in the powerhouse at the base of the dam. Recreational benefits were of secondary importance in the minds of those who conceived and built this dam. As a result the volume of water in the reservoir is continually being increased or decreased according to the requirements of the Basin States Compact and the power-grid system of which Glen Canyon Dam is a component.

The rising and falling water level entails various consequences. One of the most obvious, well known to all who have seen Lake Mead, is the "bathtub ring" left on the canyon walls after each drawdown of water, or what rangers at Glen Canyon call the Bathtub Formation. This phenomenon is perhaps of no more than aesthetic importance; yet it is sufficient to dispel any illusion one might have, in contemplating the scene, that you are looking upon a natural lake.

Of much more significance is the fact that plant life, because of the unstable water line, cannot establish itself on the shores of the reservoir. When the water is low, plant life dies of thirst; when high, it is drowned. Much of the shoreline of the reservoir consists of near-perpendicular sandstone bluffs, where very little flora ever did or ever could subsist, but the remainder includes bays, coves, sloping hills and the many side canyons, where the original plant life has been drowned and new plant life cannot get a foothold. And of course where there is little or no plant life there is little or no animal life.

The utter barrenness of the reservoir shoreline recalls by contrast the aspect of things before the dam, when Glen Canyon formed the course of the untamed Colorado. Then we had a wild and flowing river lined by boulder-strewn shores, sandy beaches, thickets of tamarisk and willow, and glades of cottonwoods.

The thickets teemed with songbirds: vireos, warblers, mockingbirds and thrushes. On the open beaches were killdeer, sandpipers, herons, ibises, egrets. Living in grottoes in the canyon walls were swallows, swifts, hawks, wrens and owls. Beaver were common if not abundant: not an evening would pass, in drifting down the river, that we did not see them or at least hear the whack of their flat tails on the water. Above the river shores were the great recessed alcoves where water seeped from the sandstone, nourishing the semitropical hanging gardens of orchid, ivy and columbine, with their associated swarms of insects and birdlife.

Up most of the side canyons, before damnation, there were springs, sometimes flowing streams, waterfalls and plunge pools—the kind of marvels you can now find only in such small-scale remnants of Glen Canyon as the Escalante area. In the rich flora of these laterals the larger mammals—mule deer, coyote, bobcat, ring-tailed cat, gray fox, kit fox, skunk, badger and others—found a home. When the river was dammed almost all of these things were lost. Crowded out—or drowned and buried under mud.

The difference between the present reservoir, with its silent sterile shores and debris-choked side canyons, and the original Glen Canyon, is the difference between death and life. Glen Canyon was alive. Lake Powell is a graveyard.

For those who may think I exaggerate the contrast between the former river canyon and the present man-made impoundment, I suggest a trip on Lake Powell followed immediately by another boat trip on the river below the dam. Take a boat from Lee's Ferry up the river to within sight of the dam, then shut off the motor and allow yourself the rare delight of a quiet, effortless drifting down the stream. In that twelve-mile stretch of living green, singing birds, flowing water and untarnished canyon walls—sights and sounds a million years older and infinitely lovelier than the roar of motorboats—you will rediscover a small and imperfect sampling of the kind of experience that was taken away from everybody when the oligarchs and politicians condemned our river for purposes of their own.

The effects of Glen Canyon Dam also extend downstream, causing changes in the character and ecology of Marble Gorge and Grand Canyon. Because the annual spring floods are now a thing of the past, the shores are becoming overgrown with brush, the rapids are getting worse where the river no longer has enough force to carry away the boulders washed down from the lateral canyons, and the beaches are disappearing, losing sand that is not replaced.

Lake Powell, though not a lake, may well be as its defenders assert the most beautiful reservoir in the world. Certainly it has a photogenic backdrop of buttes and mesas projecting above the expansive surface of stagnant waters where the speedboats, houseboats and cabin cruisers ply. But it is no longer a wilderness. It is no longer a place of natural life. It is no longer Glen Canyon.

The defenders of the dam argue that the recreational benefits available on the surface of the reservoir outweigh the loss of Indian ruins, historical sites, wildlife and wilderness adventure. Relying on the familiar quantitative logic of business and bureaucracy, they assert that whereas only a few thousand citizens ever ventured down the river through Glen Canyon, now millions can—or will—enjoy the motorized boating and hatchery fishing available on the reservoir. They will also argue that the rising waters behind the dam have made such places as Rainbow Bridge accessible by powerboat. Formerly you could get there only by walking (six miles).

This argument appeals to the wheelchair ethos of the wealthy, upper-middle-class American slob. If Rainbow Bridge is worth seeing at all, then by God it should be easily, readily, immediately available to everybody with the money to buy a big powerboat. Why should a trip to such a place be the privilege only of those who are willing to walk six miles? Or if Pikes Peak is worth getting to, then why not build a highway to the top of it so that anyone can get there? Anytime? Without effort? Or as my old man would say, "By Christ, one man's just as good as another—if not a damn sight better."

Or as ex-Commissioner Floyd Dominy of the U.S. Bureau of Reclamation pointed out poetically in his handsomely engraved and illustrated brochure *Lake Powell: Jewel of the Colorado* (produced by the U.S. Government Printing Office at our expense): "There's something about a lake which brings us a little closer to God." In this case, Lake Powell, about five hundred feet closer. Eh, Floyd?[1]

It is quite true that the flooding of Glen Canyon has opened up to the motorboat explorer parts of side canyons that formerly could be reached only by people able to walk. But the sum total of terrain visible to the eye and touchable by hand and foot has been greatly diminished, not increased. Because of the dam the river is gone, the inner canyon is gone, the best parts of the numerous side canyons are gone—all hidden beneath hundreds of feet of polluted water, accumulating silt, and mounting tons of trash. This portion of Glen Canyon—and who can estimate how many cubic miles were lost?—*is no longer accessible to anybody*. (Except scuba divers.) And this, do not

---

1. Abbey is quoting from a poem that appears transposed over photographs in *Lake Powell: Jewel of the Colorado*. In a telephone conversation with the editor on August 1, 2001, however, Dominy stated that while the photographs were his, the poem was written "by an anonymous man in Denver."—Ed.

forget, was the most valuable part of Glen Canyon, richest in scenery, archaeology, history, flora and fauna.

Not only has the heart of Glen Canyon been buried, but many of the side canyons above the fluctuating waterline are now rendered more difficult, not easier, to get into. This because the debris brought down into them by desert storms, no longer carried away by the river, must unavoidably build up in the area where flood meets reservoir. Narrow Canyon, for example, at the head of the impounded waters, is already beginning to silt up and to amass huge quantities of driftwood, some of it floating on the surface, some of it half afloat beneath the surface. Anyone who has tried to pilot a motorboat through a raft of half-sunken logs and bloated dead cows will have his own thoughts on the accessibility of these waters.

Hite Marina, at the mouth of Narrow Canyon, will probably have to be abandoned within twenty or thirty years. After that it will be the turn of Bullfrog Marina. And then Rainbow Bridge Marina. And eventually, inevitably, whether it takes ten centuries or only one, Wahweap. Lake Powell, like Lake Mead, is foredoomed sooner or later to become a solid mass of mud, and its dam a waterfall. Assuming, of course, that either one stands that long.

Second, the question of costs. It is often stated that the dam and its reservoir have opened up to the many what was formerly restricted to the few, implying in this case that what was once expensive has now been made cheap. Exactly the opposite is true.

Before the dam, a float trip down the river through Glen Canyon would cost you a minimum of seven days' time, well within anyone's vacation allotment, and a capital outlay of about forty dollars—the prevailing price of two-man rubber boat with oars, available at any army-navy surplus store. A life jacket might be useful but not required, for there were no dangerous rapids in the 150 miles of Glen Canyon. As the name implies, this stretch of the river was in fact so easy and gentle that the trip could be and was made by all sorts of amateurs: by Boy Scouts, Camp Fire Girls, stenographers, schoolteachers, students, little old ladies in inner tubes. Guides, professional boatmen, giant pontoons, outboard motors, radios, rescue equipment were not needed. The Glen Canyon float trip was an adventure anyone could enjoy, on his own, for a cost less than that of spending two days and nights in a Page motel. Even food was there, in the water: the channel catfish were easier to catch and a lot better eating than the striped bass and rainbow trout dumped by the ton into the reservoir these days. And one other thing:

at the end of the float trip you still owned your boat, usable for many more such casual and carefree expeditions.

What is the situation now? Float trips are no longer possible. The only way left for the exploration of the reservoir and what remains of Glen Canyon demands the use of a powerboat. Here you have three options: (1) buy your own boat and engine, the necessary auxiliary equipment, the fuel to keep it moving, the parts and repairs to keep it running, the permits and licenses required for legal operation, the trailer to transport it; (2) rent a boat; or (3) go on a commercial excursion boat, packed in with other sightseers, following a preplanned itinerary. This kind of play is only for the affluent.

The inescapable conclusion is that no matter how one attempts to calculate the cost in dollars and cents, a float trip down Glen Canyon was much cheaper than a powerboat tour of the reservoir. Being less expensive, as well as safer and easier, the float trip was an adventure open to far more people than will ever be able to afford motorboat excursions in the area now.

What about the "human impact" of motorized use of the Glen Canyon impoundment? We can visualize the floor of the reservoir gradually accumulating not only silt, mud, waterlogged trees and drowned cattle but also the usual debris that is left behind when the urban, industrial style of recreation is carried into the open country. There is also the problem of human wastes. The waters of the wild river were good to drink, but nobody in his senses would drink from Lake Powell. Eventually, as is already sometimes the case at Lake Mead, the stagnant waters will become too foul even for swimming. The trouble is that while some boats have what are called "self-contained" heads, the majority do not; most sewage is disposed of by simply pumping it into the water. It will take a while, but long before it becomes a solid mass of mud Lake Powell ("Jewel of the Colorado") will enjoy a passing fame as the biggest sewage lagoon in the American Southwest. Most tourists will never be able to afford a boat trip on this reservoir, but everybody within fifty miles will be able to smell it.

All of the foregoing would be nothing but a futile exercise in nostalgia (so much water over the dam) if I had nothing constructive and concrete to offer. But I do. As alternate methods of power generation are developed, such as solar, and as the nation establishes a way of life adapted to actual resources and basic needs, so that the demand for electrical power begins to diminish, we can shut down the Glen Canyon power plant, open the diversion tunnels, and drain the reservoir.

This will no doubt expose a drear and hideous scene: immense mud flats and whole plateaus of sodden garbage strewn with dead trees, sunken boats, the skeletons of long-forgotten, decomposing water-skiers. But to those who find the prospect too appalling, I say give nature a little time. In five years, at most in ten, the sun and wind and storms will cleanse and sterilize the repellent mess. The inevitable floods will soon remove all that does not belong within the canyons. Fresh green willow, box elder and red bud will reappear; and the ancient drowned cottonwoods (noble monuments to themselves) will be replaced by young of their own kind. With the renewal of plant life will come the insects, the birds, the lizards and snakes, the mammals. Within a generation—thirty years—I predict the river and canyons will bear a decent resemblance to their former selves. Within the lifetime of our children Glen Canyon and the living river, heart of the canyonlands, will be restored to us. The wilderness will again belong to God, the people and the wild things that call it home.

WALLACE STEGNER (1909–1993) was the recipient of both the Pulitzer Prize and the National Book Award. A towering figure of Western letters and an impassioned environmentalist, his works include *Beyond the Hundredth Meridian: A Biography of John Wesley Powell,* and the novels *Angle of Repose, Crossing to Safety,* and *The Big Rock Candy Mountain,* among others. "Glen Canyon Submersus" and its companion piece, "San Juan and Glen Canyon," were originally collected in *The Sound of Mountain Water* (1969). His call for the Escalante arm of Lake Powell to be closed to motorized use has yet to be heeded.

Glen Canyon Submersus

G LEN CANYON, ONCE THE MOST SERENELY BEAUTIFUL of all the canyons of the Colorado River, is now Lake Powell, impounded by the Glen Canyon Dam. It is called a great recreational resource. The Bureau of Reclamation promotes its beauty in an attempt to counter continuing criticisms of the dam itself, and the National Park Service, which manages the Recreation Area, is installing or planning facilities for all the boating, water skiing, fishing, camping, swimming, and plain sightseeing that should now ensue.

But I come back to Lake Powell reluctantly and skeptically, for I remember Glen Canyon as it used to be.

Once the river ran through Glen's two hundred miles in a twisting, many-branched stone trough eight hundred to twelve hundred feet deep, just deep enough to be impressive without being overwhelming. Awe was never Glen Canyon's province. That is for the Grand Canyon. Glen Canyon was for delight. The river that used to run here cooperated with the scenery by flowing swift and smooth, without a major rapid. Any ordinary boatman could take anyone through it. Boy Scouts made annual pilgrimages on rubber rafts. In 1947 we went through with a party that contained an old lady of seventy and a girl of ten. There was superlative camping anywhere, on sandbars furred with tamarisk and willow, under cliffs that whispered with the sound of flowing water.

Through many of those two hundred idyllic miles the view was shut in by red walls, but down straight reaches or up side canyons there would be glimpses of noble towers and buttes lifting high beyond the canyon rims, and somewhat more than halfway down there was a major confrontation where the Kaiparowits Plateau, seventy-five hundred feet high, thrust its knife-blade cliff above the north rim to face the dome of Navajo Mountain, more than ten thousand feet high, on the south side. Those two uplifts, as strikingly different as if designed to dominate some gigantic world's fair, added magnificence to the intimate colored trough of the river.

Seen from the air, the Glen Canyon country reveals itself as a bare-stone, salmon-pink tableland whose surface is a chaos of domes, knobs, beehives, baldheads, hollows, and potholes, dissected by the deep corkscrew channels of streams. Out of the platform north of the main river rise the gray-green peaks of the Henry Mountains, the last-discovered mountains in the contiguous United States. West of them is the bloody welt of the Water-pocket Fold, whose westward creeks flow into the Escalante, the last-discovered river. Northward rise the cliffs of Utah's high plateaus. South of Glen Canyon, like a great period at the foot of the fifty-mile exclamation point of the Kaiparowits, is Navajo Mountain, whose slopes apron off on every side into the stone and sand of the reservation.

When cut by streams, the Navajo sandstone which is the country rock forms monolithic cliffs with rounded rims. In straight stretches the cliffs tend to be sheer, on the curves undercut, especially in the narrow side canyons. I have measured a six-hundred-foot wall that was undercut a good five hundred feet—not a cliff at all but a musical shell for the multiplication of echoes. Into these deep scoured amphitheaters on the outside of bends, the promontories on the inside fit like thighbones into a hip socket. Often, straightening bends, creeks have cut through promontories to form bridges, as at Rainbow Bridge National Monument, Gregory Bridge in Fiftymile Canyon, and dozens of other places. And systematically, when a river cleft has exposed the rock to the lateral thrust of its own weight, fracturing begins to peel great slabs from the cliff faces. The slabs are thinner at top than at bottom, and curve together so that great alcoves form in the walls. If they are near the rim, they may break through to let a window-wink of sky down on a canyon traveler, and always they make panels of fresh pink in weathered and stained and darkened red walls.

Floating down the river one passed, every mile or two on right or left, the mouth of some side canyon, narrow, shadowed, releasing a secret stream into the taffy-colored, whirlpooled Colorado. Between the mouth of the Dirty Devil and the dam, which is a few miles above the actual foot of the Glen Canyon, there are at least three dozen such gulches on the north side, including the major canyon of the Escalante; and on the south nearly that many more, including the major canyon of the San Juan. Every such gulch used to be a little wonder, each with its multiplying branches, each as deep at the mouth as its parent canyon. Hundreds of feet deep, sometimes only a few yards wide, they wove into the rock so sinuously that all sky was shut off. The floors were smooth sand or rounded stone pavement or stone pools linked by stone gutters, and nearly every gulch ran, except in flood season, a thin clear stream. Silt pockets out of reach of flood were gardens of fern and redbud; every talus and rockslide gave footing to cottonwood and willow and single-leafed ash; ponded places were solid with watercress; maidenhair hung from seepage cracks in the cliffs.

Often these canyons, pursued upward, ended in falls, and sometimes the falls came down through a slot or a skylight in the roof of a domed chamber, to trickle down the wall into a plunge pool that made a lyrical dunk bath on a hot day. In such chambers the light was dim, reflected, richly colored. The red rock was stained with the dark manganese exudations called desert varnish, striped black to green to yellow to white along horizontal lines of seepage, patched with the chemical, sunless green of moss. One such grotto was named Music Temple by Major John Wesley Powell on his first exploration, in 1869; another is the so-called Cathedral in the Desert, at the head of Clear Water Canyon off the Escalante.

That was what Glen Canyon was like before the closing of the dam in 1963. What was flooded here was potentially a superb national park. It had its history, too, sparse but significant. Exploring the gulches, one came upon ancient chiseled footholds leading up the slickrock to mortared dwellings or storage cysts of the Basket Makers and Pueblos who once inhabited these canyons. At the mouth of Padre Creek a line of chiseled steps marked where Fathers Escalante and Dominguez, groping back toward Santa Fe in 1776, got their animals down to the fjord that was afterward known as the Crossing of the Fathers. In Music Temple men from Powell's two river expeditions had scratched their names. Here and there on the walls near the river were names and initials of men from Robert Brewster Stanton's party that surveyed a water-level railroad down the canyon in 1889–90, and miners from the abortive goldrush of the 1890's. There were Mormon echoes at Lee's Ferry, below the dam, and at the slot canyon called Hole-in-the-Rock, where a Mormon colonizing party got their wagons down the cliffs on their way to the San Juan in 1880.

Some of this is now under Lake Powell. I am interested to know how much is gone, how much left. Because I don't much like the thought of power boats and water skiers in these canyons, I come in March, before the season has properly begun, and at a time when the lake (stabilized they say because of water shortages far downriver at Lake Mead) is as high as it has ever been, but is still more than two hundred feet below its capacity level of thirty-seven hundred feet. Not everything that may eventually be drowned will be drowned yet, and there will be none of the stained walls and exposed mudflats that make a draw-down reservoir ugly at low water.

Our boat is the Park Service patrol boat, a thirty-four-foot diesel work-horse. It has a voice like a bulldozer's. As we back away from the dock and head out deserted Wahweap Bay, conversing at the tops of our lungs with our noses a foot apart, we acknowledge that we needn't have worried about motor noises among the cliffs. We couldn't have heard a Chriscraft if it had passed us with its throttle wide open.

One thing is comfortingly clear from the moment we back away from the dock at Wahweap and start out between the low walls of what used to be Wahweap Creek toward the main channel. Though they have diminished it, they haven't utterly ruined it. Though these walls are lower and tamer than they used to be, and though the whole sensation is a little like looking at a picture of Miss America that doesn't show her legs, Lake Powell *is* beautiful. It isn't Glen Canyon, but it is something in itself. The contact of deep blue water and uncompromising stone is bizarre and somehow exciting. Enough of the canyon feeling is left so that traveling up-lake one watches with a sense of discovery as every bend rotates into view new colors, new forms, new vistas: a great glowing wall with the sun on it, a slot side canyon buried to the eyes in water and inviting exploration, a half-drowned cave on whose roof dance the little flames of reflected ripples.

Moreover, since we float three hundred feet or more above the old river, the views out are much wider, and where the lake broadens, as at Padre Creek, they are superb. From the river, Navajo Mountain used to be seen only in brief, distant glimpses. From the lake it is often visible for minutes, an hour, at a time—gray-green, snow-streaked, a high mysterious bubble rising above the red world, incontrovertibly the holy mountain. And the broken country around the Crossing of the Fathers was always wild and strange as a moon landscape, but you had to climb out to see it. Now, from the bay that covers the crossing and spreads into the mouths of tributary creeks, we see Gunsight Butte, Tower Butte, and the other fantastic pinnacles of the Entrada formation surging up a sheer thousand feet above the rounding platform of the Navajo. The horizon reels with surrealist forms, dark red at the base, gray from there to rimrock, the profiles rigid and angular and carved, as different as possible from the Navajo's filigreed, ripple-marked sandstone.

We find the larger side canyons, as well as the deeper reaches of the main canyon, almost as impressive as they used to be, especially after we get far enough up-lake so that the water is shallower and the cliffs less reduced in height. Navajo Canyon is splendid despite the flooding of its green bottom that used to provide pasture for the stolen horses of raiders. Forbidden Canyon that leads to Rainbow Bridge is lessened, but still marvelous: it is like going by boat to Petra. Rainbow Bridge itself is still the place of magic that it used to be when we walked the six miles up from the river, and turned a corner to see the great arch framing the dome of Navajo Mountain. The canyon of the Escalante, with all its tortuous side canyons, is one of the stunning scenic experiences of a lifetime, and far easier to reach by lake than it used to be by foot or horseback. And all up and down these canyons, big or little, is the constantly changing, nobly repetitive spectacle of the cliffs with their contrasts of rounding and sheer, their great blackboard faces and their amphitheaters. Streaked with desert varnish, weathered and lichened and shadowed, patched with clean pink fresh-broken stone, they are as magically colored as shot silk.

And there is God's plenty of it. This lake is already a hundred and fifty miles long, with scores of tributaries. If it ever fills—which its critics guess it will not—it will have eighteen hundred miles of shoreline. Its fishing is good and apparently getting better, not only catfish and perch but rainbow trout and largemouth black bass that are periodically sown broadcast from planes. At present its supply and access points are few and far apart—at Wahweap, Hall's Crossing, and Hite—but when floating facilities are anchored in the narrows below Rainbow Bridge and when boat ramps and supply stations are developed at Warm Creek, Hole-in-the-Rock, and Bullfrog Basin, this will draw people. The prediction of a million visitors in 1965 is probably enthusiastic, but there is no question that as developed facilities extend the range of boats and multiply places of access, this will become one of the great water playgrounds.

And yet, vast and beautiful as it is, open now to anyone with a boat or the money to rent one, available soon (one supposes) to the quickie tour by float-plane and hydrofoil, democratically accessible and with its most secret beauties captured on color transparencies at infallible exposures, it strikes me, even in my exhilaration, with the consciousness of loss. In gaining the lovely and the usable, we have given up the incomparable.

The river's altitude at the dam was about 3150 feet. At 3490 we ride on 340 feet of water, and that means that much of the archaeology and most of the history, both of which were concentrated at the river's edge or near it, are as drowned as Lyonesse. We chug two hundred feet over the top of the square masonry tower that used to guard the mouth of Forbidden Canyon. The one small ruin that we see up Navajo Canyon must once have been nearly inaccessible, high in the cliff. Somehow (though we do not see them) we think it ought to have a line of footholds leading down into and under the water toward the bottom where the squash and corn gardens used to grow.

The wildlife that used to live comfortably in Glen Canyon is not there on the main lake. Except at the extreme reach of the water up side canyons, and at infrequent places where the platform of the Navajo sandstone dips down so that the lake spreads in among its hollows and baldheads, this reservoir laps vertical cliffs, and leaves no home for beaver or waterbird. The beaver have been driven up the side canyons, and have toppled whole groves of cottonwoods ahead of the rising water. While the water remains stable, they have a home; if it rises, they move upward; if it falls, the Lord knows what they do, for falling water will leave long mud flats between their water and their food. In the side canyons we see a few mergansers and redheads, and up the Escalante Arm the blue herons are now nesting on the cliffs, but as a future habitat Lake Powell is as unpromising for any of them as for the beaver.

And what has made things difficult for the wildlife makes them difficult for tourists as well. The tamarisk and willow bars are gone, and finding a campsite, or even a safe place to land a boat, is not easy. When the stiff afternoon winds sweep up the lake, small boats stay in shelter, for a swamping could leave a man clawing at a vertical cliff, a mile from any crawling-out place.

Worst of all are the places I remember that are now irretrievably gone. Surging up-lake on the second day I look over my shoulder and recognize the swamped and truncated entrance to Hidden Passage Canyon, on whose bar we camped eighteen years ago when we first came down this canyon on one of Norman Nevills' river trips. The old masked entrance is swallowed up, the water rises almost over the shoulder of the inner cliffs. Once that canyon was a pure delight to walk in; now it is only another slot with water in it, a thing to poke a motorboat into for five minutes and then roar out again. And if that is Hidden Passage, and we are this far out in the channel, then Music Temple is straight down.

The magnificent confrontation of the Kaiparowits and Navajo Mountain is still there, possibly even more magnificent because the lake has lifted us into a wider view. The splendid sweep of stained wall just below the mouth of the San Juan is there, only a little diminished. And Hole-in-the-Rock still notches the north rim, though the cove at the bottom where the Mormons camped before rafting the river and starting across the bare rock-chaos of Wilson Mesa is now a bay, with sunfish swimming among the tops of drowned trees. The last time I was here, three years ago, the river ran in a gorge three hundred feet below where our boat ties up for the night, and the descent from rim to water was a longer, harder way. The lake makes the feat of those Mormons look easier than it was, but even now, no one climbing the thousand feet of cliff to the slot will ever understand how they got their wagons down there.

A mixture of losses, diminishments, occasional gains, precariously maintained by the temporary stabilization of the lake. There are plenty of people willing to bet that there will never be enough water in the Colorado to fill both Lake Mead, now drawn far down, and Lake Powell, still 210 feet below its planned top level, much less the two additional dams proposed for Marble and Bridge canyons,[1] between these two. If there ever is—even if there is enough to raise Lake Powell fifty or a hundred feet—there will be immediate drastic losses of beauty. Walls now low, but high enough to maintain the canyon feeling, will go under, walls now high will be reduced. The wider the lake spreads, the less character it will have. Another fifty feet of water would submerge the Gregory Natural Bridge and flood the floor of the Cathedral in the Desert; a hundred feet would put both where Music Temple is; two hundred feet would bring water and silt to the very foot of Rainbow Bridge. The promontories that are now the most feasible camping places would go, as the taluses and sandbars have already gone. Then indeed the lake would be a vertical-walled fjord widening in places to a vertical-walled lake, neither as beautiful nor as usable as it still is. And the moment there is even twenty or thirty feet of drawdown, every side canyon is a slimy stinking mudflat and every cliff is defaced at the foot by a band of mud and minerals.

By all odds the best thing that could happen, so far as the recreational charm of Lake Powell is concerned, would be a permanently stabilized lake, but nobody really expects that. People who want to see it in its diminished but still remarkable beauty should go soon. And people who, as we do, remember this country before the canyons were flooded, are driven to dream of ways by which some parts of it may still be saved, or half-saved.

---

1. Since given up, at least temporarily. (Footnote by Wallace Stegner—Ed.)

The dream comes on us one evening when we are camped up the Escalante. For three days we have been deafened by the noise of our diesel engines, and even when that has been cut off there has been the steady puttering of the generator that supplies our boat with heat, light, and running water. Though we weakly submit to the comforts, we dislike the smell and noise: we hate to import into this rock-and-water wilderness the very things we have been most eager to escape from. A wilderness that must be approached by power boat is no wilderness any more, it has lost its magic. Now, with the engines cut and the generator broken down, we sit around a campfire's more primitive light and heat and reflect that the best moments of this trip have been those in which the lake and its powerboat necessities were least dominant—eating a quiet lunch on a rock in Navajo Canyon, walking the 1.7 miles of sandy trail to the Rainbow Bridge or the half mile of creek bottom to the Cathedral in the Desert, climbing up the cliff to Hole-in-the-Rock. Sitting on our promontory in the Escalante canyon without sign or sound of the mechanical gadgetry of our civilization, we feel descending on us, as gentle as evening on a blazing day, the remembered canyon silence. It is a stillness like no other I have experienced, for at the very instant of bouncing and echoing every slight noise off cliffs and around bends, the canyons swallow them. It is as if they accentuated them, briefly and with a smile, as if they said, "Wait!" and suddenly all sound has vanished, there is only a hollow ringing in the ears.

We find that whatever others may want, we would hate to come here in the full summer season and be affronted with the constant roar and wake of power boats. We are not, it seems, water-based in our pleasures; we can't get a thrill out of doing in these marvelous canyons what one can do on any resort lake. What we have most liked on this trip has been those times when ears and muscles were involved, when the foot felt sand or stone, when we could talk in low voices, or sit so still that a brilliant collared lizard would come out of a crack to look us over. For us, it is clear, Lake Powell is not a recreational resource, but only a means of access; it is the canyons themselves, or what is left of them, that we respond to.

Six or seven hundred feet above us, spreading grandly from the rim, is the Escalante Desert, a basin of unmitigated stone furrowed by branching canyons as a carving platter is furrowed by gravy channels. It is, as a subsidiary drainage basin, very like the greater basin in whose trough once lay Glen Canyon, now the lake. On the north this desert drains from the Circle Cliffs and the Aquarius Plateau, on the east from the Waterpocket Fold, on the west from the Kaiparowits. In all that waste of stone fifty miles long and twenty to thirty wide there is not a resident human being, not a building except a couple of cowboy shelter shacks, not a road except the washed-out trail that the Mormons of 1880 established from the town of Escalante to Hole-in-the-Rock. The cattle and sheep that used to run on this desert range have ruined it and gone. That ringing stillness around us is a total absence of industrial or civilized decibels.

Why not, we say, sitting in chilly fire-flushed darkness under mica stars, why not throw a boom across the mouth of the Escalante Canyon and hold this one precious arm of Lake Powell for the experiencing of silence? Why not, giving the rest of that enormous water to the motorboats and the waterskiers, keep one limited tributary as a canoe or rowboat wilderness? There is nothing in the way of law or regulation to prevent the National Park Service from managing the Recreation Area in any way it thinks best, nothing that forbids a wilderness or primitive or limited access area within the larger recreational unit. The Escalante Desert is already federal land, virtually unused. It and its canyons are accessible by packtrain from the town of Escalante, and will be accessible by boat from the facility to be developed at Hole-in-the-Rock. All down the foot of the Kaiparowits, locally called Fiftymile Mountain or Wild Horse Mesa, the old Mormon road offers stupendous views to those who from choice or necessity want only to drive to the edge of the silence and look in.

I have been in most of the side gulches off the Escalante—Coyote Gulch, Hurricane Wash, Davis Canyon, and the rest. All of them have bridges, windows, amphitheaters, grottoes, sudden pockets of green. And some of them, including the superlative Coyote Gulch down which even now it is possible to take a packtrain to the river, will never be drowned even if Lake Powell rises to its planned thirty-seven-hundred-foot level. What might have been done for Glen Canyon as a whole may still be done for the higher tributaries of the Escalante. Why not? In the name of scenery, silence, sanity, why not?

For awe pervades that desert of slashed and channeled stone overlooked by the cliffs of the Kaiparowits and the Aquarius and the distant peaks of the Henrys; and history, effaced through many of the canyons, still shows us its dim marks here: a crude *mano* discarded by an ancient campsite, a mortared wall in a cave, petroglyphs picked into a cliff face, a broken flint point glittering on its tee of sand on some blown mesa, the great rock where the Mormons danced on their way to people Desolation. This is country that does not challenge our identity as creatures, but it lets us shed most of our industrial gadgetry, and it shows us our true size.

Exploring the Escalante basin on a trip in 1961, we probed for the river through a half dozen quicksand gulches and never reached it, and never much cared because the side gulches and the rims gave us all we could hold. We saw not a soul outside our own party, encountered not a vehicle, saw no animals except a handful of cows and one mule that we scared up out of Davis Gulch when we rolled a rock over the rim. From every evening camp, when the sun was gone behind the Kaiparowits rim and the wind hung in suspension like a held breath and the Henrys northeastward and Navajo Mountain southward floated light as bubbles on the distance, we watched the eastern sky flush a pure, cloudless rose, darker at the horizon, paler above; and minute by minute the horizon's darkness defined itself as the blue-domed shadow of the earth cast on the sky, thinning at its upward arc to violet, lavender, pale lilac, but clearly defined, steadily darkening upward until it swallowed all the sky's light and the stars pierced through it. Every night we watched the earth-shadow climb the hollow sky, and every dawn we watched the same blue shadow sink down toward the Kaiparowits, to disappear at the instant when the sun splintered sparks off the rim.

In that country you cannot raise your eyes—unless you're in a canyon—without looking a hundred miles. You can hear coyotes who have somehow escaped the air-dropped poison baits designed to exterminate them. You can see in every sandy pocket the pug tracks of wildcats, and every waterpocket in the rock will give you a look backward into geologic time, for every such hole swarms with triangular crablike creatures locally called tadpoles but actually first cousins to the trilobites who left their fossil skeletons in the Paleozoic.

In the canyons you do not have the sweep of sky, the long views, the freedom of movement on foot, but you do have the protection of cliffs, the secret places, cool water, arches and bridges and caves, and the sunken canyon stillness into which, musical as water falling into a plunge pool, the canyon wrens pour their showers of notes in the mornings.

Set the Escalante Arm aside for the silence, and the boatmen and the water skiers can have the rest of that lake, which on the serene, warm, sun-smitten trip back seems more beautiful than it seemed coming up. Save this tributary and the desert back from it as wilderness, and there will be something at Lake Powell for everybody. Then it may still be possible to make expeditions as rewarding as the old, motorless river trips through Glen Canyon, and a man can make his choice between forking a horse and riding down Coyote Gulch or renting a houseboat and chugging it up somewhere near the mouth of the Escalante to be anchored and used as a base for excursions into beauty, wonder, and the sort of silence in which you can hear the swish of falling stars.

B RUCE BERGER IS THE AUTHOR of six books of nonfiction, including *The Telling Distance, A Dazzle of Hummingbirds,* and most recently, *Almost an Island: Travels in Baja California.* The following excerpt from the eponymous essay of *There Was a River: Essays on the Southwest* recounts his experiences on Katie Lee's last trip down Glen Canyon in October of 1962, and offers the reader an insight into the vexing question of why Glen Canyon Dam was built. Berger currently lives in Aspen, Colorado.

There Was a River

I T TOOK TWENTY YEARS—from the floodgate closing of 1963 to the flood
year of 1983—for the lake to fill to capacity and for Glen Canyon to finish
dying. Most who flocked to Lake Powell during the first years of its existence
were people who regretted, mourned, or were enraged by the loss of the
Colorado River. They were also impassioned or cynical enough to take
advantage of the access that the rising waters gave them to previously inaccessible caves, ledges, and side canyons. For several years after our trip, Katie
Lee explored side canyons in an outboard-powered skiff that seemed to be
called SCREWDRIVER until you noticed a small gap between the D and the R,
rendering it SCREWD RIVER. While I made numerous camping trips in the
Utah canyon country with Katie during that period, I steered clear of Glen
Canyon. I didn't want to bear witness to its end, and I put it off with the
dread of being roused from a sumptuous dream. For some canyoneers, Lake
Powell was simply a truce with reality; for others who discovered Glen
Canyon after it had already begun to fill, it was a series of fresh adventures in a
new country, new every year as the reservoir rose.

A particularly acute observer of the filling of Lake Powell was Remo
Lavagnino, whom I met in Aspen a decade after my trip through the Glen.
He had first reached Glen Canyon in 1963, the year the water started to back
up. Pulling into Wahweap in the spring of 1963, he rented a rowboat with an
18-HP outboard from Art Greene and motored to the mouth of the Escalante River without encountering another soul. He and three friends then
chipped in on a boat, kept it at Wahweap, and returned to it yearly. The lake
was still a mere bloated river and the people were like river people, mostly in
kayaks and canoes. His party documented further ecological and archaeological losses as the lake rose.

In a cave up the Escalante River, for instance, Remo found a rock inscribed, in script, "In Search of Nemo." The reference was to Everett Ruess, a twenty-year-old poet, artist, and desert explorer who disappeared in 1933 and had been the subject of a nationally publicized unsuccessful search. He had sometimes called himself Nemo, classical Greek for "no man." Inscribed in the slickrock of the same cave was another message about Nemo in French, which Remo couldn't read.

Never having heard of Everett Ruess, Remo was startled by the similarity to his own name, as if someone had been searching for *him*. Knowing the rock would be lost under the water, but fearing it would capsize his low-sided, overloaded boat, he stashed it upside down at the back of the cave with the intention of returning for it later. When he returned with a lighter load, the rock had vanished. Someone, he assumes, still has the rock, while the French inscription lies buried under Lake Powell.

When the lake level had reached some seventy-five feet, Remo took his boat into the drowned hemisphere of Music Temple and stepped into the cleft that had seemed, in 1962, a nearly imaginary canyon, one that Katie and Natalie had only dreamed of entering. To his astonishment, his party found a ledge barely protected by an overhang, full of artifacts from the pre-ceramic Basketmaker III culture. "We found moccasins, atlatl darts, quids, which were bits of yucca that had been chewed and spit out like tobacco, and a twilled ring basket that was in perfect shape. We didn't know what much of the stuff was when we found it, and half the fun was going to museums later and identifying it by matching it up with known objects. My twilled ring basket is better than the one on display at Mesa Verde. We played in that spot like it was our private sandpile. When we came back the next year, it was ten feet underwater, and everything we hadn't taken was gone."

As the lake rose and spread, Remo and friends noticed a change in the craft they encountered. There was a phase of tiny one-man skiffs, precursors of wind surfers, tacking back and forth in the widening waters. Then came the larger inboard motorboats, models that got bigger with each passing year. During this period, Remo's group was aware of accelerating erosion. Most dramatic was the undermining of sand hills that leaned against cliffs at the angle of repose and collapsed into the lake, creating round, sudsy lagoons and leaving scars where they had shielded the walls. Remo's party, camping well above the waterline in case the lake rose in the night, lay in their sleeping bags and listened to the roar of sand collapsing. By day, they saw rocks turn into islands, trapping animals. Remo found, as if in a fable, an entire island full of mice running around frantically as the water rose. When he returned later in the day, the island was gone. He saw a raccoon marooned on a ledge in a box canyon. When he saw his first rattlesnake in the wild, it was on a sandbar in front of sheer walls, with nowhere to go.

Remo's group would have kept exploring in the low-slung boat, but each year the lake seemed more dangerous. Waves smashed the cliffs and rebounded with no shrinkage in size. There were swells and whitecaps, and the kayaks and canoes had disappeared. As the wind whipped the ballooning water into wilder, more unpredictable tossings, the boats grew until they were yachts and houseboats, with dinghies for plying the side canyons. Watching watercraft broaden was like watching nonbiological evolution. Remo dates the last of his Lake Powell to a particular moment when he saw what looked like an armada bearing down on his party's frail skiff. They stared until they realized it was eight speedboats in a row, each pulling a waterskier who veered back and forth in what seemed an advancing net. "That was the end of our Lake Powell, which was a place for exploration, and its conversion into pure recreation."

By avoiding Lake Powell entirely, I missed Katie's confrontation with the loss of her river. I could only wonder that she subjected herself to that loss. Natalie took one trip with her in SCREWD RIVER, motored over Moqui steps they had taken, powered into Music Temple, and Natalie couldn't face it. "You could take a motorboat right into the place where we had spent the night in the thunderstorm," she complained. "My favorite places were just devastated." They took SCREWD RIVER as far into the side canyons as they could and hiked what was left, leaving the boat mired in a phenomenon known as Dominy Stew, after Floyd Dominy, the feisty chief of the Bureau of Reclamation. The recipe varied, but the daily special might include dead trees, outboard motor oil, styrofoam cups, filter tips, film cans, rotting animals, and the kind of mud we had once tried to claw from our legs. Natalie remembers returning from a hike, coming upon a boatload of fishermen tossing cans overboard, and Katie yelling, "Sit on your ass and catch some bass." Katie doesn't recall the incident but says that she remembers she snapped, "Up yours, dipshit!" to a drunken fisherman at Hall's Crossing with a bitterness the man may not have connected with the loss of Glen Canyon.

After her one trip in SCREWD RIVER, Natalie didn't return until nearly ten years later when the lake was almost full and didn't remind her of Glen Canyon. From 1972 to 1975 she was part owner of a boat at Bullfrog Marina, and she, too, found the lake dangerous. "It was fun but scary. The lake gets the big roller kind of waves. When it's acting up, you'd better just head for shore." It was during that period that all from Aspen who frequented Lake Powell were sobered by the fate of a deliveryman for Railway Express named Ken Ward, who had moved to Lake Powell to run the ferry between Bullfrog Marina and Hall's Crossing. No one ever quite understood what happened, but it was at night and there was a storm. Ken was alone on the ferry. The ferry was found the morning after the storm in battered condition, and Ken was never recovered.

Of the four of us who took the trip through Glen Canyon in 1962, Leo was the least affected emotionally. In fact, he didn't wait for the rising of Lake Powell to seize an opportunity. As soon as we had flown back to Hite, he took off in his Willy's for the set of *The Greatest Story Ever Told* and offered his services as an extra. "They dressed me in this fancy sheet and made me a stand-in for one of them whatcha-ma-callits that trails after Jesus."

"An apostle?" I asked.

"Yeah, an apostle. It was colder'n hell and we spent most of the time in our sheets standing around fires, burning on one side and freezing on the other, then turning around to even it up. Everyone had the flu, and pretty soon that included me."

Leo did return to the area to take more trips with Slim to prospect and look for mementos of Moqui Sam. Then he took up jade hunting in Wyoming and discovered the second largest piece of jade ever found in the United States, 2,200 pounds, for which he found no market because it lacked the cachet of Oriental jade. As to whether he felt the loss of Glen Canyon, his only reaction was, "Boy, all that new water was really sumpn." His friend Slim, however, had considered the river his refuge. As the lake rose he was forced to move into a trailer at Fry Canyon, a tiny settlement near the Happy Jack Mine. But he was not about to let the lake take his two-room house piecemeal, and as the water crept toward its foundation, he dynamited it.

No matter how bitter we felt about it, there was no avoiding Lake Powell, for the Colorado River drained the canyon country of southeast Utah, and if you followed those canyons downstream, they delivered you to the lake. I had my first encounter with Lake Powell in 1977, at a reunion of sorts fifteen years after our float through Glen Canyon, for the trip included Katie and Leo, and Slim was to collect us at Lake Powell in his motorboat. We lacked

Natalie, who had incomprehensibly defected to the game of golf, but we had gained Remo and his friends. I hadn't seen Leo in several years and was startled when he walked into the Elk Ridge Cafe in Blanding. He had acquired four new pearl-like upper front teeth that he referred to as "mah toof," giving his own larger teeth to either side the look of fangs. Excited about a new fire starter that involved a kind of brass knuckle, flint, and some exotic tinder from Mexico, he lit a small pile of napkins on the tabletop. At the age of sixty, he was still the same Leo.

For the following ten days we marched through sand that blew like white scarves down a usually damp drainage while swollen indigo clouds threatened but never delivered rain, and we were finally rewarded with idyllic limestone pools. On the last day we dealt with a tortuous descent. Rounding a bend, we came upon a stretch of shelves strewn with sticks and dirt as if ravaged by a clearcut. Lake Powell had risen here, deposited its gifts, and left. Around another bend was a rancid exhalation, a mudbank with bleaching cola cans and torn jeans, and an arm of water whose shade of green had recently been featured in *The Exorcist*. Beyond it stood Slim—his eyes glittering, his square features suppressing a grin—offering cold beers out of his tethered boat. We loaded quickly and roared into Lake Powell. Canyon walls of the sort we had just labored past with forty pounds on our backs, our very slowness compelling us to study them, flashed past like dioramas in a museum. Suddenly the sky that had withheld its moisture for ten days let loose. Lightning cracked, thunder tore through the motor's racket, and we crouched under ponchos that left only tiny folds to peer from. All I could see was the outboard itself, which, I noticed to my amusement, was a Johnson Thunderbolt. Having put it off all these years, skimming, miserable, and cold, I was baptized by Lake Powell.

The enormity that two hundred of the most beautiful river miles imaginable could be erased by one wedge of concrete has taken three decades to realize. To blame the "Wreck-the-Nation Bureau," a federal agency whose highest goal has become self-perpetuation, is too easy, too like blaming the trigger finger without questioning the brain. Even for Katie, with enough rage for all antagonists, there was a sense of bafflement, of an enemy too amorphous to target.

I made my first attempt to understand it on the river itself, reading—by flashlight in the sleeping bag, in the few moments before exhausted sleep— the *Utah Historical Quarterly* I had bought from Woody. Devoted entirely to Utah's stretch of the Colorado River, it was written by biologists, historians, and reclamationists, with an introduction by the current governor. One article would hail the replacement by water of what another had just praised. The conclusion, with mock objectivity, described "testimony generated by national conservation groups" as "bitter and emotional," while "successful efforts to secure authorization" for the dam were "an outstanding example of organized effort" by "nationwide information campaigns." Schizophrenia paraded as scholarship.

As I read more afterwards, a scenario emerged. The drainage basin of the Colorado River includes portions of Colorado, Wyoming, Utah, New Mexico, Nevada, Arizona, and California, and each began claiming its perceived share of the Colorado River from the moment of statehood. California, with its rich Imperial Valley near the Mexican border, first established a major irrigation canal. The upstream states panicked and demanded that their own water rights be established. A flood that began in 1905 and raged for sixteen months through California farms and homes—breaking through the canal that fed the Imperial Valley, creating the now toxic Salton Sea—set off a howl for flood control dams. In 1922, a pressured Congress instructed Secretary of Commerce Herbert Hoover to hold public hearings in all states involved, and the emerging Colorado River Compact was ratified. A kind of legal parting of the waters, the compact divides the river at Lee's Ferry, at the beginning of the Grand Canyon, and awards an equal 7,500,000 acre-feet to the upstream and downstream states.

The Lower Basin plunged into action and completed the massive Hoover Dam in 1935, creating Lake Mead and sending power and irrigation to southern California. The Upper Basin states watched hungrily, bickering among themselves on how to carve up their half of the water. The Bureau of Reclamation, impatient for contracts, came up with the Colorado River Storage Project and Participating Projects, with four major dams—one being Glen Canyon—and eleven minor ones. They were calculated to placate all parties, including themselves. Touted benefits included hydroelectric power, flood control, irrigation, recreation and—incomprehensibly to some—scenic enhancement.

When the plan hit Congress, not all were placated. Chief opposition was led by conservation groups because one of the projects, Echo Park Dam, was located in Dinosaur National Park. Seeing a potential threat to the entire park system, the conservationists opposed it as a dangerous precedent and achieved what may be the first nationally consolidated conservation victory. Echo Park Dam was relocated to Flaming Gorge, outside the park, and language was inserted in the Colorado River Storage Act stating: "It is the intention of Congress that no dam or reservoir constructed under the authorization of this Act shall be within any National Park or Monument." Almost all of southeast Utah, including Glen Canyon in its entirety, had once been proposed for protection by Franklin Delano Roosevelt's secretary of interior, Harold Ickes, but the proposal never passed Congress. As unthinkable as it is in retrospect, Glen Canyon was never defended by conservation groups because it had never been included in the national parks and monuments system. The Sierra Club and its allies were so intent on defending what had already been set aside that their only objection to Glen Canyon Dam was that it would back water into the tiny Rainbow Bridge National Monument. Seeing another threatening precedent, they proposed a retaining dam to protect the monument—even if that dam overwhelmed what it protected. The conservation response to the Colorado River Storage Act was entirely legalistic. It seems no one of consequence ever ventured to inspect what would be flooded, apparently assuming that if the area were so worth preserving, it would be protected already.

By the time the Storage Act passed Congress, it had swelled even beyond the Bureau of Reclamation's own dreams. Arizona wanted its own subsystem, Colorado wanted another, and each state appended projects like tipplers buying each other drinks. The whole concrete folly was chaperoned through Congress by Wayne Aspinall, who was for twenty-four years a congressional representative of Colorado's Western Slope, and for twelve of those years the powerful chairman of the House Interior Committee. The dam-loving Aspinall was particularly galling to river lovers from Aspen because he was our very own Congressman. In 1972, we took revenge by helping a law professor knock Aspinall out of Congress in a Democratic primary.

In October 1974, when Morris Udall was contemplating a run for the presidency, his brother Stewart, who was secretary of interior under Kennedy and Johnson when Glen Canyon went under, came through Aspen on a fundraising trip. I was anxious to learn what I could from one of the players, and I volunteered to drive Udall back to the airport. After answering Udall's questions about the difference between our high-altitude narrow-leaf cottonwoods and the canyon country's Fremont cottonwoods, I plunged in. "How did Glen Canyon Dam come to be? Can you tell me something of what led to its construction?"

"Well, I voted for the goddamn thing when I was in Congress," he replied in a flat, borderline sarcastic tone. "And I floated the whole Glen in 1960. There wasn't the feeling about dams then that there is now, nor the strength in the environmental movement. Goldwater had been through the Glen and voted for the dam, and he is against dams in the Grand Canyon now. The place was hard to defend because it was really unknown. Only a few hundred people—maybe a few thousand—knew about it. The book was right—it was really the place no one knew."

"Weren't there any alternatives?"

"There were other dam sites, if that's what you mean. They were all bad, of course. One site they talked about was below the confluence of the Colorado and the Green. The trouble with Glen Canyon Dam is that the river is so flat through there that the reservoir backs up for two hundred miles."

"What part did the Sierra Club play in the decision?"

"I'm afraid the Sierra Club must share some of the blame. They put all their strength in the fight against the dam at Echo Park. They had the idea from John Muir that parks were the thing, and had to be protected. Glen Canyon was much *better* than a park, but it wasn't a park. So they used up all their strength fighting the Echo Park dam, and, of course, in protecting Rainbow Bridge."

"Didn't they want to build a dam to protect Rainbow Bridge?"

"Dumbest goddamn thing I ever heard of. Anyone who really cared about Rainbow Bridge had to be against that. The monument is just a 160-acre box on the Navajo Reservation. I had to decide against them on that one. If they really wanted to save Rainbow Bridge, they should have fought Glen Canyon Dam."

"If the Sierra Club had fought Glen Canyon Dam instead of the dam at Echo Park, could the canyon have been saved?"

"It would have been a bloodier showdown."

"Hasn't David Brower had some second thoughts about the Sierra Club position on that?"

"Yeah. Dave once told me it was a mistake."

"But you favored the dam . . ." I persisted.

"When I ran for Congress twenty years ago, dams were the great thing. California was stealing our water, so we needed the Central Arizona Project. Aspinall wouldn't let us have it unless he also had his Upper Basin dams. Of course, he wanted dams at Echo Park *and* Glen Canyon."

I came now to the question that most bothered me, the one that no one seemed to ask. I could understand the case being made for dams in terms of power generation, flood control, and irrigation. I could see that recreation is used as a selling point, and while the bathtub rings of *all* reservoirs negate, for me, their scenic value, I also know that tastes in scenery vary. What I did not understand is why a state, or group of states, needed to impound water physically, merely to stake a claim. Water-measuring devices are sophisticated; laws can be passed giving credit to any state for the acre-feet it deserves; there is no reason I can conceive of why a geographical entity needs to impound water *bodily* to assert its rights. Yet even now, officials in my home state of Colorado argue that we must build more dams—drowning bottomland, destroying riparian zones—so our archenemies in Utah and Arizona won't steal our precious snowmelt. With such thoughts in mind, I asked Stewart Udall, "Couldn't they just measure the amount of water that passed Lee's Ferry and give the Upper Basin *credit* for their half of the water?"

"Sure," he said. "There were lots of other things that could have been done. But Aspinall wanted dams. He said that not to have dams would interfere with their bookkeeping system."

We had reached the airport. Udall thanked me, grabbed his bag, and ran for his plane while I sat in the jeep, playing and replaying the phrase, "not to have dams would interfere with their bookkeeping system." To preserve a bookkeeping system we are willing to destroy an ecosystem.

Ellen Meloy is the author of *Raven's Exile: A Season on the Green River* (excerpted here), *The Last Cheater's Waltz,* and *The Anthropology of Turquoise.* She is the recipient of the 1997 Whiting Foundation Writer's Award. In addition to offering an important biographical snapshot of Ken Sleight, "Travels with Seldom" elucidates the difficulty that many contemporary lovers of canyon country encounter in attempting to come to terms with Lake Powell. Meloy lives on the San Juan River in southern Utah.

Travels with Seldom

*For you cannot tame them; they are horsemen who are
born with a blue horizon in their eyes, and no matter
how fast they gallop, that horizon recedes.*
—Mark Helprin, Swan Lake

O N A CLEAR MAY MORNING, ten people board two boats near Utah's
Bullfrog Marina and roar down the "Blue Death," as writer Edward
Abbey called Lake Powell, to a base camp near the mouth of the Escalante
River. From this camp we will explore side canyons on foot for four days.
Veteran Utah guide Ken Sleight leads the trip, and it is an anomaly. Most of
the boaters we pass are engaged in strenuous water sports: microwaving
pizza, rocking out to Dirt Love Injection tapes, raking Astroturf decks,
sunbathing atop the ubiquitous houseboats that chug down the lake.

We sit several hundred feet above the Colorado River bed in Glen
Canyon, which Sleight first ran in a fat-tubed rubber military assault barge
nearly forty years before. What holds us up today are the powerboats and
Lake Powell, the vast reservoir that extends two hundred miles into Arizona
and Utah behind the Bureau of Reclamation's Glen Canyon Dam.

A few times during the ride to base camp Sleight has called Lake Powell
the Blue Death or Lake Foul, names popularized by Abbey. Mostly he calls
Lake Powell "the River," as if this inland sea of perpetual houseboat grid-
lock, visited by three million people a year, simply didn't exist. For him this is
trip number who-knows-which; he can't remember, so many times has he
traveled this piece of Colorado Plateau. Despite the lake atop the river;
despite the personal ordeals of watching Glen Canyon go under and the

death in 1989 of his friend Abbey—who Sleight believed gave voice to his own rage and grief and resistance against man's abuses of Utah's slickrock wilderness—no matter that the world has changed, Ken Sleight is still "running" Glen Canyon.

Today's pilgrimage might seem disturbing for someone who watched a river die. Instead Sleight sits in the boat grinning as if he were just caught in the attic reading cowboy novels. "I hate Lake Foul," he laughs. "But I like to come here once in a while. It makes me go back home and fight."

Sleight was the model for Seldom Seen Smith, one of the quartet of eco-guerillas in Abbey's 1975 novel *The Monkey Wrench Gang,* and its sequel, *Hayduke Lives!* Proprietor of Back of Beyond Expeditions, a jack Mormon, or apostate, but "polygamous as a rabbit," Smith was "a lanky man, lean as a rake, awkward to handle," Abbey wrote, with "a nose like a beak, a big Adam's apple, ears like the handles on a jug, sun-bleached hair like a rat's nest and a wide and generous grin." The description still fits, though Sleight is in his sixties now and has married only twice, one wife at a time. When he is not guiding, he devotes a great deal of time to environmental activism and the southern Utah guest ranch he operates with his wife, Jane. The rat's nest is gray, his hands are young and gentle, his aura of irrepressible mischief remains intact if not raised to new heights.

For me this is trip number one on the Blue Death. I was in Mickey Mouse pajamas when the hydrobinge on western rivers peaked with Glen Canyon and Flaming Gorge Dams. I knew that for conservationists Glen Canyon Dam was an act of gross vandalism. For others it is a monument to progress and human ingenuity, a recreation paradise, an economic boon, and for its energy supply, a necessity. Until this trip, however, I turned my back to Lake Powell. When there was no choice but to take the roads that skirted it, I hunched my neck, ground my fillings, riveted my eyes to the centerline, and drove around it like a crazed walnut. One exception occurred after a hide-scorching hike near Hite, a marina on Powell's upper reaches, when I waded through log debris and nervous flotillas of Styrofoam to bathe in the lake. I was joined in my swim by a large red sofa.

Sooner or later everyone must come to terms with Lake Powell's duality as hubris or techno-triumph, so I'm here to dip more than toes into the Blue Death, to travel with Sleight, who remembers pre-dam Glen Canyon better than anyone else.

I survive my first night on Lake Foul. As we motor to Rainbow Bridge, where we will hike today, I am in fact astounded by my coldly dispassionate attitude. Look at undammed Glen Canyon and Lake Powell through the different ends of binoculars, I think as we slurp over the wakes of houseboat fleets. So vast a maze of bare rock and wild river was Glen Canyon, so aloof and remote, the long-range view was far too heady. Better to pull in the details, the silt-gold river surface, crimson blossoms of a claret cup cactus, a lizard's turquoise throat, the mossy grottos, or glens, that gave the canyon its name. The beauty of Lake Powell is best seen from the end of the binoculars that distances the view: stunning azure water with a shoreline labyrinth of sensuous red, beige, and ochre sandstone domes, a lake many people call the most beautiful in the world. Up close it is a flooded river gorge lined with tons of Gulf of California-bound but dam-arrested mud, cans, bottles, batteries, stolen cars, six billion pairs of sunglasses.

Sleight and another trip companion, Bill Adams, a professional magician from California, do not have to warp their perception. They saw Glen Canyon as it was. Everywhere they look as we motor down the lake to our trailhead, they can peel back this water and remember. It is said that you can see a person's true face only in the glare of lightning. When I watch these two men remembering Glen, it is as if in lightning.

Over thirty years ago Adams shopped for outfitters in southern Utah. "I got a lot of slick brochures," he recalls. "Ken sent me a mimeo on beige paper. The lines ran together, the ink was smudged. I signed up." It was his first of ninety trips.

Sleight's guiding career began in the mountains near his boyhood home in Paris, Idaho, a farm town on the Utah border. Son of Mormon pioneers, he was the kid who rounded up friends and instigated the hikes and overnights. "I led the pack, just like I do now," he says sweetly and you know you would follow him, too. He served in Korea, earned a business degree, married, started a family, taught school, and in 1955 bought a few forty-dollar military inflatables, in which he carried Boy Scouts, youth groups, the stray flock of little old ladies through Glen Canyon. As his clientele broadened, he worked other stretches of the Colorado and Lodore and Desolation Canyons on the Green River. Off season he outfitted horsepack trips in the Escalante backcountry .

When river recreation boomed in the late 1960s, outfitters added more boats, hired more boatmen, cranked more people downriver. Federal river managers invoked a permit system giving outfitters and private boaters pieces of a pie, precariously balancing intense demand with the river's carrying capacity. Sleight kept his operation small, essentially one-man. He lobbied for a ceiling on the size of river companies, arguing that they should remain family-sized operations—businesses, not industries—suitable to their medium: the River.

For his lifelong defense of small business, Sleight has been called an anachronism and crazy. Crazy to cap the growth potential of his own enterprise, to resist the inevitable, which indeed came to pass. Commercial river running is a competitive, largely standardized recreation industry. Roughly twenty companies now run each stretch of southwestern whitewater, each carrying as many as twenty-five passengers on brief trips that maximize turnaround and profit.

Sleight turned his river business over to his son Mark in the early 1980s but continued to run Glen. "Someone has to remind the world that back when Reclamation built the dam, they promised that Lake Powell would forever remain the domain of small businesses," he asserts. Within less than twenty years of that promise, however, the Del Webb Corporation, followed by ARA Leisure Services, controlled all marinas, accommodations, and tour and boating services, a justified evolution, according to the National Park Service, which manages Glen Canyon National Recreation Area, since a single concessioner has the capital for development and can handle great numbers of people more efficiently. Several years ago the Park Service tried but failed to revoke Sleight's Glen Canyon permit on the grounds that his outfit was "too small to serve the public interest." "I enjoy being all that stands between ARA and a monopoly on Lake Powell," he says, as if he were talking about a rather pleasant game of golf.

In the summer of 1962, Glen Canyon was terminal. The river outfitters announced their "Farewell Voyages" in the July issue of *Desert* magazine, the requiem pilgrimages down a river soon to turn slack behind 800,000 tons of concrete countersunk between sheer walls of Navajo sandstone. Ken Sleight Expeditions was among the listings: group size, twelve; cost, one hundred dollars per person.

The Sierra Club and other conservation groups had resigned themselves to what they called "responsible reclamation," and much to their later horror, they virtually let Glen Canyon go. Conservation's big battle was to the north, against dams in Dinosaur National Monument. At Glen Canyon the case for mass recreation for "the common man" touted by the irascible Floyd Dominy prevailed. A pristine, inaccessible river was worthless, the developers argued, sounding a refrain that haunts environmentalists to this day: Those who want to embalm nature are elitists. "Dear God," prayed Dominy in a book about Lake Powell, "did you cast down two hundred miles of canyon and mark: 'For poets only'? Multitudes hunger for a lake in the sun."[1] Dominy's masses cameth and they are still ravenous. The waiting list for a houseboat rental on Lake Powell can be two years long.

Even without the big conservation groups, Friends of Glen Canyon, a loose assembly of boatmen and outfitters, including Sleight, made a case for damning the dam. "We hardly knew what we were doing," he remembers. "We didn't have documents to back us, we didn't know how to tell other people about the desert wilderness that would be lost. I spoke out, I said, 'This is what this place means to me.' But every politician, bureaucrat, and developer in the country wanted to dam it, and they did."

Sleight ran Glen when the dam gates closed in 1963 and the river went slack. He added motors and ran it some more, watching the reservoir rise "inch by lousy inch," an embittered witness to the disappearance of over a hundred canyons, thousands of Anasazi Indian sites, graceful sandbars, alcoves large enough to hold a symphony orchestra, grottos of gentle seeps and lush greenery, Music Temple, Cathedral in the Desert, Hidden Passage, cottonwoods, willows, saltbush, herons, snowy egrets, coyotes, deer, and millions and millions of grains of exquisite red sand. The slow inundation was a tragic personal ordeal. "I felt like I was in a straitjacket," Sleight says. "The world fell down around me and I couldn't do anything about it."

From a boat dock with floating rest rooms and a sizable pod of Dorito-addicted carp, we walk up a paved trail to Rainbow Bridge. Behind us the *Canyon Odyssey*, a sleek white multidecked tour vessel operated by ARA, pulls into the narrows, its engines idling like a lineup of 170-horsepower Cuisinarts on PUREE. "Please return to the boat in twenty minutes," commands a robo-voice over a loudspeaker, loud enough to tremble the prayer feathers atop nearby Navajo Mountain, and a large crowd shuffles obediently forward in their aloha shirts to look at the nearly three-hundred-

1. Dominy attributes the quote to Gordon Michelle; see *Lake Powell: Jewel of the Colorado* in this volume.—Ed.

foot-high, forty-foot-thick arc of sandstone. *Nonne'zoshi,* in Navajo. The stone rainbow.

"It was a six-mile hike from the river to the bridge," Sleight tells me. "A long, hot hike. Some people, before they turned the last bend and saw the bridge, were ready to strangle me. We left cans under the seeps in the canyon walls to collect water for the next batch of hikers. The creek was cool and clear, with pour-offs and pools. Redbud trees over there"—he points to the banks—"a hanging garden in each alcove. Rainbow Bridge was a monument to wild country, to solitude."

The 1956 law creating the Upper Colorado River Project contained a provision to protect Rainbow Bridge from encroachment or impairment by reservoirs. In a seven-year lawsuit, Sleight, Friends of the Earth, and the Wasatch Mountain Club fought to keep the government from breaking its own law and letting Lake Powell reach the bridge. A district judge ruled to limit the lake's height, but the Supreme Court overturned the decision, and the water crept up the canyon walls. In most years a blue tongue of Lake Powell covers the creekbed and laps the buttresses of the stone rainbow. In these recent years of low lake levels, the tongue has vanished, leaving a broad swath of lifeless, gray-brown sediment.

"We used to climb up the dome of rock on the right, then lower ourselves off a rope to the buttress and onto the top of the bridge." Sleight pauses, grins. "I think I'll do that again someday, when the rangers are here."

More tourists spill down the trail that makes Rainbow Bridge not the secluded domain of desert rats and semidehydrated Boy Scouts, but truly accessible to the motorized hundred thousand visitors per annum who won't get blisters or strangle their guide. Looking impish in his faded cowboy snap shirt, Sleight walks up to a woman in the crowd. "Want to go up there?" he asks, pointing to the top of the bridge. "I'll take you there for a hundred dollars."

After years among river people, the ones with perpetually sand-caked motleyness and a look that can be read either as supreme enlightenment or extreme horniness, I am still amazed that we call this organism "the River" when it is actually several rivers of the Colorado River system, numerous segments with no resemblance to a river, and a few more with no water in them whatsoever. Each time we say "the River" we seem to resurrect the lost wild country.

Sleight is a more proactive resurrectionist. In 1988 several hundred people gathered on the crest of Glen Canyon Dam to sing the dam's praises in its twenty-fifth year. Sleight was there, and as he walked toward the speaker's podium to present a statement with a different point of view, security guards trailed him as if he were Muammar Qaddafi strolling through the lobby of the Tel Aviv Hilton. Sleight won't let go. He simply believes there is no end to the dam's story until the Colorado River breaks loose.

Helpmeet in his battles, albeit posthumously now, is Edward Abbey, whom Sleight met in the seventies at Lee's Ferry, Arizona, when Sleight was rigging a trip down the Grand Canyon. They talked into the night, Sleight recalls, mostly about Glen Canyon Dam. In what would become a lifelong discussion, wishful thinking was epic. Some of it found its way into *The Monkey Wrench Gang.* Dynamite. ("We get three jumbo-size houseboats and some dolphins . . .") Earthquakes. (Seldom Seen kneels atop the dam and prays, "God. How about a little old *pre*-cision-type earthquake right here under this dam?") Levitation. (Abbey, Sleight, and others once circled a campfire, grabbed hands, shut their eyes, and tried to raise the dam, just a few inches, to let the water out.)

Abbey went on many Sleight trips over the years. The two "wild pre-servatives" had much common ground: belief in open government, social and environmental justice, the need to dog destructive developers and the public servants who forget whom they serve. Both were hard in their vision of a restored Glen Canyon. "Lake Powell will disappear," Abbey wrote in 1988. "Del Webb will go back to Lubbock, Texas, where he belongs."

In camp I eat breakfast alone on a shoreline ledge. Above it rises the sandy slope of camp, then a sheer eighty-foot cliff. Below this ledge, under Lake Powell, is the rest of the cliff and the old river bottom, silent in its aquarian tomb. A canyon wren sings its glissade of tender notes, and in the soft morning light the lake is lovely, not counting the thick, dirty-sock white crust of calcium carbonate directly above the water's edge: Lake Powell's bathtub ring, sixty feet high in this interminable drought. Suddenly I am weeping. I cry because I cannot smell the heady musk of cottonwoods or feel the quiet movements of water in the unlikely ribbon of paradise that curls through acres and acres of bare, baking slickrock. I cry because three million people a year love the Blue Death and I don't. I weep for Glen Canyon and I have never seen it. I am not the one who sunk his life into this place—"the heart of his river, the river of his heart," as Abbey called it. He's over there greeting each guest.

"Good morning! I see you lived another day," Sleight says to the family from Maryland.

Tears drench my shirt, my hair dangles in my salsa, a hot pain rises with such force, it blurs my vision, knocks me over, and as I hit the rock my heart splits with a loud, painful crack. I sob and mumble about dolphins and explosives.

"I sure hate to see people die on my trips," he teases. "It's such a nuisance taking them out. You have to tie them to a mule."

Later I am cheered by Bill Adams's repertoire of magic tricks and a tale of the time when, before a trip down the Grand Canyon, one of Sleight's old neoprene rafts blew up, an event forever known as "a Sleight explosion." I relish our final day of hiking, and I try hard to fill my coward's heart with the hope of Sleight, Abbey, and others for whom Glen Canyon was a tragedy but also a force around which to rally and say, No more wasting of places like Glen Canyon, no more oversized, outstripped, ultrazealous transcendence of the West's own limits, no more trying to make Utah, Arizona, New Mexico, and the rest of the desert look like upstate New York.

On our last night in camp, Sleight is laid-back, gently attentive to each guest, and speaking gross understatement. "Sure, it hurts to come back to Glen," he tells me. "I was lucky to see it, but there are lots of canyons I haven't seen." Lavender shadows etch the canyon's vermilion walls and deepen in the dusk. We recline against duffel bags on the quiet beach.

I suggest a run to Vegas for explosives. I imagine a bunch of people with terminal diseases, flinging themselves off the dam's lip with dynamite strapped to their backs, their shoes on fire. The stories of how to "do" the dam are, like the sheer catharsis they serve, epic and legendary.

For years Sleight has written letters, spoken at hearings, insisted that all sides be heard, acted to set right a wrong after everyone else gives up. While he supports environmental groups, he prefers to fight solo—Don Quixote, a friend calls him. Not long before this trip, he had ridden his horse in front of a bulldozer at a four-hundred-acre Bureau of Land Management chaining operation on a mesa near his home. (Chaining is when two bulldozers drag a ship's anchor chain between them and grind across the desert, uprooting century-old pinyon and juniper trees and all other vegetation in their path. The land is then reseeded for cattle and wildlife forage.) All avenues of public protest against chaining on the mesa had been tried. Still, Sleight felt it was wrong. He blocked one of the bulldozers, dismounted, and asked that the operation be stopped. He was wrestled aside. The bulldozers turned the desert upside down.

Sleight's style tends to mythologize him, to make him more Seldom Seen than a man whose grip on his monkey wrench is actually quite simple: unfailing truth to himself. To Utah's canyon country, to freedom, to the River, to knowing a place intimately and leading a small group of explorers into its heart, to keeping one's work well within the reach of love.

On the beach we talk of his foray into politics. He ran for a seat in the Utah legislature, lost the race, but still dreamed of the day he might ride his horse up Salt Lake City's capitol steps, followed by packhorses bearing briefcases, and "fix" a few laws. Again, humor defuses the seriousness of a tough, consuming personal endeavor.

We talk of Ed Abbey.

"He is supposed to be up there arranging that *pre*-cision earthquake." Sleight laughs. He tells me the story of the time, in Cataract Canyon, he was thrown from rowing position and yelled for Abbey to take the oars before they dropped into a maelstrom of whitewater known as Satan's Gut. "Pull, Ed, pull!" Sleight cried. Abbey pulled, there was a loud crack. The oar splintered. Abbey looked into the frothing hole, then at Sleight. "Ken," he said with a silly grin, "do we have another oar? This one seems to have an imperfection."

"With Abbey I always felt we could solve problems, we could set the world right," Sleight says. Our lakeshore camp is dark, everyone else is asleep, but we're still sitting in the sand. "On every trip together we'd try to figure out just how to do it.

"His pen was his monkey wrench. We agreed on so much, never have I felt such a kinship with another person. All my life I couldn't seem to say what I wanted to say. Abbey said it for me. He was my voice, our voice. I'm barely getting over losing him."

"Dear Ed," Sleight began in a moving letter to his friend, read during Abbey's memorial at Sleight's ranch. "Dear Ed, I wish I could rise above this."

I bid Ken good night and walk across the starlit beach to my sleeping bag. The canyons and the entombed river beside me slipped away before anyone could comprehend their wild, wild souls. Pioneers and explorers like John Wesley Powell ogled this place, never quite believed what they saw. Sleight, Abbey, and their contemporaries tasted it, its flavor barely on their tongues. Too many among those born after the "wild preservatives" do not even know that a river once flowed here. This lake, they believe, came along with everything else in the Book of Genesis.

Suddenly I remember that nearly thirty years ago this very day, Glen Canyon Dam shut off the Colorado River. I crawl into my bed by the Blue Death. I make plans to sleep tomorrow by the River, the part that still flows by and makes sounds. I try to rise above this.

A NN WEILER WALKA IS THE AUTHOR of *Waterlines: Journeys on a Desert River* and *Walking the Unknown River and Other Travels in Escalante Country* (2002), from which the following essay was developed. Walka has served as the director of various education programs for natural history and anthropology museums in the Southwest. She currently writes, teaches and leads backcountry expeditions on the Colorado Plateau.

A Far Country

THE BLUE LACCOLITHIC DOME ANGLOS named Navajo Mountain beckons like a lodestone above the Glen Canyon basin. From a distance the silhouette, both massive and as airy as rain, might be a river cobble, or the dream of a cobble, perched on the straight-edged, iron-stained mesas. Navajos know this dome as the head of Earth Woman, a powerful being who reclines across the Four Corners region. They say two sacred rivers made love at her base, the steeper-pitched San Juan covering the Colorado, their union conceiving the rain.

Another stream, the Escalante, flowed into the Colorado from the west a few miles upstream. These three rivers joined at the heart of Glen Canyon, which was, in turn, the heart of the high, dry, lonesome physiographic province called the Colorado Plateau. Lake Powell silences the confluences now, but Earth Woman—or Naatsis'áán as the mountain is called by the Navajos—still overlooks the junctions.

Most visitors now know the Glen Canyon basin as the Lake and the lakeshore, a surreal landscape as stunning in its simplicity as any modernist sculpture. In my travels here as a guide and a naturalist, I accompany folks on foot farther into the country. Walking around the flank of Navajo Mountain or up the canyons draining into the reservoir, we enter terrain that is wild enough to break us or strand us, dry us up or wash us away, terrain overlain with human hubris and travail, with stories and ceremony. Hiking away from the mirror, we discover a world as complicated as an omnipotent mind.

One May, I hike dudes from the Navajo Mountain community to Rainbow Bridge. Every morning our Navajo guides send us off to find our way while they pack camp onto their sturdy little horses. Heading around the mountain on the Rainbow Plateau, a dissected bench of Navajo sandstone, we *bilagáana* (Anglos) hardly remember that there is a reservoir down there, or even that the twenty-first century has arrived. Despite the trampling by burros and sheep, Naatsis'áán, a remote slice of the Navajo Nation, remains largely unchanged since Major Powell's men floated by in 1872.

Powell conducted his land survey in the high plateau country west of the Colorado River. Except for prospectors greedy for silver and nineteenth-century adventurers led by the locals to the fabled stone rainbow, Euro-Americans didn't often explore this side of Glen Canyon. Although tourists ogle the bridge from the lakeshore now, permission from the Navajo Nation is still required to hike this far country.

When I pester him for his stories about this other world, one of our guides grins that everyone has their own story, and all of them are true. An Anglo, I was taught these things in school: the laccolithic mountain was created by magma folding up layers of country rock, and the Navajo are newcomers who elbowed into what was Paiute territory in the 1850s, when Hoskininni and his family were harried there by Ute and New Mexican slave traders.

Local stories, though, recount how holy beings shaped the mountain around a light-filled inner form using soil brought from a previous world. And oral tradition asserts Naatsis'áán and the Rainbow Plateau, lying within the fork of two sacred rivers, as ancestral Navajo homeland. Although Paiutes did live here when the Diné arrived, the holy people had come long before, marking the territory.

Largely from scholars' re-tellings, I have gleaned that Naatsis'áán is the head of Earth Woman, a figure sprawling across the northwest corner of Dinétah; Black Mesa to the south and east is her body and Agathla, a volcanic neck near Monument Valley, her wool spindle. Monster Slayer, the son of Changing Woman and the Sun, lived for a time in a flint hogan atop the mountain. His life-and-death struggle with He Who Kicks People Off took place at Naatsis'áán. It was Monster Slayer who used his shield to stop the spruce and pine trees Black God threw this way from Dook'o'osliid (the San Francisco Peaks) and who planted them on the stony slopes.

The natural bridge at the base of the mountain is reputed here to be two rainbows, male and female. These rainbow people, the two great rivers making love nearby, and the sacred springs on the mountain all gave birth to water children, to the clouds and rain.

Anglo and Navajo histories agree that in the 1860s the number of local

Diné swelled to more than a thousand as Navajos fleeing Kit Carson's raiders disappeared into the maze of canyons at the foot of Navajo Mountain. They managed to escape the Long Walk to Fort Sumner, despite the federal troops manning the heliograph station at the summit. Local folk say that the Navajos hiding from the soldiers were protected by Earth Woman herself and by Monster Slayer's shield.

Usually I would escort my hikers all the way out of strange terrain, but today I'm riding up from the stone rainbow with our horsepacker guides. The folks who accompanied us down around the mountain jet away across the reservoir, while my boss and I wave goodbye from the Park Service's floating dock below Rainbow Bridge.

Eric, horseman, land-use planner, and the grandson of a Navajo Mountain Singer, leads the way up from the marvel this morning. My stomach clenched all night imagining this adventure, but fortunately I'm riding Frank, a wise and agile Navajo pony. Frank scrambles up slickrock pitches so steep his hooves slide, picks his hard-footed way along the sides of cliffs, jumps from ledges and kicks over cobbles. Settling deeper in the saddle, I learn to lean forward riding uphill, to lower my heels alongside Frank's chest going down.

Black hair swinging halfway to his waist, Eric sings in Navajo. From the stone rainbow where we parted from our guests, we ride up the streambed past the old horse camp—tucked into a spring-worn alcove and furnished with rusted bedsteads—where we slept last night. Eventually turning east, the disintegrating CCC trail, ball-bearinged with cobbles, heads across the canyons. We wind through sleeves of wildflowers and along sandstone cliffs that sheer now above our heads, now hundreds of feet below our ponies' feet. My fear of falling evaporates into rock-edged frames of blue sky and towering clouds, into wind gusts and stillness and the buzzing of flies in the noonday sun.

Eric tells me that before the reservoir filled, his family forded the Colorado to graze their horses in the canyons of the Escalante or to hunt or gather plants on the Kaiparowits Plateau. Although the risks inherent in crossing out of Dinétah required a protection ceremony, beyond the rivers the frontier was spacious and grass abundant. Despite the drowning of the old trails and fords, from Frank's back the Navajo world still seems endless. Apparently untroubled, Eric sings all the way to the corral.

Riding horseback around Naatsis'ááán was one of my gigs as a gray-haired backcountry guide. Avid to live an outdoor life, I left my career in museum education when I was nearly fifty to become a naturalist for outdoor adventure programs that explore the canyons of the Escalante, the lower San Juan and the Colorado rivers. Another of these guiding jobs takes me cruising on Lake Powell during the second week in October, bringing folks from Hall's Crossing to hike at the base of Navajo Mountain. I hardly ever confess this to my river friends who deplore lake boating as a sacrilege.

On windless afternoons, Lake Powell gleams like an enormous tinaja worn into stone the color of redware. The analogy suggests stillness, a stillness flecked by the lazy drone of flies or an occasional birdcall. On a warm day, though, the lake is abuzz with Sea-doos, wave runners, speedboats, and a variety of plastic putt-putts.

The Escalante River slipped through the willows and into the heart of Glen Canyon a few hundred yards beneath a white buoy that bobs in the wake of the speedboats. Powell's topographic crew christened the stream after Fray Silvestre Vélez de Escalante, the journal-keeper in a little band of ten tired compadres who were the first Europeans to stray into Glen Canyon.

On their two thousand-mile journey, Escalante named the landscape in his journal. The mouth of the Paria, where the companions stalled out for four days, became Paraja de San Benito Salsipuedes (salsipuedes means get out if you can), and their escape route up the wall of Paria canyon, Las Animas. Then came the camps of San Diego, San Carlos (where they dined on hackberry gruel), Santa Francisca Ramona, and at last at the Ute ford, La Purísima Concepción de la Virgen Santísima. When finally, by the graciousness of their Lord who decided they had learned enough, they traversed the Colorado, the country bore a new litany of sacred names.

Most of a century later, Navajos, harried by Kit Carson from their homelands to the east, named the country across the Colorado from Escalante's camps for the heroes who preceded them to their refuge: Earth Woman and Monster Slayer; Talking Rock and Spring-person, the rainbow people. Bilagáana, wandering in after the War Between the States, coming for glory or gold or solitude, mapped Music Temple, Cathedral in the Desert, Reflection Canyon, Twilight, Gunsight, Forbidding, Dungeon.

Before all of these, countless names uttered in tongues I've never imagined, unwritten or eventually approximated by Europeans with the Roman alphabet, tossed net after net of belonging across the intricate landscape. Now the reservoir erases both topography and a slice of this rich map of human experience. On one bright fall afternoon, turning east up the San Juan arm of Lake Powell, we travel fast and heedless across a featureless plane.

The next morning, under a fiesta-blue bowl of a sky, my handful of hikers, working on a project for the Navajo Nation, records rock art at the base of Navajo Mountain, in the triangle of wilderness south of the San Juan River and east of the Colorado. Our leader, a field-seasoned archeologist, arms us with maps and clipboards and sends us scattering up dry streambeds and over sandrock divides. One of our survey crew, a city guy from the Bay Area, marvels, "You feel like you're in the middle of nowhere until you find a drawing and then you know you're somewhere."

Before Glen Canyon Dam's floodgates were closed, salvage archeologists hurried over the basin recording the remains of past cultures. Fanning out along the creekbeds, they found thousands of signs of a scattered prehistoric people: piled rock, potsherds, scatters of stone flakes, the blackened earth of hearth fires. What established villages and fields the Pueblo folk left fell along the once arable, now largely drowned, terraces just off the river, but the traces of their comings and goings linger up here above the shore of the reservoir too. Like their four-legged and winged neighbors, humans here have always lived lightly, their adaptations to place so subtle and so myriad that we who embrace development on a grand scale can scarcely see them.

Our first morning we followed a sinuous channel carved into Kayenta sandstone, the layer of reworked river sands sandwiched between the lithified dunes of the Navajo and Wingate formations. On a living dune above the wash, among widely spaced clumps of Mormon tea and Indian rice grass, we discovered the spare remains of a Basketmaker gathering camp—blackened dirt and scattered slabs of sandstone, some half-buried on their edges, others worn concave from *manos* pushed back and forth across their surfaces, grinding seeds.

The Basketmakers brought corn from Mexico millennia ago. These hunting-and-gathering seasonal farmers lived frugally, accepting with equanimity and alacrity what the earth provided, never presuming to control her largesse in any serious way. The seasons of their lives were marked in the ripening of seed, the swelling of pine nuts.

The Ancestral Puebloans, descendants of the Basketmakers, hiked these canyons until they left for good in the late 1200s. Settled deeper into farming, they depended more on crops, crops that needed planting, tending, worrying over, rain. Still, "the genius of the Anasazi lay in . . . ancient foraging skills to which was added horticulture," according to Jesse Jennings, director of the salvage work done by the University of Utah. He called these people "typical backwoods Anasazi" who "specialized in gardening in marginal areas, and, by understanding water and its conservation and use (and the idiosyncrasies of their crops), extended their domain into areas where neither then nor now is gardening truly feasible."

Today we're surveying in a canyon farther up the San Juan, where the Chinle swamp deposits underlying the Wingate sandstone are exposed by the Monument Upwarp. We leave our tired-looking houseboat camp with its litter of driftwood, oil bottles, an occasional sneaker, and hike uphill to a spring beneath an enormous cottonwood, an oasis today for the Navajo's feral cows and a thousand years ago for Puebloan farmers. The rest of the day we'll wander a high terrace eroded from the clay slopes of the Chinle, searching for rock art and shade.

The high, holy, hotter-than-Hades benches offer long views ending in red escarpments, shadow mountains. The terrace is strewn with massive, straight-sided slabs, taller than houses, churches even, thrown out from sheer Wingate walls and blackened by desert varnish—slates for travelers, hunters and gatherers, Navajo cowboys.

One monolith is pecked with a lively intaglio of small figures: ducks; tracks of rabbit, deer, bear; a snake; lizard men and men with birds for heads. Pressed by my companions to "explain," I recall that ducks in pueblo myth bind together earth and sky and water; that the Zunis speak of First Man as lizard; that shamans often call upon animal helpers. But what do I know really? These people belonged deep in a magical, delicately-balanced universe, in which everything had spirit, and everyone—two-legged or four or six, scaled or feathered—was connected. Even here, up to our shins in snakeweed in this hot, brilliant light, for Lake boaters like us it's a faraway place.

Back at the boat Earth Woman's Chinle skirts are dragging in the lake. The shales are rumpled and faded in the afternoon sun, gray muslin streaked with burnt orange, as if she had been gathering clay on the muddy bank when the flood came. The dark blue water, pooled at her thighs and moving only with the wind, astonishes a mind evolved in nature. All that broken country ending abruptly at a machine-polished surface.

This surface moves up and down at the whim of human desires. Air-conditioning, city lights, and strategic water hoarding dictate Lake Powell water levels, which one year drown out established shrubs and trees and another desiccate water-lovers like willow and baccharis. Even where there is a pocket of soil, plants that evolved with the seasonal rhythms of desert rivers—spring snowmelt, summer floods, winter doldrums—have a hard time coping with this new regime.

Wild nature is prepared for drastic change, and tamarisk, an imported weed with a genius for colonizing wet sand, dominates the beach we're parked at tonight. Meanwhile up on Earth Woman's undisturbed flank, high above the reservoir, a far more intricate slice of life prowls and whispers and scavenges. On the mountainside the old patterns—the mosaic of plant forms, the shapes of the terrain, the energy of wild creatures—feel healthy and whole, despite the exotic weeds encroaching at the mountain's feet.

Averse to sleeping in houseboats, I thread my way through the tammies with my bedroll, avoiding the copses with little knots of toilet paper emerging at the roots. Forty years ago, I'd have made my bed "down there" in an untidy, many-storied aviary of cottonwood, sandbar willow and tree-sized Gooding willow, rhus and rabbitbrush and bunch grass. Tonight I sleep under the wispy branches of the tamarisk. Instead of waking to bugs buzzing and the murmurations of birds, I tiptoe down to the houseboat in an eerie stillness punctuated by the occasional thrum of a settling pontoon.

To say nothing has changed up on the flank of Naatsis'áán since Powell's day is foolish, of course. Everything has changed, change being what life is, and everything here being vibrantly alive. Comings and goings are written everywhere—half-circles inscribed by wind-tossed rice grass, a line of hand-sized bird tracks pecked on a boulder, burro trails. Two-legged footprints are uncommon, interesting in this sparsely settled human habitat. Someone came this way; how curious, what were they up to? A sandal track engraved in desert varnish centuries ago inspires the same questions.

A little band of hikers eager for a view from the rim of the cliffs rising above the burro's terraces, as well as for rock art, heads out after lunch. We follow one of the lightly traveled trails that link the Rainbow Plateau with springs and camps in the canyons. No doubt this route was pioneered thousands of years ago and improved ever so slightly by the Ancestors, a step carved here, a tree branch leaned up there.

Navajos, more recently, made it useful for cows and sheep by piling stones in dips, arranging juniper skeletons to fence a perilous curve. Elegantly simple, exactly fitted to the terrain, the path unfurls underfoot, step by mindful step. Today's route twists ingeniously up a talus slope and the sheer-faced Wingate sandstone, and tops out above a perched valley. Doubling back down the streambed, a carefully pieced stone ramp bypasses the dry waterfall and leads to the tinaja beneath it. Above the ramp a weathered, hand-turned chair leg is tucked into a cranny in the rock, helpful no doubt for urging animals down to water.

One faint set of Nike tracks, imprinted on a rare wet day, materializes now and again coming up, but we lose them on the rimrock. Most afternoons wind sweeps clean the sandy wash above the pour-over, and in the next half mile the only human sign is a few juniper logs cleverly arranged into a waist-high conical structure. Another half mile brings a handful of potsherds, strewn among a few rusted tin cans. Two or three well-placed rock piles mark a route into the next canyon.

A splash of bright orange on a little dune draws me like a magnet. A cooler? A life jacket? Ah, a plastic road cone, God knows how many desert miles from the nearest road. The latest in cairns? Not litter up here but another thread in the layers of stories, like the chair leg and the burro trails. This mountain, so familiar to generations of humankind, feels as coherent and tightly woven and full of surprises, as wild, as any place I know.

Back at the top of the Wingate, we sprawl on the slickrock rim, reluctant to leave Earth Woman's domain. From here we can revel in the far view. Mountains float above pale waves of sandstone, Naatsis'áán just yonder, and to the north and east the blue mystery of the Henrys. Almost straight down, the only dissonance: water gleaming like a fallen piece of sky.

D AVID ROSS BROWER (1912–2000) was perhaps the greatest American environmentalist of the 20th century. During his tenure as the first executive director of the Sierra Club (1952–1969), Brower transformed the organization from a regional outdoors organization of barely 7,000 members into a major force in national politics, largely through the successful battle to remove the proposed dam at Echo Park in Dinosaur National Monument from the Colorado River Storage Project legislation (1957). His public victory was accompanied by personal guilt, however—for the remainder of his life, Brower would be haunted by the notion that he could have saved Glen Canyon from inundation as well. In 1996, Brower helped launch the movement to restore Glen Canyon by convincing the Sierra Club's Board of Directors to advocate the draining of Lake Powell. The following essay summarized his position in the March 1996 issue of *Sierra* magazine.

Let the River Run Through It

"GLEN CANYON DIED, AND I WAS partly responsible for its needless death," I wrote in *The Place No One Knew,* a Sierra Club book published in 1963. "Neither you nor I, nor anyone else, knew it well enough to insist that at all costs it should endure. When we began to find out, it was too late. On January 2, 1963, the last day on which the execution of one of the planet's greatest scenic antiquities could yet have been spared, the man who theoretically had the power to save the place did not. I was within a few feet of his desk in Washington that day and witnessed how the forces long at work had their way. So a steel gate dropped, choking off the flow of the canyon's carotid artery, and from that moment the canyon's life force ebbed quickly. A huge reservoir, absolutely not needed in this century, almost certainly not needed in the next, and conceivably never to be needed at all, began to fill."

But as surely as we made a mistake years ago, we can reverse it now. We can drain Lake Powell and let the Colorado River run through the dam that created it, bringing Glen Canyon and the wonder of its side canyons back to life. We can let the river do what it needs to do downstream in the Grand Canyon itself.

We don't need to tear the dam down, however much some people would like to see it go. Together the dam's two diversion tunnels can send 200,000 cubic feet of water per second downstream, twice as much as the Colorado's highest flows. Once again Grand Canyon would make its own sounds and, if you listened carefully, you would hear it sighing with relief. The dam itself would be left as a tourist attraction, like the Pyramids, with passers-by wondering how humanity ever built it, and why.

Glen Canyon Dam was a power project pure and simple, built to provide a bank account for the Colorado River Storage Project, which financed high-cost agriculture, wasteful dams, and violated the spirit of the water-development agreement between the Colorado River states and Mexico. Hydropower dams were the darling of developers in this century's middle decades. They are now essentially irrelevant, but dam lovers don't know it yet. Except for a minor diversion at Page, Arizona, and the 30,000 acre-feet delivered annually to the nearby coal-fired power plant, all the water not lost to evaporation or leaks is diverted to users downstream at Lake Mead and below. Lake Mead's Hoover Dam can control the Colorado River without Lake Powell and can produce more power if Powell's water is stored behind it—saving massive amounts of money, water, and wild habitat. Economics and ecology are ready to team up on this one.

Beginning with the Industrial Revolution, people have been forgetting to ask what progress costs the earth and the future. Representing the Sierra Club as "not blindly opposed to progress, but opposed to blind progress," I have long been asking what kinds of growth we must have, and what kinds we can no longer afford. I got started on this while testifying—longer than anyone else—about the proposals governing the Colorado River Storage Project, including dams in Glen Canyon and Dinosaur National Monument. I was helped by Walter L. Huber, a former Sierra Club president and Eisenhower's key advisor on dams, who spotted the Bureau of Reclamation's *under*-engineering, and by U.S. Geological Survey hydrologist Luna Leopold, who spotted its *over*-engineering; by General U. S. Grant III, who pointed out miscalculations on reservoir evaporation, and by other engineers, in and out of government, who didn't wish to offend, but didn't mind if I did.

There were other key players, too, including the Sierra Club's Harold Bradley and at least four of his seven sons; Howard Zahniser, the Wilderness Society's executive secretary and tireless lobbyist; and the Izaak Walton League's Joseph W. Penfold, who gave us the great line, "Bureau of Reclamation engineers are like beaver; they can't stand the sight of running water."

While serving on the Club's board in 1949, I was persuaded to vote for two Grand Canyon dams, and for building Glen Canyon reservoir as a silt trap. In the first months of the battle for Dinosaur National Monument, I even urged the construction of a higher Glen Canyon dam as a way to save Dinosaur and reduce overall evaporation from the Colorado River Storage Project. Utah river runners straightened me out. But in 1956 the Club directors instructed me, then executive director, to end the club's opposition to the construction of the dam at Glen Canyon if the two dams proposed upstream in Dinosaur were dropped. Instead of flying home immediately and calling for a special meeting, I just sat in Washington and watched the mayhem proceed.

In a 1992 documentary in which I almost tearfully took the blame for Glen Canyon, producer John DeGraff kindly attributed my problem to my not having seen Glen before offering to give it away. I knew better: Wallace Stegner had told me, "Strictly between us, Dinosaur doesn't hold a candle to Glen." I have worn sackcloth and ashes ever since, convinced that I could have saved the place if I had simply got off my duff.

The fact is, though, Glen Canyon is still there. With that thought in mind, I've turned from regret to restoration. In 1995 I debated former Bureau of Reclamation commissioner Floyd Dominy, builder of more dams than anybody, Glen Canyon among them. When I proposed restoring Glen Canyon, Dominy was not ready to concede, but I think the audience was. I pushed the proposal harder in 1996 before 1,600 people gathered at the University of Utah. They gave enthusiastic support. The toughest question I got was about how long it would take the tamarisk, a notoriously invasive exotic, to recover. I fudged the answer: "Twenty-five minutes."

Then on November 16, 1996, an entity that had blocked my opposition to the creation of Lake Powell in 1956, the Sierra Club board, unanimously backed my motion to drain it. I suddenly felt about 30 years younger.

One of the strongest selling points comes from the Bureau of Reclamation itself. In 1996, the Bureau found that almost a million acre-feet, or 8 percent of the river's flow, disappeared between the stations recording the reservoir's inflow and outflow. Almost 600,000 acre-feet were presumed lost to evaporation. Nobody knows for sure about the rest. The Bureau said some of the loss was a gain—being stored in the banks of the reservoir—but it has no idea how much of that gain it will ever get back. Some bank storage is recoverable, but all too likely the region's downward-slanting geological strata are leading some of Powell's waters into the dark unknown. It takes only one drain to empty a bathtub, and we don't know where, when, or how the Powell tub leaks. A million acre-feet could meet the annual domestic needs of 4 million people and at today's prices are worth $435 million in the Salt Lake City area—more than a billion on my hill in Berkeley, California.

But these numbers are moving upward. As Powell rises, fills with sediment, and spreads out across the landscape (it peaked at 88 percent of capacity [in 1995]) the losses will be even larger. They could mount to 1.5 million acre-feet per year before *Sierra*'s middle-aged readers are my age (in their

80s), which won't take as long as we'd like. And what is an acre-foot likely to be worth when my grandson David Brower comes of age? When I was his age farmers objected to having to pay $5 an acre-foot. What has happened in the last decade or two is interesting, but what will happen in the next century or two is critical. (Powell is supposed to last at least three centuries, but malpractice in the Colorado's watershed—clearcutting, grazing, and other erosive forces—will shorten its life.)

Whatever the final details of Lake Powell's water losses turn out to be, the draining of the lake simply has to happen. The river and the regions dependent upon it, including Baja California and the Gulf of California, can no longer afford the unconscionable loss of water. We need to get rid immediately of the illusion that the only way to protect water rights is by wasting water in Lake Powell. We can simply let the flow reach Lee's Ferry, Arizona (the dividing point between the Upper and Lower basins), naturally, beautifully, and powered by gravity at no cost.

Draining Lake Powell means more water for the Colorado River states and Mexico, especially Colorado and Utah. The hundreds of millions of dollars now being lost, growing to billions in the future, should be enough to give even Bill Gates pause.

The sooner we begin, the sooner lost paradises will begin to recover—Cathedral in the Desert, Music Temple, Hidden Passage, Dove Canyon, Little Arch, Dungeon, and a hundred others. Glen Canyon itself can probably lose its white sidewalls in two or three decades. The tapestries can re-emerge, along the desert varnish, the exiled species of plants and animals, the pictographs and other mementos of people long gone. The canyon's music will be known again, and "the sudden poetry of springs," Wallace Stegner's beautiful phrase, will be revealed again below the sculptured walls of Navajo sandstone. The phrase "as long as the rivers shall run and the grasses grow" will regain its meaning.

The candle conservationists lit to remember the things lost in Glen Canyon can be put back on the shelf, and, let us pledge, be left there. In time, Glen Canyon will reassert itself, through the action of wind and water. And we will learn what Alexander Pope knew: "And finer forms are in the quarry / Than ever Angelo evoked." Once again, for all our time, the river can run through it.

J ARED FARMER WAS BORN AND RAISED in Provo, Utah, and educated at Utah State University, the University of Montana, and Stanford University. The author of *Glen Canyon Dammed* (1999), his work has also appeared in a number of historical journals and newspapers. Farmer's writing about Glen Canyon is enlivened by the inherent tension of finding peace in a depauperate world. The following essay originally appeared in *Western Historical Quarterly 27* (Summer 1996).

Glen Canyon and the
Persistence of Wilderness

WHEN THE COLORADO RIVER was a river, Glen Canyon was a place: 170 miles of flatwater rimmed by slickrock in southeastern Utah and far northern Arizona. The agreeably redundant place name—*Glen Canyon*—signified the Colorado's myriad tributaries. Glen Canyon was most remarkable for its side canyons. Some of these ravines, these enticing incisions in the sandstone wall, met quick and exquisite deadends, a waterfall, perhaps, trickling into a fern-decked pool. Others, by no indication of their mouths, strayed for dozens of dazzling miles. You never knew what to expect, except wonder. Every stop on a Glen Canyon river trip had potential for adventure. "Awe was never Glen Canyon's province," Wallace Stegner aptly wrote. "That is for the Grand Canyon. Glen Canyon was for delight."

In 1963, Glen Canyon and its extended family of canyons began to die. Twin diversion tunnels, the Colorado River's intravenous life support, were closed, plugged, then sealed. The water, frustrated from its course, pooled submissively blue against the concrete face of the West's last great dam. Lake Powell was born.

The same year saw the publication of a monumental book on Glen Canyon. *The Place No One Knew*, a title in the Sierra Club's celebrated Exhibit Format Series—coffee table propaganda—featured luminous photographs by Eliot Porter alongside quotes from travelers and poets. The book was an obituary, and for many, the definitive record by which the place would be remembered.

The Place No One Knew conveyed two basic messages: Glen Canyon used to be a pristine and astonishingly beautiful wilderness, and without public reckoning, that birthright was laid waste. "The best of the canyon is going or gone," lamented David Brower, executive secretary of the Sierra Club. "Some second-best beauty remains . . . but much of its meaning vanished when Glen Canyon died." Innumerable people have echoed the archdruid's weary outrage over the loss of one of earth's most glorious canyons. To many environmental activists, Glen Canyon Dam—a dam on a desert river that symbolizes overuse, in a rugged region that symbolizes wildness—remains *the* masterwork of human arrogance. Edward Abbey, that personable misanthrope and most widely read writer of the American desert, helped remake the edifice into an object of hate. In many of his works, Abbey both rhapsodized about the Glen and fantasized about the destruction of the dam.

Reading carefully the angry and wistful writing about Glen Canyon—and there's plenty of it—one realizes that people are lamenting lost opportunity as much as lost beauty. They mourn the canyon less as a place than as a wilderness in which they did or *might have* experienced something wonderful. Among the most desired experiences is discovery—that exciting feeling, as you move into a slot canyon, that you just might be the first to go here; that you have found a wild sanctuary and forsaken the world. The curious thing about discovery is its persistence. From river-running in the Place No One Knew to houseboating at the Place Everyone Knows—Glen Canyon and Lake Powell, two supposedly antithetical places—visitors and outfitters have often described and sold experiences using the same languages of discovery, exploration, and adventure.

Consider this 1941 river-trip promotional:

> Each year more people are taking advantage of this opportunity to penetrate the heretofore unreachable "Land of Mystery"; to thrill to the remote fastnesses of these spectacular great canyons. The unlimited number of really unexplored side canyons ever presents the challenge for investigation and exploration. It is like going into another World.

The author of this verbal enthusiasm was Norman Nevills. Out of his family-run lodge in tiny Mexican Hat, Utah, Nevills cranked out "Canyon Wonderland," a charmingly crude mimeographed leaflet. Nevills brought unflagging spirit to his struggle to make a living. His business was, for his time, peculiar. He floated high-paying passengers down remote fast-water river canyons. Nevills's bread-and-butter run started at Mexican Hat, on the San Juan River. He followed the San Juan on its relentlessly crooked course until it married the Colorado midway through the Glen. Nevills's week-long trips finished at Lee's Ferry, Arizona, where Glen Canyon ended and the Grand Canyon abruptly began.

Before he died in a plane crash in 1949, Nevills had established a remarkable river career. He fished for and caught notoriety. In the 1940s, national magazines, including *Life, Atlantic Monthly, National Geographic,* and the *Saturday Evening Post,* ran river-trip features. As much as any individual (one must also credit Bus Hatch of Vernal, Utah), Norman Nevills helped change the image of western river running from a daredevil sport to a legitimate vacation. With an excellent safety and satisfaction record, he could, by the late forties, attract diverse guests—women and men, old and young. The river trip was novel but not exceptional, exciting without the stigma of hazard.

As business improved, Nevills replaced his leaflet with a slick-paper brochure, complete with photographs and testimonials. What could you, the prospective guest, look forward to? SCENIC BEAUTY • EXPLORATION • SAFE ADVENTURE. "Here one may trod where no human has ever before set foot—or follow up the narrow chasm of a side canyon not knowing what the next turn will reveal. It is a thrilling world." True enough. Big sections of Utah's canyon country had yet to be mapped in detail. It was easy to feel like *voyageurs* charting the Unknown, and Nevills did his best to encourage the fantasy. A passenger in 1948 described waking to the rushing Colorado with a resonant sensation—"explorer's fever." His fever found relief: later in the trip, the Nevills expedition explored and then named a cavernous draw.

In his day, Nevills had Glen Canyon to himself. Only near the end of his career did the first competition form. Then, in the 1950s, recreational activity mushroomed; by the end of that decade, no less than eight outfits plied the river. The new entrepreneurs used WWII surplus neoprene pontoons, affordable, unsinkable rubber tubs that held more people in more comfort than Nevills's trim plywood boats. Business was good.

Private parties, too, began floating the Glen. All it took was a little cash and some leisure time—two post-war increases. No permits required. As well, starting in 1947, hundreds of boy scouts (Explorers, appropriately) from the Wasatch Front and Southern California rained on the Colorado. Though not the docile stream some have depicted—swift water, powerful eddies, and relentless wind could all cause trouble—the run in Glen Canyon was appropriate for anyone with average outdoor skills.

Most of the canyoneers put in at Hite, Utah, at the head of Glen

Canyon. Here was the only place to cross the Colorado—on an old-fashioned cable ferry—for 282 river miles. Considering its isolation, Hite (a town so small it eluded the census) began to see an impressive number of visitors. During the 1962 boating season, Woody Edgell, who ran the ferry for the state of Utah, carried some five hundred vehicles per month. Most of these dented, dust-covered cars carried river runners. "The Colorado and its tributary, the San Juan, are seeing traffic of a sort never dreamed of before," reported the *New York Times*. The prospectors in this "boating rush" sought one-of-a-kind beauty and adventure. In the late fifties and early sixties, Glen Canyon's busiest era, discovery didn't abate. In fact, it only increased.

The dominant explanation is Glen Canyon Dam. For many, the giant federal project—begun in 1956—intensified the canyon experience. A "fevered mix of discovery and farewell," essayist Bruce Berger has described it. Like a victim of horrifying disease, the canyon attracted loved ones and curiosity-seekers. Outfitters pocketed the bittersweet reward. In 1962 and early '63, riverman Harry Aleson issued the FINAL INVITATION to see "Glen Canyon and the superb beauty in the mouths of hundreds of side canyons and glens, never to be seen by man again." Call it terminal exploration. In a matter of months or even days, the Bureau of Reclamation would shut the river off. Aleson and his guests never in fact saw the dam from the Colorado; since 1957, all parties were forbidden past Kane Creek, a lonely spot 37 miles upriver, where the government had cut a road. However, the specter of the dam, like thunder from unseen clouds, could jostle the mind-set of canyoneers.

Were machine technology and exploration necessarily incompatible? One outfitter suggested not. Art Greene bucked the neoprene current. Forget about week-long float trips—starting in 1948, he used motorboats to go *up* the river. From Lee's Ferry, Greene powered passengers to Forbidding Canyon (from there, a six-mile hike to Rainbow Bridge) and back in just three days. Eventually Kane Creek became the base for the trip. Art Greene's first watercraft, a do-it-yourself beauty, featured a 450-horsepower airplane prop. The noise was deafening, but the contraption did the job. Passengers wore earplugs. This handicap, however, didn't prevent travel writer Joyce Rockwood Muench from hearing her pulse. She used heart-pounding language to describe Greene's inaugural up-river trip—another "first" for "Twentieth Century adventurers." There in Glen Canyon, "no hint of the outside world is had and with the grand feeling of isolation, the stupendous scale of the chasm, the world seems well lost."

Near the mouth of Glen Canyon, at the future dam site, Muench spotted survey flags and metal earth-moving machines. The equipment seemed "very much out of place among the wildness of the scenery." Still, if you could be an adventurer on a motorboat on a flowing river, so what about a dam? Would the impounded Colorado be that different? Ruefully anticipating the arrival of Lake Powell, one writer gave a sensible answer: A lot more would be able to see the area, "but these thousands will miss the thrills of that wilderness adventure in the slickrock solitude. . . ."

It's one of the great ironies of the reservoir, however, that many found just such a thrill. In 1962, weeks after Lake Powell started rising, a correspondent with the *Salt Lake Tribune* made an inspection tour. He reported, without a hint of regret, the demise of "one of the last great wilderness frontiers." Yet in the same article, he used words that could have described the former, "wild" Glen Canyon—a place of "breathtaking room" and "solitude" that offers "adventurous skippers and crews plenty of chances to let their exploring imaginations run wild."

Many embraced this exciting incongruity—a wilderness where you could pilot a boat, a reservoir where you could feel like Columbus. Travel articles covering nascent Lake Powell are laden with metaphors of exploration and pioneering. "Historians have called the Indian Wars the last great American adventure," wrote one Salt Laker, "but I can testify there's some left, and I've just had a taste of it." His party of six spent a long weekend at Lake Powell. Half of them had never camped before. They returned to their city homes after three delightful days as frontier adventurers.

The chance to discover was intoxicating. David Brower once labeled 1963 the "Year of the Last Look." Page, Arizona, construction town converting to tourist site, liked to call 1963 the "Year of Exploration." A characteristic traveler's report went like this:"[A]s the water reaches into mysterious canyons, creeping into areas never before seen by whitemen, it will disclose to exploring boaters exciting country seen for the first time." Before the dam, Glen Canyon's tributaries often contained impassable drop-offs or choke-stones, tantalizing barriers to the unknown. As the listless lake invaded the glens, overwhelming ferns and cottonwoods, beaver and deer, the water surpassed the rock obstacles, permitting exploration beyond. Eyes aglow, boaters propelled up canyons where perhaps even the nimble Anasazi had never been, and itinerant ravens never cared to go.

And Lake Powell offered more. Not only could you discover a specific twisting canyon, you could find solitude in the main channel. Most observers of the infant lake mentioned both the geographic isolation and the personal solitude—a week gone by without seeing another soul. Here you could really escape the world. Like any "wilderness" should be, Lake Powell was a clean slate, the marks of riverine history having been erased. *Terra incognita:* This created landscape literally had never been seen before. The new shoreline was simple—rock meets water, water reflects rock. The reservoir looked, at least while it rose, shockingly pure. Several went so far as to describe the man-made waterway as "unspoiled" and "unexploited." SCENIC LAKE POWELL proclaimed one newspaper subhead, HEART OF UTAH'S WILDERNESS.

This wasn't mere hyperbole. In the first months—even the first several years for some parts of the sprawling lake—the place did seem wild. The head-start boaters found no operating marina. For seven months after the dam gates closed, boating recreationists had to drive 23 miles of jarring dirt road to Kane Creek to put in. During the same time, at the very same spot, straggling river parties took out. In August 1963, the lake finally rose high enough to service the permanent boat ramp at Wahweap Marina, near Page. Years before, with great foresight, Art Greene had leased the state property for development. Did the Arizona business pioneer have misgivings about Lake Powell? No permanent ones. "Now a whole new breed of people can come out and be adventurers in safety," Greene told *National Geographic,* sounding like Norman Nevills two decades earlier.

Adventure it was. Before the summer of 1964, nothing save shoreline and sky existed for 150 miles beyond Wahweap. If you wanted to make it very far from the dock, you had to carry your own gas, and plenty of it. More than a few visitors got stranded or lost. There were no patrols at first, no buoys marking the maze of side channels. "Be carefree but not careless," admonished the National Park Service, the agency given charge of the reservoir. "This is a place for recreation, but it is just emerging from its wild state." Ambitious recreational developments were in the works, but they were unfinished when, just days after Lake Powell started rising, people arrived with their boats in tow.

Visitation numbers tell a story. In 1963, the year of Lake Powell's debut, an estimated 44,000 people came to look, to fish, to boat. Judging from entries in the Rainbow Bridge visitor register, the actual count on the lake was lower, but the fact that any number of people would haul a boat across hundreds of miles of desert to a reservoir with practically no developments is remarkable. Primitiveness was part of the lure. "From an exploring standpoint," explained the *Salt Lake Tribune,* "boating the lake right now is the best time."

People understood that Lake Powell's embryonic phase would be short. Now was the time to explore. In 1968, one travel writer was surprised but delighted that he couldn't find a detailed map of the reservoir. "Ahead of all who go there is mystery and discovery. Go there now, before it is all 'discovered,' and make your own map. You'll never have a chance again quite like it." These words, and others like them, sound like preparations for nostalgia. Bruce Berger tells of a friend who discovered the canyon only after the dam. On his first day on Lake Powell in 1963, he saw nobody else. He returned yearly for a "series of fresh adventures in a new country." But each subsequent year, more people appeared and more canyon disappeared. Finally, inevitably, faced with a barrage of fun-seekers, he threw in the towel: "That was the end of our Lake Powell, which was a place for exploration, and its conversion into pure recreation."

A trip through the travel literature shows that the lake has indeed become something of an aqua-park for the affluent. Contemporary travel articles tend to focus on the joys of houseboating and waterskiing. But the language of discovery survives. Even the reservoir's name, Lake Powell, evokes exploration. It honors—or dishonors, depending whom you ask— John Wesley Powell, the great scientist and bureaucrat. Travel brochures recall his famous first voyage down the Colorado River in 1869. In the remote realms of the lake, they say, you'll feel a bit like Major Powell. ARAMARK, the leisure corporation that now owns the marinas, points up the available comforts of home and luxuries of a resort, but adventure still comes with the package: "96 Canyons to Explore" at "America's Natural Playground." The concessionaire advertises various combo tours—the Houseboat Explorer, the Senior RV Rainbow Explorer, the Canyon Explorer. With its subsidiary, Wilderness River Adventure, Inc., you can experience the remnant 15 miles of Glen Canyon. Motorized float trips embark daily from the foot of the dam.

The persistence of wilderness buzz-words around places that no longer resemble "wilderness" indicates the cultural—and commercial—importance of the imagined primitive West. Glen Canyon is but one example. The words are pervasive; one should be wary of associating public language with private experience, or basing generalizations on selected sources. Not everyone who wrote about what they did in Glen Canyon used the language of discovery. Not everyone, by a long shot, wrote anything at all. And though published travels accounts do display striking correspondence, the same words don't necessarily embody identical personal meaning.

Despite these problems, the point remains: At Glen Canyon, before and after the dam, something real, something participatory, is obtainable beyond the worn-out vocabulary. Each year, as the reservoir inched upwards—Lake Powell didn't reach capacity until 1980—landforms were submerged and viewpoints revealed, creating unused exploring grounds. At full pool, Lake Powell boasts an incredible 1,960 miles of shoreline. In recent years of little rain, the reservoir dropped nearly one hundred feet, exhuming cliffs and canyons, disclosing sites never seen by most visitors. And for each individual, of course, the first trip to any canyon of Lake Powell at any time offers personal opportunity for exploration. What's more, these slickrock fjords, stained as they are by a bathtub ring and clogged with summertime tourists, *do* lead to "natural" areas, oases of solitude. Today Lake Powell receives nearly three million annual visitors (who consume some five million gallons of gas), but the surrounding territory remains as undeveloped as any in the contiguous United States. One recent guidebook described the lake as part of the last great American wilderness, a place that "offers adventure and discovery."

Many who mourn Glen Canyon have forsaken the place. They refer to its successor as Lake Foul or the Blue Death. "Put a road into wild country and the wild country is gone," elegized one conservationist in 1964. "Put a marina in wild country and again it is gone." The message? Glen Canyon has changed from sacred to desecrated. Formerly a wilderness, the place is now a playground.

In truth, the reservoir can act as both. A representative travel writer cited the "feeling of adventure following the spirit of early explorers" as an important component of his idyllic Lake Powell vacation, "but the luxury of the houseboat had to top the list." Another houseboater, after enjoying a spaghetti dinner, "slipped from familiar domesticity into a night out of time, simply by stepping off the porch of the houseboat into the silent, black solitude of the canyon." Like Norman Nevills's passengers 30 years before, she entered another world, a world for exploration—only she did it with a single step.

Accounts like these pose difficult questions. If you can have a "wilderness experience" on a houseboat (a mass of metal and plastic) on a reservoir (the result of concrete and tubing), what in the world is wilderness? Why do people cry over the lost wilderness of Glen Canyon?

Considering what Lake Powell replaced—natural bridges, nameless canyons, cliff ruins and heron rookeries, the Colorado bending round tapestried walls—it's difficult not to feel bad. The room for sorrow is spacious. One suggestion of the Glen's former glory is the size (and remarkable high caliber) of its literature—the literature of the lost.

Ironically, though, for those who have only books by which to remember, even well-placed sorrow can turn to self-pity: *I came too late.* Too late to see the unspoiled West, too late to discover Glen Canyon in its wilderness state. But imagined paradise is just imagination—not a place, but The Place No One Knew. This consecration of Glen Canyon implies inconsistent beliefs. Not enough people knew about the canyon to save it; and precisely because it was unknown, Glen Canyon was wonderful—a rock fantasy land, in other words, where you might have felt the ecstasy of exploration.

Viewing the canyon like this—seeing the true West, in the sharp words of Elliott West, as "timeless, unlayered, storyless . . . the land of No Place"— leads to heartache and short-sightedness. This viewpoint disguises the fact that exploration has and will go on at Lake Powell. It excludes the possibility that the man-made lake could possess some of the other experiential qualities—mystery, sacred beauty—so freely attributed to wilderness. Perhaps most troubling, it serves to define "wilderness experience" as essentially escaping the world and finding, however briefly, a more potent one. Discovery—with its legacies of conquest and consumerism—becomes a desired means of encountering the wild. The irony is poignant, and very human.

"[O]n a geological scale of time, the building of Glen Canyon Dam hardly mattered," Patricia Limerick has written. "If the dam was a crime, [people]—not nature itself—were the victims." One should add a clarification: Some people were victims, some beneficiaries, still others a bit of both. Nevertheless, the language, and at times even the experiences of those who mourn Glen Canyon and those who delight in Lake Powell are parallel.

And to follow that conclusion, a caveat.

Whatever meaning people give Glen Canyon, whatever reading one may give the texts on Glen Canyon, there is this humbling, inescapable fact: *Something* great is gone. Not some idea of nature, but the reality of a maidenhair fern unfurling in the quiet of a glen. Something independently real and irreplaceable—a place if not a wilderness—lies submerged beneath the wakes of passing boats.

⚜

Source Notes

"The Damnation of a Canyon," from *Beyond the Wall.* © 1971, 1976, 1977, and 1984 by Edward Abbey. Reprinted by permission of Henry Holt and Company, LLC, and of Don Congdon Associates, Inc.

"There Was a River," by Bruce Berger, from *There Was a River.* © 1994 by the Arizona Board of Regents. Reprinted by permission of The University of Arizona Press.

"Let the River Run Through It," © 1996 by David Brower. Reprinted by permission of Kenneth D. Brower, for the heirs of David Brower. Published in *Sierra* (March/April 1997).

The Domínguez-Escalante Journal, edited by Ted J. Warner, translated by Fray Angelico Chavez, © 1995 by the University of Utah Press. Reprinted by permission of the University of Utah Press.

"Forbidden Passage," by Charles Eggert. Published in *Sierra Club Bulletin* 43:9 (1958). Reprinted by permission of the author.

"Glen Canyon and the Persistence of Wilderness," by Jared Farmer. Published in *Western Historical Quarterly* 27 (Summer 1996). Reprinted by permission.

Excerpt from *Delightful Journey down the Green and Colorado Rivers,* by Barry Goldwater. Published by Arizona Historical Foundation (1970). Reprinted by permission.

"Nonnezoshe," from *Tales of Lonely Trails,* by Zane Grey. © Zane Grey, Inc. Reprinted by permission.

"Visit to a Drowning Canyon," by Frank L. Griffin. Published in *Audubon* (January 1966). Reprinted by permission of Myrthle Griffin.

Excerpts from *All My Rivers Are Gone,* © 1998 by Katie Lee. Reprinted by permission of Johnson Books.

Excerpt from "The Salvage Seasons," from *A Story That Stands Like a Dam:*

Selected Bibliography

Abbey, Edward. *Desert Solitaire: A Season in the Wilderness.* New York: McGraw-Hill, 1968.—Contains the tale of Abbey's only float down the Glen, in 1959.

——. *The Monkey Wrench Gang.* New York: McGraw-Hill, 1975.—The classic comic novel about a band of four eco-saboteurs who work diligently to save the Glen Canyon region, while dreaming of blowing up the dam.

——. *Hayduke Lives!* New York: Little, Brown and Company, 1990.— Abbey's last novel, completed days before his death.

Bowden, Charles. *Blue Desert.* Tucson: University of Arizona Press, 1986.— Includes a chapter detailing the famed Earth First! encounter with James Watt at Glen Canyon Dam in 1983.

Carothers, Steven W., and Bryan T. Brown. *The Colorado River through Grand Canyon.* Tucson: The University of Arizona Press, 1991.—A scientific analysis of many of the downriver effects of Glen Canyon Dam.

Crampton, C. Gregory. *Ghosts of Glen Canyon: History Beneath Lake Powell.* St. George, Utah: Publishers Place, 1986.—A brief history and a great series of photographs create a site-by-site guidebook to what lies beneath Lake Powell, written by the foremost expert of the Glen Canyon region. Highly recommended in a reprint by Tower Productions, Salt Lake City.

DeVoto, Bernard. "Shall We Let Them Ruin Our National Parks?" *Saturday Evening Post* 223 (22 July 1950): 17–19, 42.

Fradkin, Philip. *A River No More: The Colorado River and the West.* New York: Alfred A. Knopf, 1981.—A thorough history of the river, well-told.

Farmer, Jared. *Glen Canyon Dammed: Inventing Lake Powell and the Canyon Country.* Tucson: The University of Arizona Press, 1999.—An excellent analysis of tourism's role in transforming the Colorado Plateau.

Frost, Kent, with Rosalie Goldman. *My Canyonlands.* Moab, Utah: Canyon Country Publications, 1997.—The autobiography of one of Norm Nevills's boatmen.

Geib, Philip R. et al. *Glen Canyon Revisited.* University of Utah Anthropological Paper No. 199. Salt Lake City: University of Utah Press, 1996.—An examination of the prehistoric inhabitants of Glen Canyon, as well as a reexamination of the results of the Glen Canyon Project. Very complete, but quite scientific.

Graves, John. *Goodbye to a River: A Narrative.* New York: Ballantine Books, 1971.—Not about the Colorado River, but about the Brazos, in Texas; nonetheless, Graves reflects upon the battle for Echo Park and the personal losses that come with the damming of a favorite river.

Hannon, Steven. *Glen Canyon: A Novel.* Denver: Kokopelli Books, 1997.—The tale of four people who plot to destroy Glen Canyon Dam by smuggling a nuclear bomb out of the Ukraine.

Harvey, Mark W.T. *A Symbol of Wilderness: Echo Park and the American Conservation Movement.* Albuquerque: University of New Mexico Press, 1994.—A comprehensive history and analysis of the role of the Echo Park struggle in mainstreaming conservationism.

Hillers, Jack. *"Photographed All the Best Scenery": Jack Hillers' Diary of the Powell Expeditions, 1871–1875.* Don D. Fowler, ed. Salt Lake City: University of Utah Press, [1972].—Bereft of the purple prose of both Dellenbaugh and Powell, Hillers's journals nonetheless offer the occasional insightful passage.

Hyde, Philip. *A Glen Canyon Portfolio.* Flagstaff: Northland Press, 1979.—A collection of beautiful black-and-white photographs of Glen Canyon, accompanied by an early version (the journal entries) of Bruce Berger's "There Was a River."

Inskip, Eleanor, ed. *The Colorado River through Glen Canyon Before Lake Powell: Historic Photo Journal 1872–1964.* Moab, Utah: Inskip Ink, 1995.—A photo book that rivals Eliot Porter's, with images of the drowned canyon arranged, heartbreakingly, by Lake Powell buoy numbers.

Leydet, Francois. *Time and the River Flowing: Grand Canyon.* San Francisco: Sierra Club Books, 1964.—A book that Brower called a continuation of *The Place No One Knew,* by Eliot Porter; contains some fine photographs of both Music Temple and Cathedral in the Desert.

Limerick, Patricia Nelson. *Desert Passages: Encounters with the American Deserts.* Albuquerque: University of New Mexico Press, 1985.—A history of American attitudes toward the desert by one of the foremost historians of our day, who also happens to be a beautiful writer.

McCulley, Patrick. *Silenced Rivers: The Ecology and Politics of Large Dams.* Atlantic Highlands, New Jersey: Zed Books, 1996.—Although not explicitly about Glen Canyon, this book, published in association with the International Rivers Network, offers an excellent overview of the worldwide anti-dam movement.

Miller, David E. *Hole-in-the-Rock: An Epic in the Colonization of the Great American West.* Salt Lake City: University of Utah Press, 1959.—The story of the Mormon attempt to find a shortcut to the San Juan area via Glen Canyon.

Nichols, Tad. *Glen Canyon: Images of a Lost World.* Santa Fe: Museum of New Mexico Press, 1999.—Beautiful black-and-white photographs accompanied by recollections of more than thirty trips made through the Glen.

Porter, Eliot. *The Place No One Knew.* San Francisco: Sierra Club, 1963.— The book that started it all, Porter's failure to capture the scope of Glen Canyon makes this a disappointing photo book.

Potter, Loren D., and Charles L. Drake. *Lake Powell: Virgin Flow to Dynamo.* Albuquerque: University of New Mexico Press, 1989.—A natural history and scientific analysis of the reservoir.

Reisner, Marc. *Cadillac Desert: The American West and its Disappearing Water.* New York: Viking Penguin, Inc., 1986.—The classic and wonderfully written history of the era of big dams.

Richardson, Elmo R. "Federal Park Policy in Utah: The Escalante National Monument Controversy of 1935–1940," *Utah Historical Quarterly 33* (Spring 1965): 109–133.—A detailed history of the effort to make the Glen Canyon region a national monument.

Rusho, W.L. *Everett Ruess: A Vagabond for Beauty.* Salt Lake City: Peregrine Smith, 1983.—A good history of Ruess and his disappearance; also, a collection of his letters.

Russell, Terry, and Renny Russell. *On the Loose.* San Francisco: Sierra Club Books, 1969.—A classic, strange little book of photographs and calligraphy, detailing two brothers' impressions of the West.

Short, Vaughn. *Raging River, Lonely Trail: Tales Told by the Campfire's Glow.* Tucson: Two Horses Press, 1978.—Riotous cowboy poetry, including "Floyd's Void."

Sprang, Elizabeth. *Good-bye River.* Reseda, California: Mojave Books, 1979.—A journal of a six-week stay in Glen Canyon in the autumn of 1959, including sketches by the author.

Stanton, Robert B. *Down the Colorado.* Dwight L. Smith, ed. Norman, Oklahoma: University of Oklahoma Press, [1965].—The narrative account of Stanton's many industrial adventures along the Colorado River.

Stegner, Wallace. *Beyond the Hundredth Meridian: John Wesley Powell and the Second Opening of the West.* Boston: Houghton Mifflin, 1954.

Stegner, Wallace, ed. *This Is Dinosaur: Echo Park Country and Its Magic Rivers.* New York: Alfred A. Knopf, 1955.

Topping, Gary. *Glen Canyon and the San Juan Country.* Moscow: University of Idaho Press, 1997.—The best and most comprehensive history yet written of Glen Canyon before the dam.

Trimble, Stephen, and Terry Tempest Williams, eds. *Testimony: Writers of the West Speak on Behalf of Utah Wilderness.* Minneapolis: Milkweed Editions, 1996.—Contains Richard Shelton's fine poem, "Glen Canyon of the Colorado."

U.S. National Park Service. *A Survey of the Recreational Resources of the Colorado River Basin.* Washington, D.C.: Government Printing Office, 1950.—An interesting and somewhat frightening report on the dams once planned for the Plateau region.

Webb, Roy. *Call of the Colorado.* Moscow: University of Idaho Press, 1994.—A wonderful and somewhat-neglected look at those who made as much of an impression on the river as the river did on them; serves as a great introduction and a sort of who's-who of the Colorado River.

Zeveloff, Samuel I., L. Mikel Vause, and William H. McVaugh. *Wilderness Tapestry: An Eclectic Approach to Preservation.* Reno: University of Nevada Press, 1992.—Contains Ann Ronald's wonderful send-up of Glen Canyon writers, "Why Don't They Write About Nevada?"

About the Editor

MEL SCULLY

M ATHEW BARRETT GROSS holds degrees from the University of North Carolina, Chapel Hill, and the University of Montana. He lives in Moab, Utah.